'I soon found myself enjoying the book immensely. Indeed I was captivated by Lady Annabel's warmth and great good humour. There are lashings of jolly jokes about childhood romps and drunken cooks ... [Jimmy] Goldsmith ... here emerges as a richly comic figure ... She tackles the tragedies and dramas of her life in an admirably direct and straightforward way'

Hugh Massingberd, *Spectator*

'Her memoirs will be devoured by many: historians of the twentieth century, celebrity addicts who wish to graduate to a higher altitude than this week's issue of *Hello!*, and lovers of good English prose ... This is not a kiss-and-tell story. The chapters about love and sorrow in the family are deeply moving ... It is a rare gift to be able to write well about your innermost feelings and memories'

Claus von Bülow, *Literary Review*

'[Recalls] a world which no longer exists, a world of good manners, great fun and civilised behaviour. She writes the way she speaks. Directly and amusingly ... This is a wonderful read. Annabel stays a lady throughout – no lurid exposés and the like – yet she has a voice, and a very moving one'

Taki, *Evening Standard*

'A well-ordered, decently written book ... one can only hope for her sake that in future she steers clear of the cads and high-rollers that have provided such excellent copy for her life-story so far'

Selina Hastings, *Sunday Telegraph*

'In her maturity, she enjoys a rich and full life, surrounded by the beings she enjoys most, children and dogs, a warm and still beautiful woman whose life, despite all its tragic moments, has been a celebration of vitality, charmingly and innocently recorded in this delightful memoir, enriched by fascinating photographs'

Paul Johnson, *Spectator*

Annabel

An Unconventional Life

The memoirs of
Lady Annabel Goldsmith

PHOENIX

A PHOENIX PAPERBACK

First published in Great Britain in 2004
by Weidenfeld & Nicolson
This paperback edition published in 2005
by Phoenix,
an imprint of Orion Books Ltd,
Orion House, 5 Upper St Martin's Lane,
London WC2H 9EA

5 7 9 10 8 6 4

A CIP catalogue record for this book
is available from the British Library.

ISBN 0 75382 037 4

Typeset by Butler and Tanner Ltd, Frome and London

Printed and bound in Great Britain by
Clays Ltd, St Ives plc

www.orionbooks.co.uk

For my sister and brother,
Jane and Alastair, and for
my six children, Rupert, Robin,
India Jane, Jemima, Zac
and Ben-Ben

Contents

Illustrations

Photographs used are taken from the author's albums, except where otherwise indicated.

My sister-in-law and best friend, Nico.

My cousin Patrick Plunket, who served as the Queen's Equerry for twenty-seven years.

My cousin Dominic Elwes and John Aspinall, known to us all as Aspers.

Aspers with one of his gorillas.

In the garden at Pelham Cottage with India Jane and my nieces Sophia and Cosima.

With Jimmy in 1978.

Jimmy and me arriving at Bow Street magistrates court for the *Private Eye* libel trial in 1976.[1]

The Birley children in the small fishing boat that we rented on holiday in Porto Ercole, with Libero the boatman.

Nico with her second husband, Georgie Fame and their two sons, Tristan and James.

In Las Vegas with Mark and Liz Brocklehurst, during the early days of my relationship with Jimmy.

On holiday in Mexico in 1973.

Victoria Getty.

Jemima, my first child by Jimmy.

Zacharias, known as Zac.

Benjamin, my youngest son.

Jimmy with Margaret Thatcher at the launch of *NOW* magazine in 1987.

Jimmy in Barbados at Easter 1981 with all his children.

Ormeley Lodge.

In the garden at Ormeley, with Ben, Zac, India Jane and Jemima.

Section 3

With Jimmy and the children at Torre de Tramores, our house in Spain.

My beloved eldest son, Rupert.

Robin, in the mid-1990s.

India Jane.

With my three youngest children in my bedroom at Ormeley.

Jemima's wedding to Imran Khan, in June 1995.

Our much loved nanny, Mimi arriving at Jemima's wedding.

The inimitable and wonderful Mrs White, pictured with Sulaiman shortly after he was born.

With Jimmy and Copper the dog in 1997.

Copper, the greatest canine character I ever knew.

The cover of *Private Eye*, the week after Jimmy died.

Zac's wedding in June 1999 to Sheherezade Bentley.

Ben's wedding in September 2003 to Kate Rothschild.

The grandchildren: Sulaiman and Kasim, Uma, Thyra, James, Iris Annabel.

With my dogs at Ormeley.

With Mark at the party we hosted at Annabel's in celebration of the fortieth anniversary of the founding of the club.

The author and the publishers offer their thanks to the following for their kind permission to reproduce images:

[1]Topham Picturepoint
Adam Butler

Londonderry Family Tree

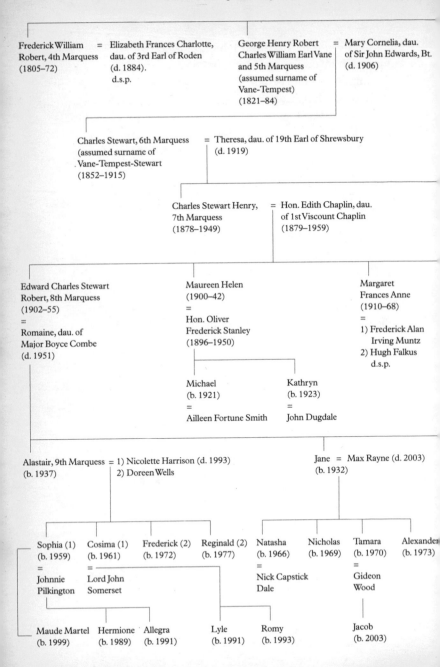

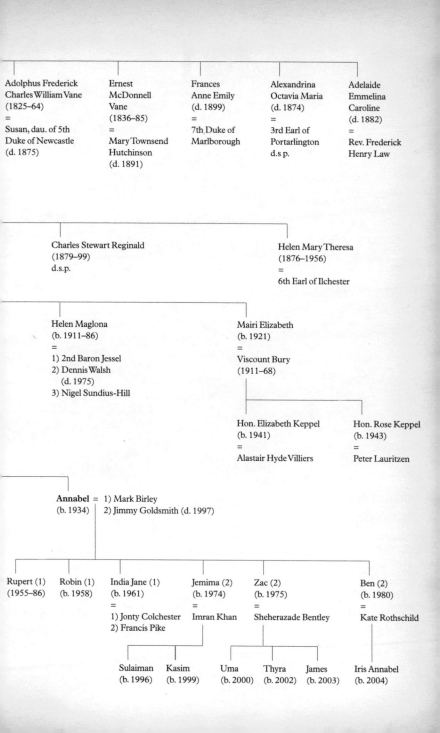

Adolphus Frederick
Charles William Vane
(1825–64)
=
Susan, dau. of 5th
Duke of Newcastle
(d. 1875)

Ernest
McDonnell
Vane
(1836–85)
=
Mary Townsend
Hutchinson
(d. 1891)

Frances
Anne Emily
(d. 1899)
=
7th Duke of
Marlborough

Alexandrina
Octavia Maria
(d. 1874)
=
3rd Earl of
Portarlington
d.s p.

Adelaide
Emmelina
Caroline
(d. 1882)
=
Rev. Frederick
Henry Law

Charles Stewart Reginald
(1879–99)
d.s.p.

Helen Mary Theresa
(1876–1956)
=
6th Earl of Ilchester

Helen Maglona
(b. 1911–86)
=
1) 2nd Baron Jessel
2) Dennis Walsh
   (d. 1975)
3) Nigel Sundius-Hill

Mairi Elizabeth
(b. 1921)
=
Viscount Bury
(1911–68)

Hon. Elizabeth Keppel
(b. 1941)
=
Alastair Hyde Villiers

Hon. Rose Keppel
(b. 1943)
=
Peter Lauritzen

Annabel = 1) Mark Birley
(b. 1934)   2) Jimmy Goldsmith (d. 1997)

Rupert (1)
(1955–86)

Robin (1)
(b. 1958)

India Jane (1)
(b. 1961)
=
1) Jonty Colchester
2) Francis Pike

Jemima (2)
(b. 1974)
=
Imran Khan

Zac (2)
(b. 1975)
=
Sheherazade Bentley

Ben (2)
(b. 1980)
=
Kate Rothschild

Sulaiman
(b. 1996)

Kasim
(b. 1999)

Uma
(b. 2000)

Thyra
(b. 2002)

James
(b. 2003)

Iris Annabel
(b. 2004)

Introduction

All my hopes for immortality were severely shaken in December 2000 by an incident which nearly wiped out three generations of my family. As usual I had spent Christmas at Ormeley, my home near London on the edge of Richmond Park, with all my five children and three grandchildren, and had planned to celebrate the New Year in a safari lodge we had rented in Kenya. On the evening of 28 December we were to fly to Nairobi and we were all in a merry mood as our large group, consisting of myself, Jemima, my younger daughter, with her two small sons Sulaiman and Kasim, their nanny Rose, Benjamin, my youngest child, and his friend James Sevier, and my niece Cosima and her two children, Lyle and Romy, checked in at Gatwick for the evening flight. Zac, my first son with Jimmy, his wife Sheherazade and their daughter Uma were spending the New Year in Mexico. The plane was delayed and we finally took off at ten at night and Jemima, her boys, Ben and James (who had been upgraded from their economy seats) and I were all in first class, and Cosima and her two children and Rose were in economy.

I usually find it hard to sleep on a plane but on this occasion I was so tired that I dozed off around midnight. I was excited about our forthcoming holiday and Jemima was looking forward to being reunited with her husband, Imran Khan, who was flying in from Dubai with his friend Jonathan Mermegan. Sulaiman fell asleep at once but Kasim took a long time to settle. I remember two early bouts of turbulence and I wondered if Jemima was all right as she was so afraid of flying. Round my neck I had been wearing the cross that Jimmy Goldsmith, my second husband and father of Jemima, Zac and Ben, had given me many years before. It is a particularly beautiful cross with rubies set in the middle and I feel rather superstitious if I am ever without it. That night for some reason I took it off and put it in my purse, but as I removed it the thought flashed through my mind that this was an unlucky thing to do as I had never taken it off on an aeroplane journey before.

In the early hours of the morning I woke up very suddenly to feel the aeroplane shaking violently and the noise of the engines stalling. I could feel the plane falling, but most eerie of all was the sound of grown men howling, not a sound I had heard men make before or one I shall ever forget. There was a short silence and then the waking nightmare started all over again. The plane plunged downwards as much as 10,000 feet, and there was a shuddering as if the pilots were trying to start the engines. Two huge hands seemed to be trying to wrench the plane apart and as it went into the last final dive I felt pure feral terror, as I knew with absolute certainty that we were all going to die, realising that this is how whole families are wiped out. There was a moment of silence, followed by renewed howling. I could hear Benjamin agitating behind me when suddenly he grabbed my hand in terror and said, 'Mum, we're all going to die.' I remember saying to him in a strange slurred voice because my mouth was so dry, 'No, Ben, we're not going to die.'

Behind him were Jemima and her sons, and because I wanted us to die as a family with our arms round each other, I wanted more than anything else to reach them, but as I struggled to undo my seat belt I realised that because of the steep angle of the plane I was pinned down and could not move. I looked at my children and grandchildren whose lives had just begun and thought, *You are all so young and there is nothing I can do to save you.*

Then I heard Jemima, telling everyone to shut up and pray. She has described the alarm she saw in Sulaiman's eyes:

Sulaiman was clinging to my neck, staring into my face. He was panicking but his eyes were focused on mine, waiting for any sign of alarm in my face. All my life I have been a coward, especially on planes, yet when my worst fears were realised I was strangely calm. Death seemed inevitable so screaming was pointless. But more than that, it was the power of the maternal instinct which enabled me to retain my composure and repeat like a mantra to my terror-stricken child, 'It's all right. Everything is OK. We are going to be fine...' while all the time I was thinking *very soon we are going to die. Please let it be quick. Please don't let his last minutes be filled with fear or pain.*

It was only then that I thought of praying and I started shouting 'Everyone pray'. I heard my brother praying 'Oh God help us'. And someone behind me praying in Arabic. Then I heard myself loudly deal-making with God: 'Oh God help us. Don't let us die now. Please save us!'

Suddenly everyone seemed to have heard Jemima and started praying aloud as the plane went into another dive and we waited for the impact. Not one person on that flight believed that they would live. The whole episode had only lasted minutes, but to us passengers it felt like hours. Then there was a lull and the captain's voice came over the speaker, shaking, almost tearful (sounding, Jemima thought, because of his Scottish accent, exactly like Sean Connery). He told us that a madman had tried to kill us all but that they had managed to regain control and that he would speak to us later when he had pulled himself together.

My first thought was relief on hearing that it was a man's doing rather than mechanical failure and then we all cried and hugged each other. I remember undoing my seat belt and going back to look for the rest of the family. I saw Rose holding Kasim tightly, with tears pouring down her cheeks and then Cosima, white-faced, with her arms round her two children. The cabin crew were unbelievably brave and good to us, because they must have thought they were going to die too.

On arrival at Nairobi the police arrested the man, a Kenyan student called Paul Mukonyi, and when I watched him leave the plane handcuffed I saw that he was a giant. I was amazed to learn later that after a short stay in the local hospital under psychiatric observation, he was allowed to fly back to France and continue his studies at Lyon University.

As planned we went on to our ranch at the foot of Mount Kenya where Imran was due to meet us. After most near-death experiences one can sometimes find something that, despite the trauma of it all, makes one laugh and today I can laugh about Jemima's reunion with Imran.

On landing at Nairobi airport from Dubai he ran into Lucy Ferry who had also been on our plane with her husband Bryan Ferry, the rock star. Still in a state of shock, she told Imran about the horrific events that had just taken place.

Imran is one of the calmest and most laid-back people I have ever met in my life. He believes that death is predestined and that if your appointed time is not up you will be spared. He also knows that Jemima and I are prone to exaggeration, although in this case no amount of imagination could have done justice to the appalling experience we had been through.

On his arrival at the ranch, Jemima flew to greet him but before she could tell him about what had happened he said, 'Well, baby, I hear you had a little turbulence. I have always told you it is better to fly PIA.' (This last remark referred to the ongoing dispute between them over whether it is better to fly British Airways or Pakistan International Airlines.)

At the time, Jemima and I were not amused. In fact, we were furious with him.

Although parts of that holiday were wonderful, most of us dreaded the return journey. We had all lost our nerve and since then flying has never been the same for any of us. Jemima finds it so traumatic she will only fly when she has to and Ben suffers as much. Even Zac, who was not even on the plane with us, now finds flying impossibly difficult because he has never recovered from the shock of nearly losing all his family in one go.

After we returned to London I met Captain Hagan, and Mark Birley, my first husband, and I arranged for him, his family and Flight Officer Philip Watson to have dinner at Annabel's, the nightclub in Berkeley Square that Mark had founded and named after me. Those two brave men were responsible for saving our lives. Had they not done so it would have been one of the worst accidents in aviation history and the world's third largest in terms of fatalities. That we survived at all was due to the courage of Hagan and Watson.

Captain Hagan described later in detail what had actually happened.

In the early morning of 29 December 2000 a British Airways jumbo jet with a total of four hundred and seven passengers and crew on board came within a whisker of crashing. In the early morning hours, as daylight was breaking, an intruder had burst into the cockpit of the Boeing 747 on route from London to Nairobi. The aircraft was over the Sudanese desert at the time. Most people on board the aircraft were still asleep and only one pilot was at the controls of the aircraft. The suicidal intruder had entered the cockpit in an attempt to seize control of the aircraft, intending to crash it. He placed his body between the solitary co-pilot and his controls in such a manner that the co-pilot had limited access to the control column. He was unable to reach the throttles and his view of his instruments was almost completely obscured. The intruder took control of the aircraft. He grabbed the control column of the aircraft so aggressively that the autopilot dropped out almost instantly. The aircraft started climbing and banking very steeply, and as the co-pilot struggled against the intruder it subsequently entered a steep dive.

Captain Hagan had been taking his rest at the time in a bunk next to the cockpit but on being disturbed by the noise, he rushed into the cockpit and tried to attack Mukonyi from behind, but because of his huge size he found it impossible to move him away from the controls. In his desperation, Captain Hagan suddenly remembered his small son asking him when they were on holiday in Australia, what he would do if he swam into a shark near the Barrier Reef. Captain Hagan had replied, 'I suppose I would go for his eyes.'

Inspired by his own advice, Captain Hagan jabbed his fingers into Mukonyi's eyes and, in momentarily stunning him, was able to wrestle Mukonyi to the ground. How Philip Watson managed to right the plane none of us will ever understand because it was about to flip on to its back and go into an irretrievable tailspin from which nothing could have saved it. For Captain Hagan it must have been an added horror to know that his wife and two children were also on board. Afterwards the passengers campaigned for locks to be put on all cockpit doors and I have wondered more than once whether the adoption of such a basic security measure might have prevented the actions of those on the more successful suicide mission of 11 September.

Bryan Ferry has said that his survival has made him anxious to get on with his life and to get things done. It made him aware that there isn't much time. After such a dreadful experience I too felt that I had to re-evaluate my life and try to make myself a better person.

For a while I found that things that had once mattered suddenly seemed quite trivial, but whether I have changed fundamentally I am not sure. I am certainly more frightened of flying, but I will not put my life on hold by refusing to get on an aeroplane just because of the insane actions of a deranged individual.

Before the incident I would not have believed that I would come to love and value my family even more than I did already. Shortly after the incident, with an awareness of how close my children and their children came to being denied their future, an understanding of the fragility of my own hold on life and a profound appreciation for my own past, I decided to write this book.

ONE

Mount Stewart

Every morning during our holidays at Mount Stewart I would sit on the bed beside my grandmother, struggling to renounce the devil. I was not quite five years old.

Despite a lifetime of unconventional behaviour my grandmother, whom we grandchildren called Mama, was most anxious that we should be raised as fully participating members of the Church of England and determined that at the earliest opportunity we should learn to recite parts of the catechism by heart.

However, my concentration would soon waver as I became distracted by the long green snake which wound its tattooed way up Mama's left leg. Mesmerised, I would gaze at the scaly coils, which began just above her ankle, tracing the spirals that looped round her calf, up to the point where they vanished beneath the folds of her blue silk dressing gown. Where did that forked tongue end, I wondered? Only my grandfather, Papa, knew the answer and I certainly never dared to ask.

To a five-year-old my formidable grandmother could be hugely mysterious. She was universally acknowledged as a famous beauty, but as a child I could not see this. I thought she looked rather like a sheep, an observation undoubtedly encouraged by my father who at church each Sunday would keep an impassively straight face during the Twenty-third Psalm, until singing out, 'We have erred and strayed from our ways like lost Mamas,' at which we three children, struggling unsuccessfully to maintain our composure, would disgrace ourselves by laughing helplessly in front of the disapproving congregation.

Years later I discovered that Edith, the seventh Marchioness of Londonderry, had acquired her incredible indelible snake in 1903 while in Japan on a second honeymoon with my grandfather. Although she does not mention the occasion in her autobiography, *Retrospect*, the procedure involved in tattooing such a large reptile without any anaesthetic must have been horribly painful. While Papa, the seventh Marquess, chose somewhat conservatively to have his regimental badge marked out on his forearm, Mama's preference was characteristically more outrageous.

For several decades her legs were covered by the floor-length dresses of the time, but in the 1930s, as skirts grew shorter, her secret was spotted by press photographers who went quite wild with excitement, mistaking the tattoo for a new fashion for patterned stockings. When I grew older I was hardly surprised to discover that many of her closest friends, including several prime ministers and members of her famous and eclectic club, the Ark, had known my grandmother as Circe, the sorceress, daughter of the witch who was famous for her heathland encounter with Macbeth.

I spent a great deal of my early childhood at my paternal grandparents' Irish home, Mount Stewart. While their other main country house, Wynyard Park near Stockton-on-Tees in the north of England, eventually became my home on the death of Papa, Mount Stewart was the magical place I visited during those early years of my life with my parents, my sister Jane and my brother Alastair.

Although my grandparents owned several large houses, they spent most of their time at Mount Stewart, the nineteenth-century Londonderry seat in Northern Ireland. The long stone house, whose forbidding dark grey façade is softened by the thick ivy that covers much of it, was built mainly in the early nineteenth century. Although some later additions were made by the third Marquess, Fighting Charlie, the main part of the house was built by the first Marquess, the father of the most famous Londonderry of all, the Foreign Secretary, Viscount Castlereagh, who in 1815 had masterminded the Congress of Vienna that concluded the Napoleonic Wars. The house was built on the edge of the waters of Strangford Lough, with the beautiful Mourne Mountains in the distance, and the greatest designers and craftsmen of the day were employed. The architect James Wyatt was responsible for the stable block, and the West Wing was the work of George Dance, Professor of Architecture at the Royal Academy in London. The red leather chairs on which the allied sovereigns sat to negotiate the historic treaty are still on display in the dining room.

My memories of Mount Stewart are of endless sunny summers. My mother was a passionate photographer and, elegant in her blue linen sailor trousers, she followed Jane, Alastair and me everywhere with her little Box Brownie camera. Once developed the pictures were reproduced in triplicate and pasted into three large bound black leather books with our initials stamped on the outside in gold. Each photograph is meticulously labelled and charts our carefree childhood lives, and my album remains one of my most treasured possessions.

During those seemingly endless pre-war summer months of the late 1930s, my brother and sister and I were always out of doors. As soon as we were old enough to escape the supervision of our nannies we spent our time running about on the lawns, sprawling on rugs, and having picnics. In later teenage holidays we built dams on the stream in the wood, climbed old wrecks and capsized boats on the beach, raced each other on our bicycles and rode our fat, shaggy black ponies. My cousin Shaun Plunket remembers hating being encouraged to ride there. He was given a pony that preferred to remain in the stable, but one morning, with Shaun on top, it slipped out of the grip of the groom and bolted for home, throwing Shaun over its head. To spare his feelings we pretended he had chickenpox, because his poor face – he landed face downwards on to the gravel – was so marked by the stones.

In a climate blessed by the Gulf Stream we rarely wore anything other than swimming costumes as we paddled in the warm waters of Strangford Lough, and were taken for the occasional supervised splash in the salt-water pool that Mama had designed and built nearby. Only once, when Jane and I were teenagers, were we invited to join Mama on her naked nocturnal swim. As part of her daily summer ritual she would cross the moonlit lawn after dinner and, removing all her clothes in the little wooden changing rooms next to the pool, she would plunge into the water. Surprised by such unorthodox behaviour in an adult and unaccustomed to the wonderful sense of freedom in swimming naked, Jane and I were overcome with badly concealed laughter and the privileged invitation was never extended to us again.

My grandmother was followed everywhere by her dogs. She had about a dozen of them, including two Irish wolfhounds, several lurchers and a kindergarten-sized pack of Pekineses. The Pekineses terrified Jane and me. Suddenly breaking into a chorus of cacophonous yapping, they would pull away from the disciplinary cordon of my grandmother's heels and rush towards us. My family has always been passionate about dogs and I have letters from my father in which he writes to me about our Aberdeen terriers with as much pride and concern as he does his children.

The sub-tropical climate of Mount Stewart provided the ideal environment for Mama to create the ninety-eight-acre garden that is now acknowledged as among the most glittering in the National Trust's possession. Here she made the formal Italian Garden, the Sunken Garden, the Spanish Garden, the Shamrock Garden in the shape of the leaf, and the Mairi

Garden where a statue of a child marks the place where Mama's youngest daughter would take her afternoon sleep. Part of the wood was given over entirely to lilies, but it was the wild garden that I particularly loved. Perhaps it was there that my own special enthusiasm for wild flowers was kindled. Or maybe it came later, at Wynyard, where my mother too made a wild garden, a place she grew to love more than any other and the place where she would eventually be buried. Whatever the influences, my own wild garden at Ormeley, with the rare species of birds and butterflies that the wild flowers attract, is a source of great joy to me.

At Mount Stewart, on a little hill about half a mile from the house is the octagonal Temple of the Winds, a romantic pavilion, overlooking the lough built in homage to the Tower of the Winds in Athens. Pre-dating the house, it had been built in 1782 for outdoor suppers, its purpose 'solely appropriate for a Junketting Retreat' as the third Marquess later described it. There was a cellar for wine and brandy beneath, but for us it provided a marvellous sanctuary for hide and seek, an appropriate activity in a place 'built for mirth and jollity'.

I can still remember the smell *inside* the house, which came from the heavy-scented lilies, brought in from the garden to fill the great rooms, and from the home-made pot-pourri for which Mama was famous. Aged five, I embarked on a lifelong love affair with the perfume of hyacinths and every winter huge baskets of the bulbs fill my own house. During the thirties the level of grandeur of life that had been established at Mount Stewart before the First World War remained intact. It was a lovely place to be invited to stay. After long late lazy lunches, the adults would go rowing on the lake in one of the eleven boats or they might be invited to join Papa to go up in the skies above Strangford Lough in one of his small planes, as the Londonderry family had an almost genetic passion for flying.

With several dozen servants, the residential staff at Mount Stewart outnumbered the family by five to one. Outside there were gardeners, grooms, groundsmen, keepers and beaters, and four chauffeurs. Inside the house the head housekeeper was in charge of the Groom of the Chambers, the butler and the under-butler, several footmen, Mama's own special footman, the nursery footman, who carried our meals upstairs to us, and the night watchman. In the kitchen there was cook, the head kitchen maid, two further kitchen maids, the scullery maid and the stillroom maid, in addition to the other staff who included two ladies' maids, Papa's valet, a couple of housemaids, a nursery maid, a schoolroom maid, several daily cleaners, a telephonist and a fully trained hospital nurse.

The Mount Stewart piper would play to the house guests after dinner and walk around the house each morning to wake us in turn. He was our personal musical alarm clock and I never fail to be moved even now whenever I hear that evocative drone of bagpipes. Footmen in livery stood behind each chair in the dining room. Gilbert, the head butler, was very tall and thin, and was particularly friendly to us children as we grew older. Later I used to see him carrying out his work at Londonderry House and noticed that he held his head at a very stiff angle and never actually looked any of the guests in the face. He had a rather supercilious air and with hindsight I realised that he was very happy in his role overseeing the duties of the beautiful young footmen.

My grandmother was the great political hostess of her day, notorious particularly for her extremely close friendship with the Labour Prime Minister, Ramsay Macdonald. They first met at a party at Buckingham Palace and this unlikely bond between a left-wing politician and a wealthy aristocrat brought them both lifelong pleasure. She tried to explain the essential nature of her great friend in *Retrospect*: 'He was an old-fashioned socialist who loved beautiful things, dignity, dinner parties and dressing up in resplendent uniforms. He was simple and naïve, the only genuine pacifist I have ever met.'

The house was always filled with distinguished friends,

including many members of Mama's idiosyncratic club, the Ark. In 1914 she had been heavily involved in her own wartime duties, as founder of the Women's Legion, for which in 1917 she was made a Dame of the British Empire. She explains in her autobiography, 'It became obvious that there was room for some organisation of women on a large scale, not only for emergency work as and when required, but for all those other duties where women could take the place of men called to the Colours.'

Members worked on the land as ambulance drivers and wherever their assistance might help to free up men for military service. But she felt it was important to provide an occasional source of amusement that would take people's minds off the intense daily political pressures of the war. Every Wednesday she gathered together a group of friends at the great London family home, Londonderry House in Park Lane. This group of distinguished people was known collectively as the Ark. To be eligible you had either to be engaged at the front or in some way involved in war work. She created an order called the Order of the Rainbow, which was the sign of hope. The glittering membership was invited to give themselves special names. In *Retrospect* Mama summarised the rules. 'The members of the Order had to bear the name of either bird, insect, beast, or reptile, or else a mythological or magical creature. The name had to begin with the first letter of the Christian name or surname, or else it had to rhyme or be funny.' Winston Churchill became Winston the Warlock, Nancy Astor Nancy the Gnat, the first Viscount Hailsham became 'the Wild Boar' because his family name was Hogg, Harold Macmillan was known by fellow members as Harold the Hummingbird. Papa became Charley the Cheetah, although whether this was a dangerously ironic nickname, given my grandfather's compulsive infidelity, I do not know. The activities at Ark parties were fairly wild, as every Wednesday evening, pillars of political and social life would meet on the top floor of Londonderry

House. Painters, writers, soldiers and cabinet ministers gathered to converse and to exchange news, but also to have some fun, inject a little gaiety into life, play silly games, act charades, tell outrageous jokes, gossip like mad, flirt with each other and drink large quantities of the delicious pre-war Londonderry champagne that was stored in the great cellars beneath Park Lane.

Prime Ministers, past and present, including Ramsay Macdonald, Neville Chamberlain and Stanley Baldwin, all joined the club, as did Sir James Barrie (Barrie the Bard) and Queen Victoria's granddaughter Princess Helena Victoria (Victoria the Vivandière). And of course Edith was Circe, the sorceress, and the female Noah at the helm of her own Ark. I remember how Jane, Alastair and I loved playing among the stone statues of the Ark animals on the Dodo Terrace in a corner of the garden at Mount Stewart, little realising that we might be riding astride the back of the Prime Minister's namesake.

Members of the Ark, and other guests such as W. B. Yeats, Bernard Shaw, the teenage Prince Rainier of Monaco, the Spanish royal family and Douglas Fairbanks Junior would sit down to a sumptuous dinner in the Mount Stewart dining room, while Jane, Alastair and I would be banished to our nursery at the top of the house, joined sometimes by our cousins the Jessels and their fierce and disapproving nanny. The Jessels were the children of my father's sister Helen and her husband Teddy. Papa, who adored Helen but was fiercely anti-Semitic, had refused to attend their wedding and my own father went instead to represent the male side of the family.

Dashing through the immense black-and-white marble hall, we would run up the domed central staircase, passing Stubbs's huge portrait of the celebrated racehorse Hamletonian, being rubbed down by his groom after a famous win at Newmarket in 1799. I also remember rushing *down* the stairs, terrified that the yapping Pekes would appear but full of nervous excitement for the few dinners that, on reaching the age of thirteen, we were allowed to stay up for. On one memorably confident occasion I appeared at the top of the great balustrade, feeling rather grand and important wearing a white organza dress, which had been my bridesmaid's dress for a cousin's wedding. Sadly, I had never actually made the wedding because I caught mumps, and Jane had to stand in for me. But I did manage to hang on to the dress.

These were pre-school, and therefore lesson-free, days and our nursery was crammed with toys. However, there was one book which we grew to know well. In 1928, when my father's youngest sister Mairi was seven, my grandmother had written a fairy tale for her. *The Magic Inkpot* is set in a fantasy land 'where there is no time' and the children have all sorts of glorious adventures with the mysterious character who lives in the pot. The story is interwoven with old Irish legends and Mama would read this to us herself, giving us a break from the catechism. The huge joy of the story for us was that it was set in and around the familiar landscape of Mount Stewart itself. Tir-n'an-Og is an enchanted place in the book which means in Irish 'land of the ever young' where in real life Mama had made a walled garden, filled with climbing roses and olive trees grown from seeds sent from the Mount of Olives in Jerusalem. Mairi's elder sister Margaret illustrated the story with her delightful watercolours and Harold Macmillan's eminent firm published it. The tale is about two children with fairy blood in their veins and their adventures with the sooty character, the Magic Inkpot, who was no ordinary inkpot. He lived in a round flat box, surrounded by a flat piece of sponge with an island in the centre. He had a real face and smiled a glassy but very friendly smile, but he also had another secret identity as Dagda Mor, one of the ancient gods of Eire. In the story Mairi is seven years old (her true age in 1929) and Robin is a fictional six, although in reality he was twenty-seven. Mairi, the youngest, was the favourite of all of Mama's and Papa's five children.

Born twenty years after her first child, for Mama her arrival confirmed the unshakeable strength of her marriage to Papa and when Mairi married in 1941 Papa wrote to his wife, 'for over twenty years she has been the star in our little universe.' In the foreword Edith explains how she justifies Robin's age-altered involvement in the book: 'Robin really was a very big brother – too big for fairies to bother with – quite a grown-up and useless except for a good romp; but as he is much too precious to be left out, he has quite simply been made young again.'

My grandmother's evident love for Daddy was at that time still very strong and there is a charming and affectionate account in her autobiography of her son's performance as a page at the coronation of George V. He was only eight years old and, while he behaved beautifully during the ceremony, the strain of it all soon took its toll. He often told me how, bored, he had picked a fight with another page. They had been about to engage in a duel with their ceremonial swords when Daddy kicked off his shoe and aimed it at the boy. His mother describes what happened next.

The shoe shot past the boy and just skimmed the ear and coronet of an aged Peeress, falling with a clatter on the Abbey floor some distance away. Her enraged spouse, encased in his robes, advanced on Robin, whose cheeks now matched the colour of his mulberry red coat. The Peer was intent on administering a sound box on the ears of the culprit, when his grandmother, Lady Londonderry, bore down on both like an angry swan, swept Robin into the folds of her robe, and withered up the aged Peer with a scornful look – after which everyone laughed, and Robin was bundled into the Londonderry state coach and taken home.

My grandfather, the seventh Marquess, was a much more shadowy figure in my childhood than my grandmother. Mama had married him at the very end of the nineteenth century in November 1899. They had five children: four daughters – Maureen, Margaret, Helen, and Mairi – and my father, Robert, always known as Robin, the only son and the future eighth Marquess of Londonderry, but he was not their favourite child. The Stewart sisters were an impressive quartet, Mairi the youngest born only a few months after the marriage of her eldest sister Maureen. Maureen married Oliver Stanley, younger son of Lord Derby, a young up-and-coming MP who served as Under-Secretary for Home Affairs during the war and she shared with my father a much praised gift for public speaking, but tragically died during the war of tuberculosis.

Margaret, the second daughter, became a well-known war correspondent and fell in love with the famous French pilot and author of *Le Petit Prince*, Antoine de Saint-Exupéry.

Helen was acknowledged as the prettiest of the four sisters and Mairi, as the youngest and my father's co-star in *The Magic Inkpot*, was the most indulged by her parents and ultimately inherited Mount Stewart.

My grandfather was tall, thin and very bony, with an oddly high forehead. Chips Channon described his appearance as 'almost theatrically eighteenth century. Slim with an elegant figure and pointed features, he was red in the face and dressed with distinction.'

He had resigned from the Northern Ireland government in 1926 to spend his time managing the coal-mining properties in Durham on which the Londonderry fortune was based. At that time he owned 27,000 acres in Ireland, and 23,000 acres in England and Wales. In addition to Mount Stewart he had a huge house in London's Park Lane and five further large country houses including Wynyard, although in 1931, a few years before my birth, the Londonderrys decided they should economise by spending most of their time at Mount Stewart. Having served in the British cabinet under Stanley Baldwin in 1928, Papa joined Ramsay Macdonald's British National

Government in 1931 as Secretary of State for Air, where he did much to preserve the standing of the Royal Air Force and devoted himself to invaluable work on the development of radar. He was also successful in promoting the Hurricane and the Spitfire, aeroplanes that would play such an important part in the winning of the Battle of Britain.

While most British Nazi sympathisers of the early thirties became disillusioned with developments in Germany, my grandfather continued to remain on friendly terms with senior Nazi officers and in 1935, after an unfortunate public remark condoning air bombing, he was abruptly dropped from Baldwin's cabinet. Undeterred, in 1936 he visited Germany and was entertained by Goering and Ribbentrop, and Hitler himself gave a dinner in his honour. The hospitality was reciprocated and Alastair still has the Wynyard guest book containing Ribbentrop's signature made during a visit there in 1936, as well as the signatures of other famous but less controversial later guests including Churchill, Macmillan, the Queen Mother, Mick Jagger and the Supremes.

As children we saw very little of Papa. I remember particularly his long blue fingers, which we used to imitate, rigid as they hit the piano keys. I wondered if he was ever able to unbend and I now find it difficult to understand how this stiff, formal man was able to justify his reputation as a great lover. Once, during the final summer before his death when I was about thirteen, he asked me to take him by boat across the lake. I had just learned to row and to please me he asked me to show off my new skill. The oars were so large and heavy that I could only steer a very rocky and uncomfortable course, catching endless 'crabs', but he managed to sit serenely all the way across. He had made a great effort during that holiday and I had felt particularly close to him. On the day we left he kissed me goodbye and surprised me by putting one of those enormous old five-pound notes into my hand, then a huge amount of money. My last sight of him was of his tall figure waving goodbye as we climbed into the car, to go to the boat that would take us back to Wynyard.

The evidence of Papa's infidelities was more glaring than I had suspected. When I was growing up, we were often joined at Mount Stewart by the three Plunket brothers, Patrick, Robin and Shaun. Although they were much older than us we adored them and only at the age of eighteen did I discover that Jane, Alastair and I shared with them, as Shaun puts it, 'a mutual kinship' and that we were all first cousins.

Early in 1899, a few months before his engagement and marriage to Edith, my philandering grandfather had an affair with an older married American actress called Fannie Ward. Fannie was one of the famous Gaiety girls, of the Gaiety Theatre in London, and although she was not recognised as a great actress, her beauty, youthful looks and slim figure drew much admiration. When she played the stage part of the principal boy in *The Shop Girl* in 1884, reviewers said that the delicacy of her tiny rosebud mouth was only rivalled by the glory of her long slim legs. Always vague about her exact age, she was born in St Louis some time in the 1870s and hit the boards at about the age of fifteen. She was famous for being Cecil B. de Mille's (the early master of cinema) leading lady in his film *The Cheat* made in 1915 and she attributed her youthful appearance to a diet highly unusual in the Edwardian age of excess. 'Avoid sugar, fats, white bread, use ice for your complexion and go to sleep lying on the right side,' she advised. In her famous novel of 1925, *Gentlemen Prefer Blondes*, in which she satirises the sirens of the jazz age, Anita Loos was referring to Fannie when she wrote, 'When a girl is cute for fifty years it really gets to be history.' When Fannie's movie career finally came to an end she opened a beauty shop in Paris appropriately called the Fountain of Youth.

After Fannie's death in 1952 a Hollywood producer wanted to make a movie based on her memoirs and Lee Remick was chosen to play the lead. Unfortunately, a disreputable companion of her later years stole the manuscript and disappeared, together with all her jewellery, and the film was never made.

In 1899 Papa became smitten with Fannie when he saw her in a play called *The Cuckoo* and by the time Papa met Mama, Fannie had been Papa's mistress for several months. Six weeks after my grandparents' marriage at St Peter's Eaton Square, Fannie gave birth to a daughter, Dorothe. There was an unmistakable Londonderry look about the beautiful baby, but when Mama found out about her she was remarkably forgiving, her love for Papa overriding all other reactions of anger and jealousy. She even suggested adopting the child as their own. Over the years, Mama grew to accept her husband's repeated infidelities which, despite Papa's protestations of remorse, continued throughout their long marriage. When Dorothe's rich Air Force husband died suddenly of flu in 1918, he left a wealthy, beautiful, eighteen-year-old widow and my convention-defying grandmother rushed to comfort her. None of the five Londonderry children was told that she was their sister but Mama became devoted to her. So, unfortunately, did my father who was then sixteen years old. Unaware of the incestuous nature of his passion for this lovely young widow, he had to be gently discouraged. In 1922, Dorothe married as her second husband Teddy Plunket, an Irish baron from a neighbouring landowning family and a dashing serving soldier, the match having been much promoted by Mama. Their three sons, Patrick, Robin (now Lord Plunket) and Shaun grew up at Mount Stewart.

My grandfather was demonstratively fond of his grandsons, encouraging them in their cricket and promising them cash rewards if they should score in a match. To us three Stewarts they were the most glamorous human beings on this earth.

But there was to be a terrible tragedy. In 1938 Dorothe and Teddy were on holiday in California and, against all advice, they could not resist boarding a tiny private aeroplane to accept an invitation from Randolph Hearst to visit him at his ranch. As had been forecast, a blindingly thick coastal mist rolled in, causing the pilot to miss the runway, and Teddy and Dorothe were killed. My own parents and the Plunkets had been an inseparable and devoted foursome and, devastated by the accident, my parents never flew again.

After the death of his daughter, Papa became the legal guardian to the Plunket boys and the relationship between the cousins and their grandfather's wife grew very close. Shaun remembers asking 'Aunt Edie' if he and his elder brother Patrick could borrow the dining room at Londonderry House for a smart dinner party and how she agreed in affectionate approval when he told her that Patrick's date would be Princess Margaret, and that he would be bringing the actress Elizabeth Taylor.

My father's own early romantic adventures were a source of amusement for his parents. In 1928, when visiting a friend in Paris, he met a Frenchwoman whose morals were not exactly irreproachable. After a few days of fun together, during which she had apparently not been told his full name, Daddy prepared to return to London. The French lady asked for his address and, anticipating the disapproval of his parents should she follow him to Londonderry House, Daddy put his hand in his pocket and produced a visiting card. 'I would be delighted to see you again at this address,' he said as he gave her the card face down, and left. Daddy never discovered whether she followed up the invitation, knowing that on turning over the card, she would read the Right Hon. Stanley Baldwin, 10 Downing Street, London SW1.

In 1930 he fell in love with my mother. She was the daughter of Major Boyce Combe, an army officer, and his wife Gladys Combe. The Combes had two sons, Uncle Tony and Uncle Simon, and two daughters, Aunt Kitty and Mummy. They were a close, jolly, middle-class family with a terrific zest for life.

Uncle Tony was a magical figure, a tall, good-looking, strapping man who had served in the Royal Navy at the Battle of Jutland. He was a particular favourite with us because he had a wooden leg, which he had acquired in the most courageous way. Grandmother Combe had won on the Irish sweepstakes and divided up her winnings among her children. Uncle Tony used his money to go on a big game hunt in Rhodesia and, striding through the bush, he shot but failed to kill a lion. Following the strict jungle rule of never abandoning a wounded lion, he plunged back into the jungle to finish off the job. Suddenly the animal charged and as the bearers ran away in terror, the lion knocked Uncle Tony to the ground and managed to wrench off his leg. Displaying immense bravery, Uncle Tony fought back, shoving his hand down the lion's throat and eventually a beater, called Chinwara, came to the rescue and shot the lion dead, saving Uncle Tony's life. When he had recovered from his appalling injuries, Uncle Tony returned to Rhodesia and built his own ranch, which he named Chinwara, giving the position of overseer to Chinwara himself. We used to love the funny hollow noise his false leg made when we tapped it and I worshipped Uncle Tony, to whom I was as close as I was to my own father.

Uncle Simon was as handsome as his elder brother, with a long Combe nose but a much sterner manner. He had a very distinguished war record, having been a prisoner of war twice. He started his working life by rolling the barrels in the brewery of Watney Combe and Reid, and ended up as the chairman. He married Lady Silvia Coke, the sister of the fifth Earl of Leicester, and they had two children, Robin and Rowena.

Aunt Kitty, the youngest Combe, was Mummy's closest friend and was always staying with us. My father used to tease her unmercifully although he adored her. Kitty never married but she had many suitors. One of them, a Mr Nat Allgood, was extremely short in stature. Daddy would wait until she was sitting in the drawing room with Mummy and then get the butler to announce that a gentleman had come to call for Miss Kitty. Kitty would become quite agitated and start to fluff up her hair. The drawing-room door would be flung open to reveal not Mr Nat Allgood but Daddy, crawling in on all fours. 'Oh *Robin!*' Kitty would cry, half laughing and trying to hide her disappointment.

Mama had unsuccessfully floated a few infantas and daughters of senior peers past Daddy as potential wives, so in my grandparents' view the daughter of these warm, normal, worthy Combes did not amount to satisfactory marchioness material. However pretty and amusing Mummy may have been, she was not the dynastic bride that Mama had had in mind for her only son and heir. Even so, I cannot understand why they were quite so snobbish about Mummy. An injection of Combe blood was the best thing that ever happened to the Londonderry men who, given their women's inclination to dominate, had a tendency to weakness.

My parents met in October 1930 at Dunrobin, my grandmother's childhood home, a dramatically beautiful castle, with white turrets reminiscent of the great chateaux of the Loire. It is the largest house in the northern Highlands, balanced on the top of a cliff overlooking the North Sea in Sutherland. Dunrobin is allegedly the oldest inhabited house in Scotland and the Dukes of Sutherland have lived on this site since the first castle was built in 1235. Dunrobin was nearly destroyed by a dreadful fire in 1915 but the entire castle had been beautifully restored by the time Mummy knew it. She had been invited to stay there more than once by Maureen, Daddy's eldest sister, and she loved the huge romantic place with its gardens modelled on those at Versailles. I remember a time during the war when, unsure of what the future held, she told me sadly she could not imagine us ever having such fun as she had had at Dunrobin. On one of her visits there she met my own future father-in-law, the well-known painter Oswald Birley, and his beautiful wife Rhoda, who were fellow guests, while Oswald was painting the Duke of Sutherland.

Soon after their first meeting, Daddy invited Mummy to dinner at Londonderry House. Their courtship is recorded in extremely loving letters, which I still have. His are written in his careful neat hand while hers are more confident, even flamboyant, often in pencil, spilling over the edges of the Sussex Square notepaper. They fell quickly and passionately in love with each other and he left notes to be carried up with the breakfast tray, urging her to 'stay in bed and I will be there in a minute'. In the summer of 1931 he wrote, 'I am so much in love with you that I have got into a sort of moonstruck state. I have slept with your letters under my pillow.'

As their relationship developed, the authoritative concern that Mummy was to feel for Daddy until her death was already becoming apparent. She urged him to 'get fatter' and not to skip breakfast, and had a particular distaste for his occasional habit of drinking too much. Her father was nicknamed 'Boozer Combe' and, teetotal herself, she had no intention of marrying a man who drank. In contrast, Daddy's lack of self-regard, sense of inadequacy and dependence on her is quite clear in his letters to her: 'I do hope your family don't think I am too awful. They probably do and they are quite right. I could never understand why an angel like you could ever love something like me.'

As early as his schooldays at Eton Daddy had failed to establish an affectionate relationship with his father, disappointing him with his lack of interest in sport, particularly in cricket, riding and hunting. Things did not improve when he was nearly expelled for the prankish crime of stealing cigarettes. As my father grew older, and began to form his own political views, he withdrew even further from Papa, inheriting a deep social conscience from his mother.

Hints of the displeasure that the Londonderrys felt about their only son's increasingly serious romantic relationship soon began to emerge. My mother was referred to with withering condescension as 'little Miss Combe from Farnham'. Daddy revealed his apprehension on 8 July 1931 in a letter written to Mummy while on his way to Ireland to announce his engagement to his mother: 'I wrote a rather snappy letter to my father, the merry old marquis, saying that you and I thought it rather a good idea to get married. I added I should make a similar communication tomorrow to Edie, the messy old marchioness.' This bravado is followed by a jokey couple of lines: 'Everyone thinks you are an angel. What *your* family will think I don't know. They probably realise I am a moderate character and definitely not socially OK and that may be a snag.' On the same day Mummy writes nervously, 'I hope everything will run smoothly for us.'

But when Daddy arrived at Mount Stewart on 9 July his mother did not give him the sort of welcome he hoped for: 'There were the usual stock remarks that as both of us had liked other people before one had to be quite certain.'

By return of post, Mummy tried to comfort him: 'Poor darling. I hope you haven't been having too hard a time with the family all through me – I really feel badly about it – but I love you so much that nothing in this world matters really does it?'

Two weeks before the wedding, the mood had not improved, as Daddy wrote from Mount Stewart, 'I shall be overjoyed to leave this mournful atmosphere. The sooner we can get married and out of that domineering circle the better for all.' And a week later, an even more revealing letter: 'I fail to understand and am furious that my mother has made things so unpleasant for you. In future the more time we spend away from L. House the better, as mother is such a blasted busy body and will try and ruin everything. Father is all right at heart. Mother is different . . . I don't suppose any girl has ever been put in such a position by her prospective in-laws.'

I do not remember this prejudice being aired openly, but years later Mummy's maid, Rhoda, would hint darkly and sadly to me that my grandparents had not always been kind to my mother. She may have been exaggerating but after my mother's death the bitterness my father felt at their treatment of Mummy grew worse and when Papa lay dying Mama continued to keep Daddy at a distance, which he minded desperately although he did attend Papa's funeral in 1949 at Mount Stewart with the rest of the family. Not long before her own death I asked Mama about the feud but even then the answers she gave me continued to be evasive.

My parents were married on 31 October 1931 in London at St-Martin-in-the-Fields. Three of my four Londonderry aunts – Margaret, Helen and Mairi – were bridesmaids and Robin Plunket carried the ivory velvet train. Edith gave them exquisite sets of Irish linen sheets in every different colour and they moved straight away into 101 Park Street in Mayfair, a couple of hundred yards from Londonderry House. The following year my sister Jane Antonia Frances was born and two years after that my mother discovered she was having another baby.

TWO

My Arrival, the War
and the Brown House

Thunderstorms no longer seem to me as theatrical as they were when I was a child. On the night of my birth, after a stuffy, heavy summer's day, there was a tremendous and dramatic storm. The sky above the tall London town houses of Mayfair was floodlit by brilliant forks of lightning that flickered across the black sky, illuminating the midsummer darkness like the splayed fingers of some giant electrical hand. Years later my mother could still describe for me the long unforgettable drum roll that preceded the crash of each thunderclap.

Inside 101 Park Street on 11 June 1934 the tense atmosphere that accompanies any home birth was unusually heightened. The principal players in the drama, already the parents of a two-year-old girl, were, like most dynastic families, eagerly awaiting the arrival of a son and heir. But this particular birth held an even deeper significance for my father who hoped that by producing a son and fulfilling his dynastic responsibilities he would alleviate some of the displeasure his parents felt in him for marrying Mummy. The arrival of a second daughter, delivered by the family doctor and attended by Sister Doris, must have been a blow, although my parents never spoke to me of their disappointment, always taking care to emphasise what a very pretty baby I had been. They had prepared a weighty directory of names for their son. He was to have been called Alexander Charles Robert Stewart. For me they chose just one, as I was named Annabel after my mother's favourite song, 'Miss Annabel Lee', a hugely popular hit of the 1930s with a refrain that went 'She's wonderful, she's beautiful, Miss Annabel Lee'. My godfather Hughie Northumberland (the Duke of Northumberland) loved the song so much that I can remember my mother playing it for him when he came to visit us during the war.

I was christened at Mount Stewart by the Primate, the premier bishop of Northern Ireland, and the photographs that open the album my mother made for me show a rather grim scene as all the guests are dressed in black except for Mummy and me. However, when I look at the pictures of Jane's and Alastair's christenings, the guests at those occasions look equally serious, the current obligatory wide toothy smile not then a requirement for family poses. In the photographs the dog-collared Primate appears very grand and splendid, with his neat-cropped white beard. Beneath his black-waisted gown and frock coat he is wearing tight black leggings, which are neatly buttoned at the side from thigh to ankle and from which his black patent leather spats emerge. Mummy is beside him, elegant, beautiful, nervous, in white wool, her shoes tied at the front with a bow, and she is holding me, although I am almost invisible under the folds of the lacy Londonderry christening gown. Mama sits beside her, a black feather in her hair, with Jane perched uncomfortably on her knee and, from the alarmed expression on Jane's face, rather too close to the great wet nose of one of Mama's enormous lurchers. Standing behind them is a very stiff-looking Daddy with his three rather stern-faced sisters, Margaret, Mairi and Helen. There is not a Combe in sight.

My godparents were Patsy Ward, Hughie Northumberland and Billy Ednam (Viscount Ednam). Patsy Ward was Eric Dudley's (the Earl of Dudley) sister, one of my mother's best friends and I adored her. Hughie was one of my father's greatest friends and after the war Daddy was best man at his marriage to the beautiful Elizabeth Montagu Douglas Scott, the daughter of the Duke of Buccleuch.

My third godparent, Billy Ednam, was only fourteen and had been invited to become a godfather for a not altogether godly reason. Although my father enjoyed shooting, he always hated the stalking and killing of stags, much to the disappointment and contempt of Papa. One weekend, shortly after my birth, Daddy and Billy Ednam, son of Eric Dudley, Daddy's cousin (and nephew of Patsy Ward), were staying at Dunrobin Castle and Daddy realised that by conspiring with the willing young Billy he would be able to get out of a disagreeable and arduous day's stalking. Leaving the house with the other guns in the morning, Daddy shoved his sandwiches in one pocket and a book in the other. As soon as he got out on to the moor he threw himself down in the heather and spent the day happily reading his book and eating his sandwiches, well away from the sound of the guns until it was time to come home. Billy, who had thoroughly enjoyed his day, shot two stags, attributing one to Daddy. As a reward for his co-operation, Daddy and Mummy asked Billy to be my godfather, and Billy and his family have remained great friends of mine.

Despite Daddy's antipathy for stalking, in all other ways he was a man of the countryside and we were certainly brought up as country children. Not until after leaving school did I show any inclination, nor was I given the opportunity, to spend much time in London. However, I do have one very early London memory when Jane and I went to tea at Buckingham Palace. We had been invited to a large party given by George VI and Queen Elizabeth. We were taken by our parents and, dressed in our best clothes, queued up to meet the King and Queen. I was beside myself with excitement because I was convinced that I was going to meet the kind of king I had heard about in fairy stories. This was a televisionless age, so we had no idea what the King looked like in real life and I thought he would be wearing cloth of gold, preferably hard gold resembling the cloak that Rumpelstiltskin had transformed from straw for the unfortunate queen, and that he would have a gleaming gold crown on his head. Suddenly I found myself in front of a small, grey-suited man. My mother nudged me to curtsy but I found myself unable to move, as I stared at him in amazement. 'Are *you* the King?' I asked in a loud, clear and thoroughly puzzled voice. There was silence, followed by quite a few laughs. I was too young to be embarrassed, but my parents must have been mortified.

Although we spent many glorious days at Mount Stewart, until Papa's death in 1949 we did not officially have a country house of our own. We never went abroad and I remember several summer holidays in a wonderful hotel at Hunstanton on the Norfolk coast, near my Uncle Simon and his family at Blakeney. But even before Papa officially left Wynyard to my father in his will, we would spend time there and it was the place I grew to love most. While Mount Stewart offered every childhood luxury imaginable, Wynyard, in County Durham, although in some ways no less grand, was the place where we were allowed to run free.

On one early visit to Wynyard, in the late summer of 1936, my sister and I joined our parents there, accompanied by our nanny, Bella Fraser, and Ruth, the nursery maid. Mummy was heavily pregnant and was already at Wynyard, awaiting the birth of Alastair. Somewhere along the route our car, which must have been going rather fast, drove head-on into another car and a large hay wagon. The impact threw us all into a chaotic jumble on top of each other on to the car floor. I only have very vague recollections of the accident itself, which was so serious that two people in the other car were killed, but it made a great impression on me, and for years afterwards I would become hysterical at the sight of hay wagons and lorries carrying hay. I had terrible nightmares about them and for some unknown reason I named these hay wagons Boswell Hazy.

Ruth was badly bruised and cut in the accident and so

was Bella Fraser, but while Jane seemed quite unscathed, I screamed every time anyone touched me. The doctor who examined me could not find anything wrong with me and years later Mummy told me that he had been drunk. I continued screaming all night and an X-ray the next day revealed that my hip was very badly fractured. Although the memory of the pain has dimmed, I do remember the Boswell Hazy nightmares and being pushed around in a wheelchair. I have photographs of myself lying in bed at Wynyard with my leg in a huge plaster cast stretching from my hip to my knee. For a child aged two and a half, who had only recently revelled in the newfound skill of walking and running, it must have been a dreadful thing to endure. Sister Doris, who had looked after my mother during and after the home births of the three of us, always seemed to be present at critical moments throughout my young life and, ever reliable, she appeared to nurse me after the Boswell Hazy accident and to try to encourage me to eat. Fifteen years after Boswell Hazy it would be Sister Doris to whom the task fell of breaking the news to me of my mother's death.

When I was only five those early holidays at Wynyard were interrupted by the outbreak of war. No-one was prepared for the devastation that the air raids and the Blitz would bring. During these raids, which usually took place at night following the siren's warning, everyone would hurry to the bomb shelters and sit out the bombardment. Emerging exhausted and anxious in the morning after the 'all clear' siren had sounded, it was not uncommon to find your own house or that of your neighbour completely flattened. Many friends of my parents' generation, who were unable or unwilling to leave London because of their war work, have described to me very vividly what the raids were like, with the skies lit up and the heavy assault from the artillery guns returning fire on the German planes, which relentlessly shelled the City. As well as the fear and the fatigue, because no one ever seemed to get a good night's sleep, there was a great feeling of camaraderie and sharing of tea and sandwiches among those people who were crowded together in the shelters and the Underground stations.

In common with other very large houses, Wynyard was requisitioned by the army and turned into a teachers' training college as soon as war broke out. Mount Stewart was also denied us during those six years as Ireland was too far and too dangerous to visit, but as an immediate threat was imposed on those living in cities my parents were anxious to move us out of London to the comparative safety of the country. Most city children were evacuated to the country and London railway stations were suddenly filled with young evacuees getting on to trains, luggage labels tied round their necks, many going to live with complete strangers who had offered to look after them for the duration of the war. It must have been heartbreaking for both parents and children who knew it might be many months before they saw each other again. But we were particularly fortunate as, when our family moved away from London, we remained together.

My parents set about trying to find a suitable house although between 1939 and 1942, until we finally settled at the Brown House, we travelled around the country from rented house to house, memories of which are enhanced by the masses of little black-and-white photographs, painstakingly recorded and stuck into the albums by my mother. In 1940 we were at Askham Hall near Penrith in Cumbria, and in 1941 at Ramsbeck, in Cumbria on Lake Ullswater, where my mother took some enchanting pictures of Alastair with a mop of golden curls, wearing a miniature army uniform. The dogs came everywhere with us, as did our governess Melle and, at the beginning, our nanny Bella Fraser, the youngest daughter of the head gamekeeper at Wynyard who had come to work for us when Jane was born. I have one surviving picture of her, taken when she was holding Alastair at his christening at

Wynyard, a tiny figure, dwarfed by Papa standing behind her. At Ramsbeck she became seriously ill and, although forbidden to do so, I remember peeping into her bedroom and seeing her lying there looking very pale and tired. She beckoned to me to come and talk to her, but I refused as I was too afraid of defying Melle to go in and a little while later Bella Fraser died of cancer.

After Ramsbeck we moved to Hill House on Richmond Hill in Yorkshire, and I have never experienced such cold as I did there. Some mornings there would be icicles hanging from the windows *inside* Jane's and my bedroom, and we were made to wear liberty bodices over our vests, which were intended to provide insulation but were horribly uncomfortable and so restricting that they achieved the opposite of their proud claim. Melle, a fresh-air fiend, would drag us out for long walks in the snow, but despite the exercise we never seemed to feel warm.

Finally my parents found the Brown House in what is now known as the stockbroker belt, on Worpleston Hill in Brookwood, Surrey. Lying on the edge of a golf course, it was only a short railway journey from London for my father. Many of the army camps were nearby, as well as the Military Academy at Sandhurst and all the men in Mummy's photograph albums are dressed in army uniform, including a very bored-looking Patrick Plunket with Jane and me clinging to his arm.

In a curious link with my future husband, I discovered later that the house was owned by Jimmy Goldsmith's uncle and as a young subaltern Jimmy would stay there, exhausted when on leave, sleeping for forty-eight hours at a time. He grew up hearing stories of 'those dreadful Castlereagh children', a just assessment because Jane, Alastair and I had enjoyed using a large painting of Jimmy's paternal grandmother for bow and arrow target practice. Mrs Goldsmith was a formidable-looking lady who had a well-rounded décolletage, at which we would let fly a volley of arrows. The point of the game was to try to place your arrow between her breasts, not a difficult task for a good shot, owing to the size of her bosom, but to us inexpert archers accuracy was a challenge and most of the portrait soon became pitted with tiny holes. Subsequently, in order to reduce the unsightly scarring of the Goldsmith ancestral chest, the painting had to be cut down to a quarter of its original size. Years later the story of the destruction of the portrait became one of Jimmy's favourites and Alastair used to beg Jimmy to tell it again and again, never tiring of the repetition.

For the greater part of the war the Brown House was our home and as a small child the house seemed to me rather large. A typical turn-of-the-century 'villa' on a golf course, its Edwardian wooden beams supplied the obvious name, although it was a house filled with such happiness that I never associated the name with darkness or gloom. The schoolroom was next door to the drawing room and there were french windows leading on to the lawn at the front. There was also a veranda, on which I can still vividly see Uncle Tony and Aunt Kitty bending near to share each other's conversation, their heads thrown back in laughter, Uncle Tony's bull terrier between them at their feet.

Behind the house there was a large wood where Jane and Alastair and I built wigwams and pretend houses, and there was a big kitchen garden where we grew our own vegetables although the imagination of any cook must have been very stretched to come up with good menus during rationing. However, there was a bustling black market, and sugar and the occasional bar of chocolate would be slipped our way, as well as the odd pair of silk stockings for Mummy.

In our least favourite part of the garden there was a chicken run where we were made to feed the chickens, our hands wet and cold, developing chilblains before our eyes. There was no sentimental reason for keeping these chickens as their eggs were crucial during rationing and sometimes we ate them roasted for lunch, and there were also rabbits that Melle would fatten up for the pot. On one of their visits my grandparents brought us each a pet bantam. Jane and I were given little black hen females and Alastair received a cockerel with magnificent gold plumage. I called my bantam Josie, but when Alastair named his cockerel 'Jesus' my grandmother said she would take it away unless he changed his sacrilegious choice. Alastair declared himself adamant and threw a tantrum, while Jane and I managed to assure Mama that we would persuade him to change the name as soon as she had gone. But Alastair refused to be budged and Jesus spent his war strutting around the chicken pen keeping a beady eye on his harem.

Before the war we had lived a very outdoor life and, in the absence of our ponies, Mummy was anxious that we should continue to have some formal exercise. She recruited a Sergeant from one of the local army camps to come to the Brown House twice a week to give gym classes and build up our muscles. The Sergeant would line us up and put us through our paces. On hot days everyone was allowed to take their vests off, with the exception of me because Melle thought I was too skinny. One day our sessions with the Sergeant abruptly stopped. I never questioned why at the time because I was only too relieved to be let off the hook from these physical exertions, but years later I was told he had been sacked for turning us upside down by our ankles and dangling us like little Lolitas with our knickers showing.

Another visitor from the army base was an American, Harley P. Mosley, whom for obvious reasons we nicknamed Baldhead. He was rather taken aback after Alastair asked him one day at lunch, 'How old are you?' Followed by, 'Has your mother got a beard?' He was not to know that for a time Alastair asked every man he met the same two questions.

Shortly after we moved into the Brown House an efficient lady in uniform came down to discuss the blackout and to show us how to tape the windows. Because of the dangers of flying glass from bomb blasts, windows were taped in a criss-cross fashion in every room. Black blinds had to be pulled down at lighting-up time. After dusk it was strictly against the rules for any window in the land to allow even a chink of light to show through and there were regular visits from wardens who came to make sure the total blackout was enforced.

In the beginning, war seemed to us children like an adventure and we were too young to take much interest in the radio or in reading newspapers. However, I was to become increasingly aware of the seriousness of events.

Although we were safely out of central London, we were near enough for the occasional German aircraft to fly overhead and in June 1944 the Germans started a campaign involving pilotless flying bombs known as Doodle Bugs. Their destination was London but occasionally the programming went wrong and they fell in the middle of the countryside, short of their target. Resembling conventional dull-grey aeroplanes, but distinguished by the brilliant orange streak of flame pouring from the back, they passed over the Brown House several times during that summer. Flying at 400 miles an hour, they made a terrifying staccato roaring and rattling sound, like an enormous motorbike whose muffler had dropped off the exhaust. Even more frightening than the noise was the silence after the engine had cut out because then you knew they would drop like a giant bird wherever they were. I remember with intense clarity being woken one night by the sound of one of them directly above me. Instinctively trying to take cover, I dived under the bed, where I shook with terror as the engine fell silent, certain that the bomb was going to land on our house. I was not far wrong, as it landed less than a mile away on a garage and the next day we all went to look at the vast crater it had made. From that moment I began to realise that I was not living through an adventure at all.

As a result of the sudden mass employment in the war effort, the hierarchy changed in any house that employed domestic staff and ours was no exception. Thus war became a great leveller of society, even for those few who for various reasons were not called up. Instead of serving lunch, servants were serving their country and countesses were said to have milked cows while earls ploughed the fields. Lady Diana Cooper kept her own cow called Princess at her farm in Bognor, causing something of a local stir by painstakingly milking it herself.

By 1943, because of the absence of so many men abroad, almost 90 per cent of single and 80 per cent of married women were employed in some sort of war work as nearly everyone was required by an act of Parliament to do their duty. (Mummy, although officially exempt as the mother of three young children, was involved in working for the local Red Cross.) Thousands of women joined the auxiliary services as WRNs in the Navy, WAAFs in the Air Force and ATS in the Territorial Army, others went to work in the munitions, tank and aircraft factories, and many became nurses. Some even took jobs driving trains and operating anti-aircraft guns, employment that had until then traditionally been 'men's work'. Many joined the Women's Voluntary Service, helping in a variety of emergency services at home, and the Women's Land Army provided much needed help on British farms while thousands more joined my grandmother's successful effort to reactivate her Women's Legion of the First World War.

Our governess, Mademoiselle Cretegny, known to us as Melle, had arrived in our lives in 1938 and stayed until all three of us had left to go away to boarding school, but with the outbreak of war Melle's circumstances also altered. Having been the family governess, waited on hand and foot, she suddenly found herself doing a bit of everything, from helping in the kitchen to, eventually, taking over the nannying duties of Bella Fraser who was by then very frail. Melle was small and round, and rather brown-skinned, who not only *looked* like a brown bun but wore her hair in one. She had very long black hair and she would let it down when she went to bed and carefully pin it all up again by breakfast. She became increasingly authoritarian, much to the disapproval of Bella Fraser who could have done with a lot less strictness, and fewer of the airs and graces that Melle felt went with her rather senior position in the household.

Melle's disciplinary tactics included our only experience of corporal punishment, for neither of my parents ever smacked us, preferring to reprimand us far more effectively through an altered tone of voice or a withering comment. Melle had commandeered for her own purposes a rather beautiful small green Spanish riding whip that had originally been given to me as a birthday present by a cousin. An act of rebelliousness would result in a sharp slap of the whip from Melle on the backs of our legs, which particularly hurt when our legs were wet from the bath. After we had been tucked up in bed for the night we would creep out on to the landing, but Melle's ears were very sharp and, hearing the creaking floorboards, she would come flying up the stairs whip in hand, by which time I would have jumped into bed, leaving Alastair to take the punishment. One day Jane, more confident than us having spent a few terms at boarding school, managed to steal the green riding whip and hurl it over a hedge in the garden where thankfully it remained, lost for ever.

As the eldest, Jane was given the most onerous tasks by Melle, not the least of which was to keep an eye on Alastair and me. This was not easy as we were very unruly, but she accepted her responsibilities willingly and the same qualities that are inherent in her now were apparent in her as a small girl. Instinctively caring and honest, although only ten years old herself when we arrived at the Brown House, Jane's early experience caring for her younger siblings was invaluable when later she became the motherly figure on whom Alastair and I grew to rely.

Only when I went to boarding school did I realise what a truly good teacher Melle had been. I arrived at school academically a year ahead of my contemporaries, excelling at French, even though I spoke it with the slight Swiss-German accent we had picked up from Melle.

But the lessons I learned from her went far beyond the academic. For it was Melle who taught me how to sew lavender bags and, in a time of scarcity during the war, it was she who showed me how to appreciate the value of things home-made rather than shop-bought, in particular a memorably favourite birthday present of a farmyard made from cardboard. She had a skilful way of making me believe that I yearned for things that were in reality necessities: a new dressing gown to replace the old holey one became a genuine object of desire. She showed me the fun to be had from blackberrying and she even tried to teach me to knit, although I was hopeless at it. She was in charge of the rabbits and, in cleverly disguised self-interest, managed to persuade me that all I wanted for Christmas was a new rabbit hutch. She taught me things I never learned from anyone else.

Melle was also responsible for the nightly transformation of our lank hair into a mass of curls. Every evening she would sit Jane and me down on chairs and, using the hard brown wartime loo paper, would roll our hair round the paper into a series of knobbly parcels. In the morning she would remove the paper to reveal the curls. Sleeping in these home-made rollers was at first torture, but in common with straight-haired little girls up and down the land, we soon got used to them although we were always relieved on Melle's night off when Mummy was in charge as we knew she could not be bothered with the hated rollers. We were certainly in awe of Melle and she was undeniably strict, but despite the odd whacks, we all adored her.

When she arrived to be our governess, she brought her blue budgerigar, Gary, with her, and carried him around everywhere in his cage. She absolutely worshipped Gary and he was

41

rather engaging, especially as he was very tame and could say 'hello'. Occasionally, maddened by his incessant chirping, Jane and I would surreptitiously shove a pillow over his cage to muffle him. But when Gary became ill, Melle carried him everywhere in her hand, tears rolling down her cheeks and she was inconsolable when he died a few days later. Today I would probably cry with her, but then I remember Jane and me finding the idea of such grief shown over a little bird rather funny. There was something enduringly safe about Melle and when eventually we went away to school and she left us to look after the children of Bernard Norfolk's (the Duke of Norfolk) sister, we missed her dreadfully, although she would come back to help us for the odd holiday by which time she had mellowed greatly.

Melle and my mother were the pivots around which we existed and for me the years at the Brown House were exceptionally golden. Despite the seriousness of the political situation, nothing could diminish the air of gaiety and laughter that surrounded our mother. Born in 1904, two years younger than Daddy, she was thirty-five when war broke out and as soon as the immensely grand trappings of Mount Stewart, Wynyard and even, to an extent, Park Street were left behind her she allowed herself to breathe freely. By the time she was living at the Brown House, a happily married mother of three, she had found her self-confidence. She was very flirtatious, with a speaking voice that was shot through with irrepressible merriment and gaiety. She thrived on being surrounded by people, and people, especially men, found her irresistible.

There is an angularity and severity about the contemporary photographs of her which disguise her beauty but Edmund Brock's lovely portrait comes closest to capturing her vitality and luminosity. The painting, almost life-size, hangs today on the staircase at Ormeley. Large, wide-apart brown eyes look down from a gently pointed, rather olive-skinned face.

Conscious of taking care of her complexion, she had written to Daddy a month before they got married, 'I'm longing to sunbathe, but dare not because of my wedding day appearance.' She would always say to me that she considered it prettier to 'go gold not brown', although my own children tease me about my passion for the sun, which I obviously did not inherit from her. In the painting she is wearing a pale peachy pink coat which falls in folds over a cream silk evening dress and there is no suggestion of a timid 'little Miss Combe'. On the contrary, a self-assured young woman, with slightly wavy side-parted brown hair, her hand on her hip, looks out at you, determined and yet with an eminently kissable mouth.

Despite the battering that she had taken from Mama and Papa as the fiancée and young bride to their son, she managed to survive their criticism and by the end of her life Mama had become rather fond of her. Jane clearly remembers listening to a conversation between Mama and Mummy a little while before the wedding of Mairi, Daddy's youngest sister, in 1941. They were discussing the wedding dress and Mama was clearly close enough to Mummy to ask her opinion on whether the cut of the neck should be round or square. I believe that my grandparents grew to respect her and be grateful for her influence over their son, as they came to recognise that Daddy's sobriety depended on the support and encouragement he received from Mummy. She was, they finally acknowledged, a force for the good.

Motherhood suited her. For a woman of her generation she was the most hands-on mother I have ever heard of. One of my very earliest memories is at Mount Stewart when, although there were dozens of nannies and maids employed to care for us, it was Mummy I chose to rush to, burying my head in her lap as I poured out my woes. We lived a life unusually liberal for those days. She delighted in the company of her children and encouraged us to join in the adult world, in a manner far removed from the rigidity and formality of the Mount Stewart environment. Ours was an inclusive rather than exclusive wartime existence, unusual during a time which was so divisive for so many others.

We were instinctively infected by her sense of freedom, and found ourselves shrugging off childhood inhibitions and shyness as we were encouraged to join the large parties of friends who would come to fill the big lawn in front of the house. Many came down from London, and there were others like us who had escaped the city and were living nearby including Pat Wilson (later Laycock) and her three children. She had previously been married to Lord Jersey, by whom she had one daughter, Caroline Child-Villiers, who became a great friend of mine. Other visitors included David Ogilvy (later Lord Airlie), and Peter and Victory Ducane, and their three children, Diana, Margaret-Anne and Charles.

Before her illness Mummy could make us laugh till we cried. When a persistent bore would telephone, she would pick up the receiver and, adopting a cockney accent, pretend to be the daily. 'Lady Castlereagh's not in at the moment. And I'm busy doing the cleaning.' Continuing, 'I'm busy cleaning the stairs now. I'm the daily.' And then, hardly bothering to disguise her voice, 'I'm down on my knees, scrubbing away. I've got one set of steps to do and then the other set,' and, seeing us doubled up with laughter she would go on, 'Then it's the basins,' by which time we all knew that the person on the other end of the telephone must have seen through her. 'That foxed them!' she would say triumphantly, hanging up. In addition to her sense of fun, there was a calmness and serenity about my mother, a dependability that reassured all those who knew her. This inner quiet, as well as her powerful faith in God, must have sustained her in the terrible long years of her illness.

As if taking the lead from Mummy, Daddy was also happy during those years. He would visit the Brown House as often as he could, although he was frequently abroad with the Royal

Artillery, having been largely exempted from his duties as Conservative Member of Parliament for County Down. During the time we were at Hill House and Ramsbeck he was away at sea, in Trinidad, and in 1942 he was based in Baghdad. Later when we were at the Brown House he was in the Middle East and I remember the rather exotic carved wooden bracelets he brought us on one of his visits. He missed us all dreadfully when he was away and I have many of the yearning letters he wrote to my mother, although unfortunately her replies have not survived. In August 1941 after a brief visit home he wrote to her, 'It was lovely seeing you and saying goodbye was lousy. It is sad to think I shall not see you or the children for so long. You look exactly the same age as when I first saw you, but the children change so quickly. I hardly recognise them and they won't know me. You must look after yourself and three very sweet children. I am miserable at the separation.'

Throughout his life my father adored children and having a rather childish side to his character he was brilliant at inventing games guaranteed to amuse us, which used to take place the moment we were put to bed by Melle supposedly for lights off and sleep. She was very disapproving of these games and would wander around with pursed lips muttering under her breath in French. Daddy would first go to Alastair who slept with Melle in the room next door to Jane and me. One of these entertainments involved a fictional character called Mr Barber, the principal of St Asaph's School, interviewing Alastair as a prospective candidate. Daddy would play Mr Barber and would ask Alastair a series of questions to which Alastair would answer in nonsensical sentences like 'To mit to ra'. Inevitably the 'interview' would end up with a pillow fight and shrieks of laughter. By this time Melle would be tearing out her hair but did not dare to interrupt.

The best game of all was Dr Jekyll and Mr Hyde. Daddy would drag a large German shell up the stairs, which he had somehow acquired during the war, bringing with him a wooden cooking spoon for a gong. First he would play the role of Dr Jekyll doing the rounds of the room as if at a cocktail party, unctuously moving between our beds saying, 'Ah my dear Duchess, how charming you look this evening,' or, 'Countess, how wonderful to see you again.' Then he would turn off the lights, beating the wooden spoon on the German shell twelve times to announce that it was midnight and time for the transformation. We would shiver with excitement and anticipation as he suddenly turned into Mr Hyde and pretended to murder us. All this was very unsuitable for children who were theoretically settled for the night but it was such fun. Sometimes Daddy would read to us, choosing one of Grimm's fairy tales, or one of Rudyard Kipling's short stories or, as we got slightly older, passages from our favourite writer Saki. He also took us regularly on to the golf course where we were all given golf lessons. None of us became good enough to play with him but we would follow him around adoringly.

These halcyon days were not entirely cloudless as we were well aware that Daddy himself could be as changeable as Dr Jekyll and that if he was in a bad mood, or, as we later discovered, if he had been drinking, he would become very stern and irritable. Although at that stage his tempers were infrequent, he was undoubtedly capable of frightening us.

But far worse than the unpredictability of Daddy's moods was the gradual awareness that all was not well with our mother. There came a time, well before the end of the war, when she began to take the train up to London. None of us children was told the reason for her absences, but we gathered it was something to do with her health. Between us we concluded at first that she was going to have a baby and we were terribly excited, waiting for the news. But no news came and no one wanted to talk to us about Mummy's illness. With time the illness became a mystery that we accepted and never challenged although we were aware that it was something to do with her mouth and 'Mummy's

Mouth' became a condition we learned to live with. But as we watched our vibrant life-enhancing mother begin slowly to withdraw from people and into the loneliness of the illness that in those days dared not speak its name, the sound of laughter seemed to fade from our lives.

THREE

Boarding School

I was eleven in September 1945 when I arrived at Southover Manor, a boarding school on the edge of the South Downs in Lewes in East Sussex. I was quite small, rather plain and very thin, with lank, brownish hair. The uniform of chocolate-coloured shifts and burnt-custard-yellow shirts made even the most beautiful girls hideous and certainly did nothing to improve my own appearance. But although my upbringing had so far been rather insular, I was a confident child, excited if a little apprehensive at the prospect of being with so many girls of my own age and of joining my sister Jane, who had already been at the school for two years. I was irrepressibly high-spirited and people probably thought me bumptious. War was over and at times I regarded the whole idea of school as my next great adventure although, having heard some of Jane's experiences, I had also been dreading leaving home for well over a year. Little did I know how grim some of the school experience would indeed prove to be.

As feared, I never did get over my homesickness and would sob when Jane and I were put on the Lewes train at Victoria Station at the beginning of every term. I missed my mother dreadfully. I do not remember her ever visiting me while I was at Southover, although I am sure she would have come had she not feared showing her mouth in public. She once managed to go and see Alastair at his prep school, Ludgrove, and he has a photograph taken on that day, at a school cricket match where she is wearing dark glasses and covering her mouth with her hand, trying to draw away from the camera as it intrudes on the sight of the ugly scabbing that covered her lips.

Once, when I was ill myself, confined to bed in the school san with glandular fever, a letter came from Daddy saying that Mummy had gone into hospital for yet another operation, and asking me if I would write to cheer her up. I never liked to let anyone see me cry, but that time my usual resilience deserted me and I felt deeply depressed after receiving Daddy's letter. Glandular fever does tend to depress one anyway but Mummy's illness began to sound hopeless to me. Unaware of the true gravity of the case, I could not understand why her mouth had not improved. I began to ask myself for the first time whether she would ever be well. I longed for life to go back to the way it used to be when Mummy was happy and well. If anybody had asked me what I wished for most in the world I would have told them that I wanted Mummy's mouth to get better.

My father would try to come down once or twice a term to take Jane and me out to lunch in Brighton. The excitement that built up in advance of these visits was enormous and they never failed to live up to expectations. We would explore the inexhaustible delights of the two great Victorian piers, the West Pier (parts of which in 2003 were not only destroyed by fire but also collapsed into the sea after a particularly fierce storm) and the Palace Pier, with the ghost train and the bumper cars and the choc ices, all followed by an enormous lunch at the Metropole Hotel on the seafront. At the end of the day out I would get that familiar sinking feeling as we drove back to Lewes, knowing I would not see Daddy for weeks. Daddy always hated tears but I was unable to stop them flowing at the final hug.

Tiredness, too, must have exacerbated my longing for home. The school was in the centre of the town and somewhere outside my dormitory window there was a church bell, which chimed on the hour every hour, day and night. Some nights, perhaps once or twice a term, I would lie in the dark, tearfully counting the rings at two, three and four in the morning. On these occasional sleep-deprived nights, the only child awake in a crowded dormitory, I felt intensely lonely. My desperation for sleep became an obsession and I remember very clearly the anxiety I felt at the prospect of being exhausted yet again by the time morning lessons arrived. My frustration was increased by the teachers' refusal to believe me, and by their expectation and assumption that at night-time children slept. The sound of church bells has depressed me ever since.

Many people of my generation remember their post-war schooldays as far harsher than life today in an open prison. There was minimal central heating and we were always cold. We wore jerseys and socks in bed, and the only radiators that seemed to work were in the cloakrooms. There we would warm our chilblained fingers for as long as we could tolerate the overwhelming stench of the loos. There was no carpeting, no privacy and the food was revolting as rationing removed all the enjoyment of eating. Nonetheless, food was the highlight of most of the girls' lives and our days were punctuated by meals. For me they brought no pleasure, either gastronomic or social, and I dreaded the sound of the bell summoning us to the stark dining room with its long central trestle table. I was very underweight, which greatly concerned my father, and he wrote to the school requesting that my meals should be eaten under supervision. For a while I was made to sit next to matron and became quite ingenious at dropping food into my napkin without being spotted. By the end of the meal, sticky lumps of porridge, and grey powdered scrambled egg were all secretly and glutinously piled on my lap.

Occasionally we were given the great treat of a long iced bun for tea and a few sweets were handed out each week by the prefects. I would eat all mine immediately and I was maddened by the self-control shown by some girls, who managed to spin out their supply until bedtime, and I would bribe girls into giving me their entire ration in return for doing their French homework. Under rationing rules, cakes and sweets were only sent from home on our birthdays. But girls were allowed to receive butter in the post. Most girls were sent shop butter, but mine came straight from the Wynyard Farm estate. Normally this butter would have been far more delicious than its commercial equivalent but home-made butter lacks preservatives and has to be eaten within two days. By the time it reached me at school it had invariably turned rancid.

Breakfast was followed by Assembly, after which we would rush to the hall to see if we had any letters or parcels. I would feel a little guilty at my disappointment when I saw the oblong shape in its brown wrapper waiting for me on the hall table, knowing that it would contain nothing more exciting than the weekly slab of inedible butter.

But I wanted to fit in and to be popular with my fellow pupils, and I learned quickly to draw approving attention to myself by being naughty because I knew it made the other girls laugh. One day I persuaded a couple of members of my gang to help me steal the school bell. It was a vast, unwieldy, gunmetal-grey object, which reached as high as my knees, and this cumbersome timekeeper controlled the school routine. Somehow we managed, unseen, to lug it up the backstairs and hide it in the dormitory clothes cupboard. With the school at a standstill the headmistress, Miss Aspden, threatened every pupil with serious punishment unless someone owned up. Not wanting to get my friends into any more trouble, I moved the bell by myself to what I considered a less incriminating hiding place. Girls were not allowed in the staff lavatory, but by suspending the bell from the indoor handle I could be certain that as soon as a teacher opened the door the bell would be jostled and begin to clang. This prank established me as one of the school comedians and gave me everlasting notoriety as the only girl there ever to receive corporal punishment with a smack on the hand.

My naughtiness grew by increments and soon it had blossomed into a rebellious courage. When I was about fifteen I was mad about the film star Gregory Peck and to my delight I discovered that *Captain Hornblower*, starring my pin-up, was playing at the cinema in Lewes. I had, with considerable foresight, joined the Girl Guides and in the absence of any other applicants for the position had appointed myself Leader of the Bullfinch Patrol. During our interminable banner-wielding marches outside the school grounds I would abandon my group, run into the local bakers and, with saved-up pocket money, buy myself the sublime treat of a Fuller's Walnut Cake as, although there was only a solitary walnut embedded in the centre, the entire point of the cake to a sugar-starved schoolgirl was the deliciously thick white icing. While out on one of these expeditions I found the perfect opportunity to sideline my troupe into marching past the door of the cinema to find out the show times of *Captain Hornblower*. A few days later, with a mixture of exhilaration and terror, I climbed over the garden wall and belted the short distance down Lewes High Street into the dark anonymous sanctuary of the Lewes Odeon. Three subsequent dashes and three solitary visits later meant I was much envied for having seen my heart-throb in his starring role, albeit in interrupted instalments.

I don't think there were any male teachers at Southover, or if there were I have quite forgotten them. And I don't think I had even heard the word 'boyfriend'. I certainly knew very little of the act of love and, unlike some other girls' boarding schools at the time, Southover was not a place that encouraged younger pupils to have crushes on those in the forms above. Years later I discovered that some of the older girls were convinced that two of the teachers were having an affair with the gym mistress but I remained oblivious at the time to the alleged resident lesbians among us. I don't think we ever talked much about sex in the dormitory after lights out, because we were so innocent that no one would have known what to talk about.

But I was a witness to the Man on the Train. Next to the tennis courts, on the perimeter of the school grounds, ran the London-to-Brighton railway line. Twice a day the Victoria-to-Brighton Express would pass through Lewes without stopping, but as it approached the station, the train would slow down and we would interrupt our tennis game to watch the train go by. One day, as the train slowed to pass, we saw a man standing in the open doorway of a carriage. He was waving to us with one hand while from the other swayed his unbuttoned, fully exposed genitalia. We thought he was being funny as we had no concept of perverts and had he stuck his bottom out of the carriage window we would have been equally entertained, interpreting his display as nothing more than lavatorial high jinks. So intrigued were we by this unexpected sideshow during tennis that a few days later we stopped our game early in anticipation of the sound of the train's arrival, hoping that the man would appear again. Sure enough, as the train neared there he was, in all his waving and smiling glory. After three conclusive sightings we went to tell Miss Aspden, innocent of the seriousness of our account. Clearly horrified at our amused description of the man's willy, she cautioned us in her sternest voice that under no circumstances were we ever to laugh if we saw this sort of behaviour again.

In 1949 my grandfather, Papa, had a stroke. I had been aware from recent letters from my father that he was very ill and that his death was imminent. One morning Miss Aspden sent for me. I knew I had not committed any crime recently, so the summons could only mean bad news.

Although I loved my grandparents, I had not seen them very often during the post-war years, so the immediacy of Papa's presence in my life had faded a little. I knew that I should be feeling sadder than I did and that this time tears were expected of me. But I also knew that when I heard the news I might laugh, precisely because I was conscious of the fact that it would be wrong to do so. I have always had an uncontrollable desire to laugh during awkward situations and the more serious the circumstances, the more I have to try to control myself. There was a time, in our early twenties, when Alastair and I could not attend funerals together because we knew we would set each other off, however sad we felt. Even now I have to fight to control myself at the twice-yearly trustee meetings I have to attend with the family. The mere sight of all the serious faces of the trustees, accountants and lawyers, sitting round a long table discussing figures which I cannot pretend to understand, is enough to get me going. I have been known to drift into a sort of daydream in which I imagine some of the senior trustees as rats or other furry creatures and then I really do start laughing, joined quickly by my children. I am aware that this behaviour is very childish and irresponsible, but I cannot help it.

When Papa died I was more frightened of my unreliable reaction to the news than of the news itself. 'Come in, my ducky,' Miss Aspden called, as I clung tightly to the doorknob willing it to calm me. But I could feel myself begin to shake inside. Having barely succeeded in maintaining control while in the study as she gave me the news, my first and urgent thought was to write immediately to my family. With the death of my grandfather my name had automatically changed from 'The Hon. Annabel' to 'Lady Annabel' and this seemed to me quite ridiculous as none of the other girls in the school had titles. Of infinitely more urgent concern was my sense of how important it was to conform and fit in, and not to be different or stand out at all from my peers, a preoccupation that can affect one at any age but acutely so when one is a teenager. What was I going to do? Life as the sole Hon. in the school had gone largely unnoticed and the prospect of being a Lady appalled me. My only hope of avoiding attention was to keep the whole thing a secret. Sitting on the school bench, I scribbled letters to my mother, father, grandmother, sister, brother, Melle and to everyone I could think of who wrote to me at school begging them all not to put my new title on their envelopes.

A few mornings after Papa's death I walked into the hall and saw a lot of girls crowding around the pigeon-holes. I heard their excited whispers, but they fell silent when they saw me. As they moved away I saw my familiar weekly butter parcel lying on the table and suddenly remembered that I had forgotten to alert the Wynyard Farm estate office about addressing my butter parcel in the usual way. My fellow pupils did not realise that the title was as alien to me as it was to them and, odd as it may seem, I had never really anticipated the effect the new title would have on me or on my relationships at school. Some girls were openly hostile, some were impressed, most soon forgot all about it. But it was the reaction of my English teacher that shocked me most. A short while after getting my new name, I had been running through the main hall, a contravention of one of Southover's strictest rules, when Miss Cheryl grabbed me quite violently by the arm and said, 'If I did not already know who you are, I would not have believed it, judging by your wild behaviour.' The unfairness of this remark enraged me, and I went straight to Miss Aspden's study and repeated the offending comment. I said that I quite understood that when I grew up and became, for example, a magistrate I would be required to set an example to others. At that moment, however, I argued, I was just a schoolgirl and should receive the same treatment as everyone else. Unhesitatingly Miss Aspden took the side of Miss Cheryl and in so doing, all respect I held for them both vanished instantly. Miss Cheryl's remark was my first lesson in the damage snobbery and prejudice can do, and it made a lasting impression on me.

Arriving back home for the school holidays was the moment I longed for during term-time but all school terms, even unbearable ones, do eventually end. The almost uncontainable excitement I felt aboard the train from Lewes to London was followed by the wonderful reunion with my parents and the dogs, and after only a day or two in London for visits to the dentist and the hairdresser we were all longing to head north. Because I was car sick, I travelled by train with our cook, Mrs Smith, a Latvian maid called Mrs Kausin, who had briefly cooked for us in the war at the Brown House, Rhoda Rich, Mummy's own maid and, of course, the dogs. I would sit in my carriage with a packet of Mrs Smith's chicken sandwiches (positively the best I have ever eaten) and my book, and in no time we would arrive at Darlington station to be met there by George the chauffeur. There were no motorways then so the journey for the rest of the family, with Daddy at the wheel, took most of the day but soon we were all reunited and the holidays had begun.

FOUR

Wynyard

Four years before his death my grandfather, who had already moved permanently to Mount Stewart, made Wynyard over to my father for his lifetime and the house in which I had always been happiest at last became not only our home but remained the focus of all our lives for many years.

Wynyard means 'enclosed meadow' in Anglo-Saxon and from the moment we drove through the formal Golden Gates, so called for their shiny gold-plated tips, and as the car followed the gently winding two-mile drive, I never failed to be amazed by the grandeur and beauty of the place. Halfway down the drive on the right was the towering grey stone Wellington monument, exactly 127 feet high, built to commemorate the Duke's visit to Wynyard in 1827 at the invitation of the third Marquess of Londonderry, Fighting Charlie. Nearing the house I would catch my first glimpse of the unusual curved lake on the left, then I would feel and hear the rattle as the car crossed the grids over the Lion Bridge and arrived at the grand porticoed façade of the front of the house. I can still rerun in my mind every yard of that journey. There was no question of spending even part of the holidays with friends and we never went abroad, partly because Daddy would not dream of spending holidays anywhere other than at Wynyard but also because we children had no desire to go anywhere else. The place was sheer magic.

Wynyard was designed by Phillip Wyatt, son of the renowned architect James, and took nineteen years to build, but when the work was finally completed, in 1841, a fire broke out in an overheated flue and destroyed two-thirds of the house. It was rebuilt immediately in an even grander manner, with impressively opulent decoration. There were doors of Siena marble and floors of white marble and lapis lazuli. When Disraeli saw the newly restored house he called it 'a startling resurrection'. Had it not been my much loved home, it would not have pleased me architecturally, as it is far too stark and austere for my taste, and rather reminded me of Buckingham Palace. And indeed, in the glory days of the Edwardian age Wynyard was grand enough to play host to the royal family six times between 1890 and 1903. Elizabeth Countess of Fingall, a great friend of Theresa Londonderry, Daddy's grandmother, describes in her diary the experience of being a houseguest at Wynyard while Queen Victoria was still on the throne: 'Theresa lived and ruled at Wynyard like a very benevolent monarch. Once from there I went to Stockton races with my hosts and our reception as we drove on to the course was such as might be given to royalty.' Whenever a tenant was ill Theresa would visit them at home fully decked out in Londonderry jewels, knowing that the tenants appreciated such a dazzling show from their mistress. A feudal sense continued well into the next century as I can clearly remember tenants dropping a curtsy to my own parents.

However regal and luxurious life may have been then, thanks to Mrs Smith, our own meals nearly half a century later were almost certainly more delicious than those served in 1900. The sixth Lord Londonderry, Daddy's grandfather, was uninterested in food and in the etiquette of eating, considering the whole procedure rather a waste of time. The Countess of Fingall was disappointed to record that her host had 'instituted short meals instead of the immensely long ones to which we had been accustomed. Half an hour was the time allowed for dinner, a footman stood behind nearly every chair and plates were often whipped away from the guests before they had finished. If you stopped to talk you would get nothing to eat at all.' He also introduced cold entrées and with evident distaste she adds, 'It was a new idea to be offered ham at dinner' and when on one occasion she found herself sitting beside the Lord Mayor she recorded that on sight of the ham 'his endurance gave out and he expressed his feelings to me. "I don't call this a dinner at all," he said, "I call it a rush" and, eyeing the ham, "Cheap too!"'

Before Wynyard was requisitioned for the war the kitchen staff, under the direction of my parents' cook Mrs Smith, would prepare mouth-watering meals and one of the things I missed most at Southover was the wonderful food I got at home. When Mrs Smith finally retired many years later and went to live in a little house in Fulham I would take my own children to have tea with her and she would produce for them the same delicious little dishes of scrambled eggs, home-made cakes and scones, and meringues that she had for me when I was a child. Mrs Smith's pre-war kitchen was stocked almost entirely from the estate, game was reared and shot on Wynyard land, all the vegetables were grown in the garden, butter was churned in the dairy, and milk and cream came fresh from the cows each morning. I remember going into the dairy as a small child to be given cream to drink by the chief dairymaid and I would watch the golden butter being paddled with huge wooden spoons. The dairymaid actually looked like a big pat of butter with her smooth, velvety cheeks, and she smelt so delicious that I wanted to lick her.

After the war, when our own family took up residence, Mrs Smith returned to preside over the kitchen, and a series of butlers came and went. One of them, Johnson, was rather thin and cadaverous, and he would float around the table at mealtimes looking pale and wan. I noticed that Daddy and his cousin Neil Chaplin were always laughing and joking about him, and one day I heard Neil telling Daddy that he thought Johnson had something called VD. Plucking up my courage and risking being told to mind my own business, I asked Daddy what VD meant. Trying to keep a straight face, he explained that bits of Johnson's body would probably start to fall off and there was a strong possibility that he might lose his nose, which would in all likelihood fall into my soup. I was horrified at the prospect and could not resist giving Johnson's perfectly secure-looking nose surreptitious glances whenever he put my plate in front of me. Johnson was replaced by Robert who, I believed, had a wife tucked away in the south, but this did not deter him from having a romance with Flo, the parlourmaid. He later divorced his wife and married Flo. Although Robert was devoted to Daddy I never trusted him myself because he was a sneak and would listen in on Jane's and my phone calls, passing on anything of interest directly to Daddy. There was also a handyman called Watson who sometimes helped Robert out. He was known to us as Wendy Mouse Badger as he had an uncanny resemblance to all three, especially Wendy, one of our small Scottish terriers.

By moving to Wynyard my father found a way of life he had always longed for – a country estate of his own, a place where he was in charge, where he could establish an independence and newfound confidence away from the controlling influence and disapproval of his parents. Although he was still financially restricted by Papa and kept on a limited allowance, those few years at Wynyard, before the death of my mother, were some of the happiest of his life.

My father was tall and well-built, with large bespectacled grey eyes and I always thought his face looked naked without his glasses. He had dark hair and a rather mobile mouth, ideal for pulling faces behind backs to make us laugh. He was not good-looking in the conventional sense but he had such charisma and was so funny that most people, particularly women, found him delightful. He was an erudite man and acknowledged without exception by all who heard him as an extraordinarily gifted public speaker. He was also the best company in the world, the kind of person you would love to sit next to at a dinner party and, most of the time, the kind of man you would consider yourself lucky to have as a father. Despite his gift for oratory, his formal political ambition was not as strong as his father would have wished and in 1945, after fourteen years as the Conservative member for County Down, he did not stand again at the General Election. But when he moved to Wynyard Daddy was at last able to put into practice the social conscience that had been preoccupying him for years.

The marriage of Daddy's ancestor, the third Marquess, to a young heiress who owned vast coal-mining estates at Seaham, near Wynyard, had ensured the wealth of the Londonderrys for many generations. But my father's attitude towards the miners was at variance with his predecessors. As early as 1928, in response to the terrible outcome of the General Strike in which the miners were left poorer while working longer hours, my father observed scathingly, 'Half the owners don't know a colliery from a cow pat. I am not a very good Conservative at heart.' Although the coal mines were finally nationalised in 1947, Daddy understood the appalling working conditions and distinguished himself by bothering to take time down the mines himself, something that many previous Castlereaghs and Londonderrys, including his own father, had failed to do. Alastair remembers once going down the mineshaft with him and recognising even as a schoolboy how highly Daddy was regarded by the men. In an article Daddy wrote for the *Spectator* in February 1946, a few months before the bill for nationalisation was passed, he gave an excellent description of contemporary life down the mines and the piece gives more of an insight into my father's character than anything else on record. It also goes some way to highlighting the extent of the gulf in opinion between his humanitarian sympathies and those of his father.

Before the last war over half of all industrial disputes were to do with coalmining. The average owner is rarely seen by his men, the miner can hardly be blamed for regarding his employer as a man who is more interested in profits than welfare ... If I had been a mine owner I should have concentrated my energies on the human aspect. I should have gone down the pit regularly and talked to as many men as possible so as to learn their views. My wife would have visited their house and heard about the problems confronting their wives and children ... As the miner is a keen sportsman, these men would have assisted in all activities of this nature, while every year I should have organised a picnic or gala especially for the miners' children. I cannot help feeling that if more attention had been paid to the human as opposed to the purely economic element, there would have been a happier atmosphere prevailing in the mines today.

From the moment we moved permanently to Wynyard, Daddy set about improving the living conditions of the tenants and estate workers, as many of their cottages were without electricity and still had outdoor privies. Gradually he developed a strong and sympathetic bond with the miners, and took great trouble to learn everything about their lives, their health and their children. He knew most of the men by their Christian names and would often invite them to Wynyard, never missing the Wynyard cricket matches which used to take place against a local team over most weekends during the summer.

As well as Daddy's first-hand experience down the mines and his eagerness to understand the real nature of life as a miner, a book called *The Stars Look Down* by A. J. Cronin (an author more famous now for his stories about Dr Finlay) had made a great impression on him. Cronin's book, drawing on his own experiences of life in the Welsh coal valleys, followed in the tradition of D. H. Lawrence's great mining novels of twenty years earlier and Daddy urged us all to read it. Loosely based on a true coal-mining disaster that took place in the north of England, the hero of Cronin's book is David Fenwick, whose father worked in a pit. The villain is Joe Gowlan whose father also worked in a pit but Gowlan cheats his way up the professional ladder eventually to stand as a parliamentary candidate for the Conservative Party. David Fenwick, a bookish and clever young man who had risen from the pits to become a teacher, is also persuaded to stand as a candidate for the Labour Party. In the end, Fenwick is defeated by Gowlan, who is elected to Parliament while Fenwick ends up once more down the pit where as a boy he had begun his working life. There was no question with which of Cronin's main characters Daddy's sympathies lay. Several decades after Daddy's impassioned defence of the miners he would probably have been surprised but pleased to know that Wynyard itself would be bought in 1987 by Sir John Hall, himself a former miner, who became an important and successful businessman in the northeast, as well as a major shareholder in Newcastle United football club.

However, despite my father's mildly socialist views we lived in undeniable luxury. There were roughly 140 rooms filled with glorious furniture and paintings, most of which thankfully had escaped the great fire of the last century. At the heart of the main house was the statue gallery, 120 feet long, with a 60-foot central dome built to allow the daylight to fall on the many marble figures beneath it. I particularly loved the Lawrences in our drawing room and Hoppner's beautiful painting of Miranda. But the house was so vast that we only occupied the wing on the left of the great portico and our drawing room, with its magnificent view, looked out on to a great gravel terrace to the lake beyond and down towards the wild garden.

There were lots of hiding places at Wynyard, but although we thought we knew every corner of the house, it was not until the 1960s that Alastair made the thrilling discovery of a perfectly preserved darkroom left untouched since the Victorian age. Alastair, who was passionately interested in photography himself, was told one day by the odd job man, Ernie Stephenson, who had worked at Wynyard since the 1930s, about a locked room off a rickety back staircase that was used only by staff. To Alastair's amazement, on opening the door he found a treasure trove: 'It looked as if the photographer had walked out for a moment, even though over seventy years had passed since the door had closed.'

In that forgotten room he found a collection of perfectly preserved photographic equipment belonging to our nineteenth-century ancestor, Lord Reginald Vane-Tempest-Stewart, and his mother, Theresa, Marchioness of Londonderry. Reginald's collection of photographs included not only portraits of the royal family (Edward VII, sometimes accompanied by his wife and sometimes by his mistress Mrs Keppel), the leading politicians and aristocracy (Balfour, Salisbury and Lady Randolph Churchill) but also detailed studies of dairymaids, gardeners, gamekeepers and miners who fuelled the easy life above stairs, giving us unrivalled documentation of what life at Wynyard was really like in the late nineteenth and early twentieth century.

Alastair showed the pictures to the world-famous photographer David Bailey, who immediately compared Reginald's work with that of Lartigue, the great French photographer, and in 1976 Beatrix Miller, then editor of *Vogue*, on hearing about the collection and impressed by Bailey's high praise, commissioned Brian Masters to write a story for her about the find.

Despite the huge number of rooms, through choice I had always shared a bedroom with Jane, which was wonderful for me as I was prone to nightmares, but as poor Jane had to sit up for many a night trying to console me, after Mummy had redecorated Wynyard I agreed to have a bedroom of my own.

It was painted pink with tall windows which I never dared open, because outside there was a wild bees' nest. Luckily Jane slept next door and I would bang on the wall if I thought the odd wild bee had found its way in. Wild bees were a bad enough cause for alarm but I have had a lifelong phobia of wasps inherited from my mother who fell off a tree into a wasps' nest as a child. She would try to disguise from Daddy her own terror by telling us that if we sat calmly the wasp would ignore us. Of course that didn't work and sitting at lunch she would flap wildly with her napkin, driving the wasp and Daddy mad with fury. Even now, the mere hint of a buzz is enough to send me rushing from the room, and the sight of those little yellow and black bodies fills me with revulsion. My idea of hell would be to be locked up in a room crawling with wasps. I am ashamed to admit, animal and wildlife lover that I am, that I once captured a wasp and cut it in half with a pair of scissors. To my horror, both halves of the wasp crawled off in opposite directions, and for days I avoided the room where I had committed this cruel dissection, in case the wasp had joined itself together and was waiting to get me. Years later on hearing this story my son Ben called me a murderer.

After the eventual departure of Melle a string of tutors were engaged for us. The two I remember best were June Vining, an ex Wren, who tried to keep some control over us three children as Mummy was so ill, and Mr Greenup who came to give Alastair coaching during the holidays. I disliked them both and ganged up with Alastair against them.

Poor June Vining had a dreadful time. Although she was very bossy and dictatorial, she did try to devise ways to amuse us on rainy days. I remember one afternoon when she sat the three of us down at the schoolroom table and suggested we try to compose a few rhymes. This was asking for trouble and as the rhymes grew increasingly lavatorial she finally snapped, warning us that if we wrote one more rude rhyme we would be sent to our rooms for the remainder of the day. My own little masterpiece that resulted in banishment went like this:

> Oh how I loathe you Miss June Vining,
> Your seated stance showing knicker lining
> Your beefy legs and big fat rear,
> I long to make you disappear.

I would have hoped that after the number of books I had read and the excellence of the standards of English literature to which I had been introduced I would have been able to produce something a little more weighty, but such is the mind of a twelve-year-old girl. Well, mine at least.

Mr Greenup (predictably known by us as Mr Brownup), a chaplain at Eton making a little extra cash by tutoring in the holidays, was essentially a decent man who tried his best to win me over, but I begrudged him the demands he made on Alastair's time, which took him away from our outdoor life of adventure. Poor Mr Greenup must have hated me as I did everything I could to keep Alastair away from him. Alastair had also taken violently against him because Mr Greenup didn't like *The Wind in the Willows*, one of Alastair's favourite books. Mr Greenup slept in part of the house known as the Horseshoe Wing, which had a bathroom with a little secret annexe attached to it and you had to go into the bathroom to get into the annexe. He was a creature of habit and would always take his bath at seven, prior to dinner at eight, and I once persuaded Alastair to creep into the annexe and hide with me behind the dividing curtain, to wait until Mr Greenup was in the bath. The plan was to spring into the bathroom and embarrass him but as we crouched in the little annexe listening to him running his bath, the curtains were suddenly wrenched apart and there stood Mr Greenup in his dressing gown. He was extremely angry and reported us to our parents, who gave us a very sound telling off.

★

But no figure of academic authority was needed to coerce me into the glorious Wynyard library, a huge room, shelved all round, crammed with leather-bound books which provided me with a lifetime's source of literature. There I discovered the classics, and was particularly entranced by the novels and poetry of Hardy and Kipling. My love of books began when I was read to as a very young child, and I rejoice now that there was no diversionary television in those days and that we were encouraged to use our imagination to conjure up pictures of the stories that were read to us. I find it disheartening to hear children say they love *The Wind in the Willows*, *The Secret Garden* or *The Little Princess*, when they really mean they have seen the film without reading the book. However good a film is, it cannot ever replace the book. I must have read *The Wind in the Willows* hundreds of times without tiring of it. Both Ratty and Mole became personal friends, as did the characters in E. Nesbit's *The Phoenix and the Carpet*, *The Cuckoo Clock* by Mrs Molesworth and Oscar Wilde's *The Happy Prince*. As soon as I could read for myself I devoured books. I loved everything by Kipling, the satirical short stories of H. H. Munro (known as Saki), most of Thomas Hardy and later on one of Daddy's favourite authors, A. J. Cronin. On rereading *Tess of the D'Urbervilles* the other day, I wondered how I could possibly have understood it at such a young age. Much to my shame, I read much less now than I did as a child and do most of my reading on holiday where I am not so distracted by television, especially my favourite and addictive programme *EastEnders*. However, I never switch off my light at night without reading at least a few chapters of a novel or a biography.

At Southover my interest in literature developed with the encouragement of good teachers, a wonderful library and a flourishing drama department. Once a year each form produced a play of their own choice, and at the end of the year the two best plays were shown to parents. I would take sole charge of these plays, which I wrote and produced, giving myself the leading role not because of any delusions about my acting ability but because I felt only I understood how the part should be played properly. Aged eleven, I produced my first play, *Black Jake*, which was about a bank robber, much to the disappointment of the rest of the class who would have preferred something safer like *Babes in the Wood*. My double desk was used as a getaway car and, amid a great deal of noise and giggling, I rushed around the stage dressed as Black Jake, with a long black beard that I had found in the dressing-up box at Wynyard stuck to my chin and brandishing a toy cap pistol borrowed from Alastair. Although *Black Jake* was not chosen for Parents' Evening, it succeeded in both amusing and displeasing the teachers. Some used phrases like 'imaginative', others said it was 'quite unsuitable' and I suppose it was rather a violent play for an eleven-year-old to write.

My next and more successful venture in the thespian world came after reading a story about a very haughty lady of the manor who owned fields of corn and had many downtrodden tenants. My own stage adaptation of this story had a pleasing moral twist because the cruelty and heartlessness of the lady was punished when all her cornfields were destroyed and she lost everything. *This* play was a huge success as it was shown on both of the Parents' Evenings. Alas, my own parents were not present but I revelled in the applause. I must have been so confident in those days.

All Southover girls were set an annual creative project, to be judged at the end of the school year. The project could be anything from sewing to painting, knitting, or pottery but despite Melle's teaching, I was still hopeless at all those kinds of things, so I decided to write a book instead. Inspired by my Irish roots, I wrote a story about a tinker boy who lived in a caravan in Ireland and had all sorts of adventures. At the end of term the headmistress, Miss Aspden, to my surprise and delight awarded my book 'Highly commended', congratulating me with her favourite words of praise: 'Well done, my ducky.'

I took the book home and showed it to my parents, and my father was so impressed that he sent it to my grandmother in Ireland where it may still be sitting in an attic at Mount Stewart.

My second book, *Beowulf*, was about a schizophrenic dog, sensitive to those who loved it and savage to everyone else, and it also involved a married couple who were always quarrelling over Beowulf and in one of their arguments the husband said 'Damn', which I thought was very daring of me although I do not think it was a very good book.

My early career as a playwright was not confined to term-time, as I continued to write plays at Wynyard, which were produced by Mrs Worsley, the vicar's wife, and performed during the Christmas holidays. When Wynyard became a temporary teaching college in the war, one of the three ballrooms, the Bath Ballroom, acquired a stage at one end with proper theatrical curtains, so we were able to boast that we had our own real theatre. The most memorable play we did was my version of *Rumpelstiltskin* in which I played the king, Jane the beautiful but hapless girl who had to sew straw into gold; Alastair was Rumpelstiltskin and Louisa, Mrs Worsley's daughter, played a courtier and a messenger. During rehearsals, which were taken very seriously, our producer Mrs Worsley would sit in front of the stage on a small hard-backed chair with the script in her hand. Mrs Worsley was Canadian, very animated and highly intelligent. She was also extremely ugly and it was difficult to tell when she was addressing you as she had a bad squint, with one eye pointing in the wrong direction. If she was talking to me I would instinctively glance to my left to see if she was addressing someone else. Once I had finished my own lines I would distract Jane and Alastair from theirs by creeping up behind Mrs Worsley and, choosing the side of her where the eye was looking elsewhere, I would pull down my pants and place my bare bottom an inch from her cheek. If she turned I was able quickly to pull up my pants and pretend to be looking at the script over her shoulder so she never could guess what Jane and Alastair were laughing at. In a bid to get his own back for being made to laugh on stage Alastair found a fire bucket in the wings, into which he would pee, making such a loud pinging noise that it would then be my turn to try to keep a straight face.

The plays were always performed one evening shortly before Christmas and on the day of the show we would dress up in the outfits that Mummy hired from Nathans, the theatrical costumiers in London, each costume beautifully chosen complete with every period detail in the right sizes to suit the right characters, with matching wigs. The moment the large boxes arrived, Mummy would insist on baking the costumes for a few minutes in the oven, convinced that we would all catch crabs if we wore them before they were treated. On the big night we invited all the tenants to come and watch, and have tea afterwards although in retrospect I doubt whether they really wanted to come and only did so out of a sense of duty. At the end of the performance the tenants clapped politely and we took our bows at the front of the stage. Then, as the applause died away, we would all shout 'Three cheers for Mrs Worsley' and Mrs Worsley would squirm with pleasure.

Mrs Worsley's husband, the Reverend Pennyman Worsley, also a Canadian, had applied for the job as vicar of Thorpe Thewles and domestic chaplain to the Marquess of Londonderry at Wynyard Park in 1948. There had been a chaplain associated with Wynyard land for centuries, in the tradition of all the grandest English houses, and many continued to have their own personal chaplains until very recently. The chapel had been consecrated in 1849 and a weekly service was held there every Sunday until 2002. Only illness would prevent us or any of the more devout tenants from attending. You reached the chapel by walking through the Monument Wing, an eerily beautiful room dominated by the glistening white marble of the life-size recumbent effigy of the third Marquess, Fighting

Charlie, who died in 1854. All around the walls the names of the battles in which he fought are inscribed in gold and the whole impression is one of immense splendour and the-atricality. The chapel is surprisingly large for a private place of worship, capable of seating 150 people and there is a tre-mendous nineteenth-century organ, and the family pew was just beneath the pulpit. This building became Reverend Pen-nyman Worsley's special domain.

I have rarely met a stranger or more ill-matched couple than Mr and Mrs Worsley. They were both religious fanatics and he took his calling well beyond the acceptable bounds of evangelism. Mrs Worsley could be quite charming and rather jolly, and when she was with us she laughed a lot. The vicar was another matter. He was tall and demonic-looking, and while delivering a sermon he would twist his face into a series of extraordinary contortions. 'The vicar was in great grimacing form,' Daddy would announce, returning from a church service. His sermons were bellowed in a tone threatening fire and brimstone, promising all sorts of terrible things awaiting us in hell into which he obviously envisaged the Londonderry children descending.

'This is a synARRpsis of a synARRpsis,' I remember he would roar in his strange r-rolled Canadian accent. Nor did he manage to make heaven sound much of an inviting alternative. The Worsleys must have found us spoilt and badly behaved, and although Mrs Worsley was careful never to show her disapproval, Mr Worsley made it quite clear what he thought of us. Although we had to listen to his sermons in church, most of the time we thankfully had very little to do with him. Mrs Worsley, although a great help with our plays, must have been terrifying as a mother and Louisa was noticeably petrified of her, to the extent that she was clearly afraid to speak or to express any opinion. Both parents treated Louisa appallingly, well overstepping the maxim that children should be seen and not heard, undermining her confidence at every turn. They had a strict Victorian attitude towards parenthood and by today's standards they would probably have been labelled as mentally abusive. I shudder to think what emotional intimidation went on behind the closed doors of the Thorpe Thewles vicarage. Louisa later confided in me that although I would offer her bigger parts in the plays, she had been firmly instructed by her mother only to accept the humbler roles. Years later, when there was a terrible fracas in my family over my hasty elopement with Mark Birley and Mr Worsley had a stroke, which Mrs Worsley unjustly attributed to his shock at the terrible ungodly way in which I had behaved, I became great friends with Louisa who was only a year older than me. I cherished her friendship because, due to Mummy's mouth, I never felt comfortable inviting any friends from school to stay. (No one explicitly forbade me from having guests but it was certainly not encouraged, although occasionally my cousins Diana Beaumont and Caroline Combe did come to visit as they were family and therefore less of a threat.)

In a recent letter from Louisa she wrote to tell me how at Wynyard she discovered an escape route from the humourless rigidity of life at the vicarage and time spent with us was 'the only really happy phase of my girlhood'. Touchingly she added, 'You, Jane and Alastair became my only friends. Your mother welcomed me with open arms and great kindness. And there was laughter. I don't believe I had ever laughed before. It was all so young, so gay, so innocent.'

By a coincidence, several years before she left her 'lonely and studious childhood in Canada' for County Durham, Louisa had been given a copy of Mama's book, *The Magic Inkpot*, and arriving at Wynyard she found it hard to believe that the real-life character of my father in this magical book had come into her life. She wrote to me, 'Wynyard was indeed for me suffused with the magic of the inkpot.' She was thrown into a world which was part enchantment, but which must also have been unnerving and terrifying. Both Mr and Mrs Worsley respected my parents but I am not sure whether they would have felt the same way had they seen what Louisa got up to when she was with us. My mother, who loved Louisa, nick-named her Pisa and used to tease her, looking at Louisa from under her eyelashes, tring to make her laugh. She would ask her whether the Vicar ever farted and whether she had ever seen him in the bath. Louisa, who had never heard such shocking questions, particularly coming from a grown-up, was amazed at such audacity. These conversations were the source of a delicious illicit thrill for Louisa who knew that if she ever dared to mention such talk at home she would be punished by never being allowed to set foot in Wynyard again.

I tried to teach Louisa to ride a bicycle, but without much success as I would start her off at the top of the hill heading directly for the water's edge so she frequently steered herself straight into the lake. Gamely she would clamber out, soaking wet but touchingly eager to try again. I also tried to teach her to ride one of our ponies, equally ineffectually, as my pony Judy would buck her off as soon as Louisa mounted her. But although Louisa was useless at these outdoor activities, intellectually she was truly brilliant, a real bluestocking and far cleverer than any of us, and later she won a scholarship to Oxford.

Alastair and I enjoyed ourselves most when we were outside and after breakfast we would bicycle off to our favourite places. There were little temples dotted throughout the grounds and I remember a lovely pink rose near the dairy, which had been planted by Theresa Londonderry in 1899. She had put a plaque beneath it saying 'Planted in one century, flowered in the next'. We particularly loved the wild garden and the steep wooded valley, through which a small river ran fed by the lake. Behind the house there was a huge walled kitchen garden where peaches and nectarines grew along the old stone wall as well as vines laden in summer with Muscat grapes so delicious that when we finally left Wynyard both Jane and Alastair took cuttings to grow in their own gardens.

Visible from the house at the top of the drive was the elegant eighteenth-century Lion Bridge, reputedly haunted by the Grey Lady, a housemaid whose unrequited love for one of the footmen had compelled her to throw herself in despair off the bridge into the water. Some of the tenants used to swear they would still see her standing forlornly on the bridge, gazing at the house waiting in vain for her lover. I never saw her myself although I used to frighten the girls in the dormitory at school by pretending I had.

Often we took the dogs with us on our bike rides and Winkle, Wanda, Wendy and Winston loved Wynyard as much as we did. The very first time they came up there, in their excitement they ran off down the valley, which was alive with rabbits, and did not return. Mummy and I searched for them throughout that day, convinced we would never see them again. However, the following morning four very tired and dirty black dogs appeared one by one, and after a few useless attempts at trying to keep them in we gave up, knowing not only that their desire to go hunting was instinctive and impossible to curb, but also that they would always return in time for tea.

In 1953 their pleasure was cut short by the arrival of myxomatosis. This terrible disease had travelled from Australia across to Europe and crossed the Channel, killing 99 per cent of all rabbits that encountered it and by the end of 1955 it had wiped out most of the wild rabbit population of England. If a rabbit is lucky it will be dead within three days of contracting the disease, but some lingered on in agony for up to three weeks and we dreaded coming across these pathetic creatures with their appalling bulging eyes, their ears hanging pendulously, their breathing laboured and their small bodies paralysed by a sightless fear.

Sometimes we would bicycle over to one of the farms, and on one occasion we released all the pigs who hurtled themselves out of their pens to freedom at such a gallop that they sent us both flying. George Douglas, the gamekeeper's, house was another part of the estate I loved to visit, where he allowed me to play with the labradors and terriers that were under his care in the kennels. Daddy had a particularly strong bond with George and together they took enormous pride in the managing of the famous weekend shoots.

I often went out riding on my own for hours on my pony Judy. My passion for horses had started with the tiny Shetlands I had ridden in Ireland as a small child and at Wynyard I was given my first pony. Judy was a shaggy Exmoor and although she was not particularly beautiful, I adored her. On Judy I learned to ride properly and I was safe enough on her to be allowed to ride all over the estate on my own, and while cantering down the gallops past the fields where my father's racing mares and foals were grazing I had a wonderful sense of freedom. One summer Mr Tinkler, the groom at Wynyard, took me to a small horse show near Stockton-on-Tees. It was a very hot day and Mr Tinkler and I nearly melted with the heat. Loving Judy as much as I did, I failed to notice that she was shaggier and less well groomed than the other ponies, and undeterred I entered her for several of the events, enjoying myself hugely even though we remained quite unnoticed by the class judges. During the line-up in one of the classes I noticed a pretty little girl of about my age, with an enviably long blonde plait hanging down her back and a beautifully turned-out pony. Both pony and child gleamed with good grooming and they were the kind of duo that would automatically scoop up a rosette for 'Best Condition and Turnout'. This immaculate pair seemed to be winning red rosettes after every class while I failed as usual to be selected.

A few months later my father told me that he had arranged for Mr Eric Wilson, the local Master of Foxhounds, to take me hunting. Mr Wilson, who lived in Norton, a small town nearby, arrived one autumn morning, accompanied by the same girl with the plait and the immaculate pony. She was Mr Wilson's daughter Angie and we immediately became great friends. Angie and I rode out together most days and we also hunted together. Judy had become a little too small for me so she was retired and with Mr Wilson's help my father bought me a beautiful three-year-old grey mare from Connemara in Ireland called Colleen. Angie always won first prize in the horse shows although I sometimes came second or third and we spent a great deal of time together, both at Wynyard and more often at her own house nearby. When I was about fifteen I used to get in the car to drive over to see her. The local policeman would arrive at our front door saying, 'I think Lady Annabel has been spotted at the wheel of the Hillman again,' but in those days no one seemed to mind very much that I was far too young to hold a driving licence.

I used to love going to Angie's house where the atmosphere was much more relaxed than in mine. Her mother had died when she was very young and she and her half-sister had been brought up by her stepmother and doting father. It was a relief to get away to a place where I could put my worries about Mummy to one side and where I did not have to talk about her illness. Sometimes we would go to the cinema and once we intentionally dropped chocolates on to the bald head of a man sitting below us, which got us into terrible trouble with the manager. Even though we were separated each term by boarding and later by finishing schools, Angie and I remained friends and I would ring her the moment I arrived at Wynyard to arrange to meet up. We continued to see each other whenever we could, although by 1955 after the death of my father I did not spend so much time at Wynyard, and eventually marriage and motherhood intervened for us both.

FIVE

Cuffy's Tutorial College and Mummy's Illness

In the summer of 1950 my prospects for passing the School Certificate seemed remote. A few days before I was due to sit the exams, I went down with whooping cough and was confined to the Southover sanatorium, an invigilator at the end of my bed for the duration of the exam period, to make sure that I and a fellow whooper did not cheat. I had done little revision and my form mistress at Southover was depressingly unenthusiastic about my chances of success. Unlike the individual subjects one takes in today's public exams, the School Certificate, incorporating at least five topics, had to be passed as a whole, but somehow I managed to pass reasonably well and was delighted to be able to leave Southover for ever.

In the autumn of that year I arrived at Cuffy's, a tutorial college in the centre of Oxford. My parents had wanted to send me to a finishing school and the idea filled me with horror, but Cuffy's turned out not to be a finishing school at all, but a serious institution of further education specialising in French literature and French history. The principal was a Swiss lady called Mademoiselle Hubler, known for some long forgotten reason as Cuffy. She was a famous figure in Oxford and her house at number 22 Merton Street was something of a Mecca for Oxford luminaries. The celebrated don David Cecil (Lord David Cecil) was among the distinguished people who came to call in the evenings and I sometimes attended his English Literature lectures when I returned to Oxford the following year.

Cuffy was no beauty, but a little horsy-looking and she seemed quite old to me although she must only have been in her early fifties. She had never married but it was rumoured that she had a past and there was an elderly professor who occasionally stayed at the house called Foxy and we used to speculate on whether he was Cuffy's lover. She was very warm and protective towards me as at sixteen I was the youngest girl there and she further won my heart by allowing me to take her precious two poodles for walks. Cuffy made French literature enthralling. She took us through the classic works of Racine, Molière, and Corneille, reading them aloud to us and bringing the characters in the plays to life. We would sit round a wooden table with Cuffy at the head, pausing for elevenses, when she would bring in slices of toast covered with pâté or plates of delicious sausages and mugs of tea. It was exactly like staying in a well-run French household. There were only six or eight girls, including Katharine Worsley, the future Duchess of Kent, whom I remember as popular and vivacious, and very kind to me. As the youngest student I was not allowed to go out in the evening, unlike the older girls, but sometimes Cuffy invited some young people to tea and we were entertained by these special guests who she deemed her '*Jeunes Gens de Qualité*'.

I remember going one afternoon with a fellow student from Cuffy's to visit her undergraduate cousin at Christ Church for tea. Stretched out in an armchair was a tall, thin, good-looking but languid young man whom I would not have noticed at all had it not been for his evident lack of manners as he made no effort to stand up when we came in. I remember thinking that he clearly believed himself far too superior to bother acknowledging a scruffy schoolgirl. His name was Mark Birley. For hours my friends and I would play the teenage game of speculating on the identity of our future husbands, wondering whether we had in fact already met him but little did I know that within three years I would become the wife of this indifferent young man. Mark only spent one year at Oxford and admits now that lacking a sense of direction, and then uncertain what he wanted to do with his life, he did not work hard enough to complete his degree. The next time I saw him was the year I came out when as I watched him dancing with all the most beautiful debutantes, I knew he was still far beyond my reach.

After I had completed an idyllically happy year at Cuffy's, my parents sent me to Paris to spend the summer with a French family in the unlikely hope that I might acquire a bit of polish.

The idea of Paris terrified me, particularly as I had never been abroad before, nor had I ever flown, so Mrs Johnson, my grand-parents' secretary, who also worked for my father, accompanied me on the journey. She was a large lady who had been married several times and we would often visit her in her office in Londonderry House, where she was to be found sitting at her desk, legs wide apart, a cigarette dangling from her crimson lipsticked mouth and a bottle of whisky within easy reach.

When I left for the airport I was tearful and nervous. To me Paris seemed so far away that I might as well have been flying to China. We flew first class which, as a novice flyer, meant nothing to me, but for Mrs Johnson it was a big bonus as it meant she could drink as much champagne as she wanted. Glass after lipstick-stained glass was emptied and then removed by the air hostess from her tray, and I was alarmed to notice that Mrs Johnson's face was turning bright red. By the time we landed in Paris I realised she was completely pissed. Somehow we managed to find the Marquis and Marquise de Baudry d'Asson's large elegant apartment in the pretty chestnut-tree-lined Avenue President Wilson, which was to be my home for the summer, and having met my stylish French host and hostess we all stood about rather awkwardly in the salon as Mrs Johnson swayed from side to side puffing smoke into the face of an increasingly bewildered Madame Baudry d'Asson.

That afternoon, having been misguidedly asked by my mother to help me find some suitably smart clothes, Mrs Johnson took me to visit Madame Baudry d'Asson's dressmaker. My chaperone had by this time fallen down the dressmaker's stairs and was far too inebriated to give any advice at all. I have rarely been more embarrassed and, fearing that Mrs Johnson was on the point of passing out, we left. I was more than relieved when she finally headed for the airport.

Clothes continued to be a problem for the rest of my stay in Paris. At my mother's urging, I did return half-heartedly and alone to the dressmaker but with no one to guide me and no dress sense at all, I did not have a clue what to order. You need your mother for that sort of advice and Mummy did write frequently to enquire how I was handling the problem as she was always beautifully dressed herself and fascinated by the latest fashions. 'Surely your new summer dress has been finished by now?' she wrote anxiously. 'You ought to have enough money to have a dark blue silk dress run up for you as you have £50 in travellers cheques left after the spotted dress is made.' And then, 'Perhaps you could get a dark blue plain taffeta dress, as they are always so useful. Maybe Galleries Lafayette has them.'

During my time in Paris the only thing I managed to buy for myself was my first pair of blue jeans and when I got home late that summer I remember Mummy, ill as she was, hinting that she wished I had bought some for her, and I kicked myself, wishing I had.

In the mornings I was supposed to attend French classes with a small group of English friends who included Caroline Child-Villiers (the daughter of Pat Laycock, a great friend of Mummy's who had lived near us during the war at the Brown House), Arabella Stuart, who became the celebrated cookbook writer and married the cartoonist Mark Boxer, and Rosemary Stockdale, to whom I became particularly close and who married Anthony Tennant, Chairman of Guinness and later Chairman of the Trustees of the Royal Academy.

But I confess I hardly bothered to go to the classes as I realised I would pick up more French by spending time with the six Baudry d'Asson children. Their ages ranged from sixteen to the four-year-old twin boys with whom I had fallen in love at first sight. Their pretty mother was charming and on the evidence of my descriptions in letters that I sent home, my father concluded that the Marquise must have been '*un morceau de tout droit*'. Sustained by my parents' loving letters, the homesickness went away and while Mummy would offer practical advice about money and arrangements, Daddy's letters were always amusing and often quite mad. And he would write pages about his escapades at Wynyard which he knew would make me feel less far away: 'Two black doggies are having a truly wonderful time here. They were ever so good in the car and enjoyed their chicken sandwiches. Every morning they disappear up the steps and are to be found near the dairy, waiting for someone to leave the garden gate open. As I dried Wiggle yesterday, I whipped the burrs out of his beard before he guessed what I was doing.'

It was a strange summer and although I enjoyed Paris I did not learn to love or appreciate the city's great beauty until many years later when I began to know it well on visits there with my husbands Mark and Jimmy.

In 1951 my days went largely unmonitored and I wandered around Paris in a bit of a daze, going endlessly with my friends to cinemas and galleries, and eating ice creams. I learned how to buy a carnet to travel on the Métro, but I almost never went out in the evenings although one night Madame Baudry d'Asson took me to a ball. God knows what I wore but I loathed every minute of it and wall-flowered throughout. The only person who danced with me was the Marquis and in my letters home I obviously put on a convincingly brave face for the occasion, as Mummy wrote back to say she was glad to hear how much I had enjoyed the ball. In the late summer when Paris became very hot the Baudry d'Asson family took me to their chateau in Vaucluse near Vendôme. It was a beautiful place and we spent most of the time out of doors having delicious picnics, and I stayed there until it was time to go back to England.

Although I am generous by nature and love giving presents, for some reason I returned home giftless. I did remember to buy chocolate bars for Daddy because rationing meant that chocolate was still scarce in Britain, but I had nothing, not even the much coveted blue jeans, for Mummy. However, I was delighted to be back at Wynyard and reunited with my family, my pony Colleen and of course all the dogs.

I had been so happy at Cuffy's that on my return from Paris I went back to Oxford to continue studying English and History with various specialist tutors. I stayed in digs with a Mrs Williams who lived in a small house off the Woodstock Road and I had my own room. I soon developed a crush on her youngest son, Charles, who was a don. Charles was my first boyfriend and we would go to the cinema together, and occasionally to the theatre, but we never took the relationship further than having the occasional kiss whenever Mrs Williams wasn't looking.

Anne Dreydel, my English Literature tutor, was a wonderful and inspirational woman who had been paralysed from the waist down when a bomb had fallen directly on to her house during the war and she had been confined to a wheelchair ever since. Many years later when my sister-in-law, Nico Londonderry, was looking for somewhere in Oxford for her daughter Cosima to do her A levels she met Anne Dreydel, who by this time was Principal of St Clare's College. The daughter of a German, she had co-founded St Clare's in 1953 with the intention of establishing between young students of different nationalities a harmony that had been disrupted by the war.

Presenting an award for bravery to Captain Hagan, the pilot who heroically tackled the passenger who seized the controls of the jumbo jet on which I was travelling to Nairobi with my family for the Christmas holidays in December 2000.

Left: My paternal grandparents, whom we grandchildren called Mama and Papa, at the coronation of King George V in 1911.

Below left: My father, Robin Castlereagh, pictured in the thirties.

Below right: My mother, Romaine Castlereagh.

My parents fell quickly and passionately in love with each other, and were married on 31 October 1931 at St-Martin-in-the Fields in London.

My christening at Mount Stewart – I am almost invisible under the folds of the lacy Londonderry christening gown. My sister Jane, perched uncomfortably on Mama's knee, looks rather alarmed by the proximity of one of Mama's enormous lurchers.

Below, across page: Pages from the album that my mother created – each photograph is meticulously labelled and charts our carefree childhood lives, and my album remains one of my most treasured possessions. At the top left of the album page is a photograph of the portrait of my mother by Edmund Brock.

Left: A portrait taken of my mother with Jane, me and Alastair in the late 1930s.

Overleaf right: A photograph taken by my mother at Ramsbeck, on Lake Ullswater in Cumbria, where we lived for a time during the war, of Alastair with his mop of golden curls, wearing a miniature army uniform.

Overleaf far right: Jane, Alastair and me with our cousin, Patrick Plunket in his army uniform, at the Brown House during the war.

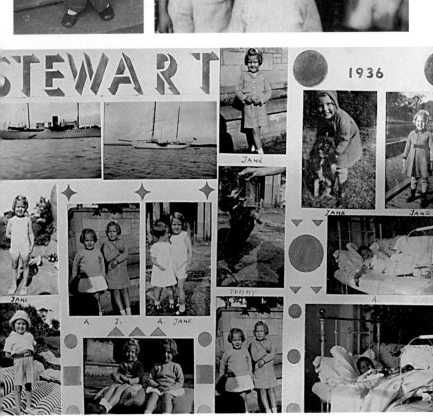

STEWART 1936

JANE

JANE

JANE

JANE

TOMMY

A.

A. J.

A. JANE

Winkle and me at Wynyard in 1949.

Jane was asked to be one of the Queen's maids of honour at the coronation in June 1953, along with five other girls. For years after the coronation, the pictures of the six girls standing next to the Queen on the balcony would be shown again and again. It was always easy to pick out Jane, partly because she was at the front next to the Queen and also because to my mind she was by far the prettiest.

My wedding to Mark Birley in 1954, at Caxton Hall in Westminster. I wore what the papers called 'a clerical grey spring suit'. It was certainly an unconventional outfit for the daughter of a marquess to get married in. After the ceremony, we emerged into the London sunshine to the cheering of the crowds and the strange experience of facing a bank of cameras from the press.

With this headline the *Daily Despatch* from Manchester indicated their disappointment that there had not been more of a show.

For a Marquess's daughter—no orange blossom

Lady Annabel's wedding

It could have been the "Society Wedding of the Year." Instead they chose a simple, quiet, civic ceremony at Caxton Hall, London, with no top hats, no satin, no orange blossom.

The bride was Lady Annabel Vene Tempest Stewart, daughter of the late Marchioness of Londonderry and the late Marchioness.

The bridegroom was Mr. Mark Birley, an advertising agent, son of the late Sir Oswald Birley, the painter, and of Lady Birley.

Even so, the event was not quite so quiet as the 19-year-old bride and her 23-year-old 'groom expected. Nearly 200 people, mostly women, crowded round the massive steps of Caxton Hall to watch the arrivals and departures.

They saw the bridegroom, a red carnation in the jacket of his blue-grey suit, leap up the steps two at a time. They pressed forward to see the bride walk quickly in, escorted by her father.

Lady Annabel, tall, slim and chestnut-haired, wore a close-fitting suit of dark blue-grey, a white blouse, a red hat, and spray of white camellias. Her jewellery was a double string of pearls and sapphire and diamond earrings, which belonged to her mother.

After a 15-minute wedding ceremony, conducted by the Chief Superintendent Registrar, in the flower-filled wedding "room," the newly-married couple came out again into the sunshine.

The "Caxton Hall wedding of the year" was over.

Anne remembered me well, telling Nico that she wished I had been able to stay on at Oxford and go to the university which was impossible as I had not passed maths at School Certificate, a condition of acceptance into Oxford at that time.

Occasionally my grandmother would come down from London with her chauffeur, Mr Page, in her Rolls-Royce and take me out to lunch at the Randolph Hotel. These visits may have been prompted by her awareness of Mummy's illness and a feeling that she wanted to become more involved in the lives of her grandchildren. She was sometimes a little tipsy but I always enjoyed the lunch and at the end she would give me a fiver, handing me another to send on to Alastair at Eton. Although I would unfailingly forward Alastair's note to him, when she gave him one to hand on to me he was less scrupulous. These little tips were extremely welcome as although at Wynyard we still lived in a world of butlers and cooks, there was never any spare cash as Daddy was still kept on an allowance, with the bulk of the Londonderry fortune in trust to Alastair.

Apart from the limited time spent in my romance with Charles Williams I conducted quite a grown-up social life at the time. Some weekends I would bicycle over from Mrs Williams's house to have tea with Cuffy and once I remember Jane's great friend, Tom Egerton, taking me to the Cottage at Badminton to have lunch with Caroline and David Somerset (now the Duke of Beaufort). David used to call Caroline Thisbe and referred to the child she was expecting as Pyramus, although when he was born he became known as Bunter. Sometimes David Ogilvy would drive me back to Oxford after a weekend in London. David was madly in love with Jane and as he drove he would discuss the chances of Jane returning his feelings. I was secretly hopelessly in love with him myself, so would willingly endure all this talk about Jane if it meant I could spend hours just sitting next to him in the car. Shortly afterwards he met and fell in love with an enchanting and highly intelligent American girl called Virginia (Ginny) Ryan. She was small, pretty and vivacious, and she and David have remained happily married to this day, with a large family.

Wholly absorbed in my new way of life at Oxford, and having spent the summer in Paris, I had seen little of Mummy during the year and even less during that autumn term. I had not been at all homesick at Cuffy's as by this time although I was unaware, Mummy had slowly but deliberately begun to distance herself from us as a way of preparing us for the time when she would no longer be there. For the preceding five years her illness had cast a permanent shadow over my life and I found it hard to remember when I had not been aware of a dull ache of uneasy thought that perhaps her mouth would never improve. When I was at Wynyard I was always a little on edge, fearing that if Angie Wilson and I ran into her, we might surprise and embarrass her. Just as I had sought refuge in Angie's house, free from the tensions at home, so I had found the same relief in the relaxed atmosphere at Cuffy's.

In the dining room at Wynyard, Mummy used to sit at the head of the table eating calves' foot jelly with a spoon and drinking through a straw as the inside of her mouth was covered in blisters. Mrs Smith would make little mousses, and milk shakes, and vegetable broths for her because she was unable to chew proper food.

Occasionally Mummy would say, as if in jest, that she did not think she was long for this earth and we would massage her feet, which she liked us to do, and we laughed at this ridiculous notion. 'Don't be silly, Mummalung,' we would say. She had made the idea of not living sound so absurd. I remember how impatient I could be with her. 'Everybody on the estate says you don't go out any more,' I complained with appalling but unintentional insensitivity. 'You don't go and visit the tenants at all and you should at least make the effort to see everyone in church on Sundays.' She had a special lipstick, a red-coloured concealing ointment, and I used to watch her looking into a small hand mirror as she would dip her finger into a little pot and carefully cover her lips with the medically approved healing cream.

In 1950 Jane came out as a debutante and Mummy felt she must make a tremendous effort and go to Jane's ball at Londonderry House in Park Lane in London. Elizabeth Arden, one of the best-known cosmetic beauty firms of those days, sent one of their staff round to the house to make her up for the party and to try to disguise her mouth. I was away at school but Jane told me that she looked marvellous that night. Only my father and her doctor, Sir Stanford Kade, the leading cancer surgeon of the day, really knew how ill she was.

On my occasional weekend visits up to London from Oxford her bedroom door would often be closed. One day when I went in to see her I was wearing a navy-blue skirt with a matching sweater and I could tell, as I stood at the end of her bed, that she liked the sweater and that she liked my look, and was trying to say so, but I couldn't understand a single word she was saying. I didn't know what to do, so I stood there, shifting from foot to foot, unable to go near her, too frightened to go up and kiss her, watching in horror as she mouthed words soundlessly. No one had told me that, in a latest attempt to cure her illness, the cobalt radiation having failed to work, they had cut out her tongue.

Even then I failed to recognise the true severity of her condition. But Jane was aware that something was terribly wrong, as well-meaning friends had started saying to her how sorry they were to hear how ill Mummy had become. At the end of the autumn term, just a few weeks before Christmas, Daddy sent Jane and me up to Wynyard alone on the train, having asked Jane to prepare me to accept that Mummy might not have long to live, but although she had tried very hard to make me understand, Jane knew I had not really absorbed the truth. When we arrived back at Park Street at the end of the weekend, I asked if I could go and see Mummy but was told I could not and a few days later I was woken at seven in the morning by Sister Doris tapping me on the shoulder. 'Annabel, I've got to break some news to you.' She was speaking briskly. 'Your dear mother passed away peacefully last night.'

Unable to believe what she was telling me, I was absolutely amazed at her words. I am not sure if I had ever heard the word 'cancer' and if I had, I would probably have associated it with a huge growth in the stomach rather than bad blisters in the mouth. And mothers didn't die.

As I burst into tears, Sister Doris started to hush me. 'Now, now. We don't want any of that,' she said. 'Brace up. Here's a cup of tea.' Later that morning, in something of the same abrupt tone of voice, Daddy told us that he didn't want to see us crying or snivelling, and that he wanted everybody to be very collected and to 'knuckle down'. With an enormous effort, I managed to do as he wished in front of him, but when he left the room, I went to find Melle, who had come back to Park Street to help nurse Mummy and, confused and angry, I fired questions at her. I couldn't understand why we had been kept so much in the dark. If we had known Mummy was that ill we could have done little things for her. We could have brought her flowers. We would have taken her bunches of violets. We could have been given the chance to be more considerate to her, to do loving things for her. Gently Melle tried to explain that it was Mummy herself who had insisted that we were not told the truth but I have never forgotten how much I minded not having the chance to say goodbye properly.

In December 1951, on the afternoon of Mummy's death, Alastair was breaking up from Eton for the Christmas holidays and Daddy had asked Neil Chaplin to meet him at Paddington. Neil, a large portly man, was Daddy's best friend and first cousin. He practically lived at Wynyard and helped run the shoot there, and Alastair knew him well. However, Alastair had been badly bullied that term and as a result he had not done well academically. He had not yet told Mummy or Daddy how miserable he was and had been particularly looking forward to the end of term and to being comforted by his mother. He had had no sense of imminent tragedy as he, like me, had become accustomed to the constant presence in his life of Mummy's illness. When Neil Chaplin broke the news to him at the platform barrier at Paddington he was as deeply shocked as I had been.

Later that day Sister Doris took Alastair and me in to see Mummy lying in her bed. I have mixed feelings about whether you should see people dead. I have seen several dead bodies and, although I recognise that it might help in the process of acceptance, I never think death is a particularly lovely sight. As Sister Doris pulled back the sheet I saw that Mummy's face had already become as smooth and waxy as a statue, and when she observed how beautiful and peaceful she looked, Alastair and I both noticed with astonishment that all the sores seemed to have disappeared from around her mouth and that her face was no longer marked. In death she seemed finally to have been cured. Leaving the room, Alastair touched her one last time. He put his hand on her feet but they were stiff and cold. These were not the feet, nor was this the face, of the mother he loved. The announcement in the paper of the tragically early death of the beautiful Marchioness of Londonderry at the age of forty-seven stated pneumonia as the cause. The conspiracy surrounding the true nature of her illness continued to the end.

Aunt Kitty took Jane and Alastair and me up to Wynyard for the funeral. I remember Jane and I thinking how important it was to make Christmas all right for Alastair and Daddy, so as soon as we arrived we decorated the tree. Daddy had kept the details of the funeral private from everyone except the family, so of all Mummy's friends, only Patsy Ward, my godmother, was there.

During the service in the chapel I noticed that the tenants

were in tears. As we left the chapel Rhoda, Mummy's maid, brought the four Aberdeen terriers to me on their leads. Black bows had been tied round their collars and I led them up the steps at the side of the house to the wild garden. There, in Mummy's favourite place at Wynyard, was a beautiful magnolia tree, and the earth beneath it, at Daddy's request, had been consecrated by Michael Ramsay, the Bishop of Durham who was later to become the Archbishop of Canterbury. We stood at the side of the grave, in the bitter cold December air, beneath the magnolia tree, and Kitty clutched my hand so tightly that it hurt. As the coffin was lowered, to everyone's horror Wendy, one of the dogs, made a dash for the grave and fell in. I don't think she was aware of the coffin, but was simply overcome with the excitement of spotting a giant rabbit hole. At the time I didn't think it was funny at all.

Daddy put a glorious pink Italian marble stone at her grave, but when Wynyard was sold in 1987 and Alastair heard of plans to build a hotel overlooking the wild garden, he had Mummy exhumed and buried in the family vault at Long Newton near Wynyard where now the third, sixth and her own husband, the eighth Marquess of Londonderry are buried.

During those unhappy holidays we all reacted in different ways. Every evening Alastair seemed reluctant to go up to bed, and I would come out of the drawing room and find him sitting on the stairs waiting for me, too frightened to go to bed alone. Although Jane and I tried our best to comfort and support him, he felt utterly abandoned. Had Mummy survived, he believes she would have prevented him from making the mistakes of his later life and remains convinced that she was the only person who ever really understood him. She in her turn had adored him and had died with a photograph of Alastair wearing his Eton uniform tied round her wrist.

Almost immediately after Mummy's death Jane assumed the maternal role and perhaps that responsibility helped her in the beginning as a distraction from her own distress.

For me, although I was profoundly affected I had not been able to get close to Mummy for many months, so her death did not involve the agonising physical wrench that I was to feel eventually in years to come with the loss of my son Rupert.

For a while, in order to preserve some continuity and routine in Alastair's shaken world, the holidays remained sacrosanct and we continued to spend those weeks at Wynyard. However, in London I went about quite unchaperoned and no one paid any attention or cared what I got up to.

But it was not Jane's or my future, or even Alastair's well-being that truly worried Mummy as she lay dying because she sensed that as children, young and resilient, we would manage. But she did confess to Melle that her greatest fear was for my father. Her fears were realised. With her death the temptation to drink, which he had fought successfully while Mummy was alive, finally overwhelmed him and as he began quickly to sink into a state of terrible drunken despair, we children were in effect orphaned.

SIX

Coming Out

I returned to Mrs Williams's digs in the January following Mummy's death, having spent one of the saddest Christmases of my life. Initially people in Oxford, shocked by this unexpected news, were uncertain how to behave towards someone who had lost her mother at such a young age. However, my father had thoughtfully written to my tutor, Anne Dreydel, asking her to give me enough work to take my mind off my mother's death, and with her sympathetic support the term passed quickly and uneventfully, lightened by the odd romantic moment with Charles Williams.

Meanwhile Jane, just two years older than me, was trying to provide some sort of comfort and structure for Alastair who was only fourteen. She was meticulous in planning his holidays, making sure she was there for all his exeats from school and she never failed to maintain the family tradition of taking a picnic down to Eton for the Fourth of June celebrations.

At the same time she was running Wynyard for Daddy and arranging the elaborate shooting weekends there; Jane herself was considered, with Debo Devonshire (the Duchess of Devonshire), one of the two best shots in the country. She had already begun to carry out a few public appearances when Mummy had become too ill to perform them herself and had opened the summer fête in 1951 at Thorpe Thewles, as Mummy had told her that it would be 'good practice'. At the time she did not realise that she was being prepared gently for a demanding future role as a surrogate wife to Daddy, when she would become a leading figure in the local Women's Institute and the Mothers' Union. There was even a suggestion, luckily abandoned, that Jane should become the Mayoress of Durham to Daddy's Mayor. These experiences were to prove helpful to her when she became well known for her charity work in the East End of London and, after her marriage, for her support and chairmanship of the charities Refuge, the Jewish Welfare Board and the Chicken Shed Theatre Company.

Jane fulfilled willingly the dual roles of acting wife and mother, although worse than the relentless organisational demands imposed upon her were the endless weekdays *without* any house guests when she would simply stay up at Wynyard to keep Daddy company. At times when he was often drunk and she was there without friends of her own age, they were both very lonely. Many years later Jane admitted to me that she was sometimes struck by the unfairness of her responsibilities and envious of her carefree contemporaries, and still feels a little regretful that a part of her youthful freedom was denied her. But her loyalty was unassailable and she says it would have been unthinkable to abandon her role.

As a young girl Jane had been known by the family as Podge, but suddenly, at the age of seventeen she had become a raving beauty. Most of the eligible young men in London were in love with her and I swung between the feelings of passionate jealousy and deep affection. On weekend visits to London from Oxford Jane would occasionally give a dinner party, generously saying to all her friends, 'Just wait till you see my sister,' giving them the idea that they were about to meet rather a knockout. As I was a particularly late flowerer, being awkward and gawky, I saw at once the disappointment on their faces when they did finally meet me.

Although Daddy's drinking was already beginning to spin out of his control, weekends at Wynyard could still be lively and fun. During Mummy's illness almost no one came to stay but to Daddy's surprise and delight, in addition to her new responsibilities, Jane seemed to have inherited from Mama all the talents of a natural hostess. Suddenly the guest rooms at Wynyard were once again filled with dozens of young people who came up to County Durham for what became a much coveted invitation to shoot and from the gunroom to the kitchen, no tiny detail that might contribute to their comfort was overlooked. In consultation with Mrs Smith, Jane would devise mouth-watering menus for the weekend meals, and carefully check the guest bedrooms and bathrooms, making sure nothing had been forgotten. Each evening she would ensure that there were enough card tables for those guests who wanted to play canasta, the card game that was all the rage in the 1950s. Occasionally we organised charades and I used to look forward to these weekends with great excitement.

Hugh Fraser (who was to marry Antonia Pakenham) and my young godfather Billy Dudley were among many others who would come to stay, and there was always a regular and popular guest in our nearest neighbour, Tony Lambton (Lord Lambton). Tony was very much a one-off, both eccentric and beautiful, rather like I imagined the young Byron to be, and I was wildly in love with him from the moment I met him aged thirteen. Twelve years older than me, he looked like a nineteenth-century figure dressed in a bright green corduroy coat that he wore for shooting. He was a brilliant shot but his temper was erratic and if he occasionally missed a bird or if his loader was slow, he would throw himself on the ground in a fury and, chewing on the grass, would fling away his gun in a rage. After these episodes he would return to the house and Mummy would give him a good talking to. My parents had known Tony since he was a boy, and he adored my mother and always listened to her.

At the time I imagined that most of the young men who were at those weekends were more than a little in love with Jane who, since the age of eighteen, had always been surrounded by admirers. However, most of them were kept at arm's length, much to my disappointment as I longed to be a bridesmaid. However, Tony Lambton's love for her did not go unrequited and for many years they were deeply in love.

Occasionally Jane and I were invited to stay for the odd ten days with David Ogilvy's parents, the Airlies, at Cortachy Castle in Scotland. These short breaks were a welcome escape from the demands made on Jane at Wynyard and although Lord and Lady Airlie were rather frightening, I liked them. They had six children who were mostly much older than us but were often there during our visits. There were three daughters, of whom one, Margaret, had been a great friend of my parents and who frequently came to the Brown House during the war. She had been engaged at that time to an American but later she met and married Ian Tennant who had served time as a prisoner of war and Alastair, whether unable to pronounce her name or simply through mischief, used to call her Cigarette. David was the oldest of the three Airlie boys, Angus was the middle son who married Princess Alexandra, and lastly there was James who was my age and whom I had known since we were both at boarding school, when we had exchanged mildly flirtatious letters. But summer was approaching and with it the inevitable Season. I was rather dreading the prospect of 'coming out' and all that it entailed. The idea of going to endless balls and meeting a lot of new people was abhorrent to me, but in those days, even six months after the death of a mother, there was no question of being allowed to back out.

King George VI had died in February, plunging the country into three months of official court mourning. This inconvenience might have played havoc with the Season, which was forced to cut short its usual twelve-week-long party and racing festival, and cram it into an unpopular eight-week period. The society magazine *Tatler* initially responded solemnly and splendidly to the news of the King's death by banishing their habitual red-and-white cover advertisements for Duff Gordon Sherries and Crawford Cream Crackers, and replacing them with a black-and-white picture of the King captioned 'The King is Dead. Long Live the Queen'.

However the resilient social life of the aristocracy burst its way through into print. Although the columnist Jennifer revealed herself to be most put out by the fact that 'due to the unavoidable circumstances' hostesses had been forced to organise more than one dance per night, the lists of parties and balls and race meetings were published as usual in the March issues. Jennifer reported that 'some very attractive Debutantes in the Bud are making their debut this season'.

The editor was clearly delighted fortuitously to have been presented with a new slogan for promoting the leading girls by dubbing them 'The Elizabethan Debutantes', thus injecting a further note of royalty and grandeur into the proceedings in honour of the new Queen. It was announced that Gertrude, Lady Howard de Walden, would be pleased that year to accept the invitation to preside over Queen Charlotte's Ball.

I found the whole rigmarole of the Season to be rather strenuous because I seemed to be the only debutante without a mother. On 14 May I was featured as one of the 'Elizabethans', pictured in a pose by Bassano, who was in effect *Tatler*'s house photographer. I was wearing a tight black jersey, two strings of pearls and I had a very soignée hairdo, and although I did not usually go to the hairdresser or the manicurist as other girls did, on that occasion I think I must have been given a little professional help. My three-line biography informed the reader that I had been 'finished' in Paris and that I was a 'keen rider to hounds'. At that stage there didn't seem to be much more to say.

I had no idea what to wear to any of these parties and although Daddy had enlisted the advice of a friend of Mummy's, Bettine Abingdon (the Countess of Abingdon) she was not much help and I was not very co-operative. Together we chose some rather unsuitable clothes for Ascot from the couturier Jacquemar, but I cannot remember her helping me to buy any ball gowns. Pat Laycock, the mother of Caroline Child-Villiers, the great friend who had been in Paris with me, was also roped in to help this skinny, gauche young girl, but although she was very sweet to me I secretly felt, maybe unfairly, that I was being used as the perfect foil to the blonde prettiness of her daughter. Maybe I wore the same dress to every party as the clothes question undoubtedly contributed in part to the total absence of pleasure I felt for any ball. In fact, I can barely remember a single one, including mine, that I enjoyed. However, I do remember the dress I wore to my own party. It was sleeveless and made of white brocade, and had belonged to Mummy. I think it was the dress she had worn for Jane's coming-out ball, so it was almost new but as I was very slim indeed, it had to be cut down for me. Even so I don't remember feeling very beautiful in it. The dance took place at Londonderry House and I shared it with my cousin Carey Coke, the daughter of Tommy and Elizabeth Leicester (the Earl and Countess of Leicester). Elizabeth Leicester was a lady-in-waiting to the Queen and her elder daughter, Carey's sister Anne, was one of the six maids of honour with my own sister Jane, at the coronation the following year. This royal connection gave our ball the distinction of being the first private party to be attended by the Queen and Prince Philip since the death of her father the King. I particularly remember how friendly they both were to me although it was the first time I had met the Queen since my invitation to tea at Buckingham Palace when I was three.

Otherwise I have rather hazy recollections of the evening. I know that I watched Mark Birley, still as good-looking as I remembered from that first meeting at Oxford, swirling deb after deb round the dance floor, and wearing a dark mourning armband round the sleeve of his evening jacket as a mark of respect for his father, Oswald Birley, who had recently died.

Carey says that I was so unengaged in the dance that I actually left Londonderry House halfway through the party although I cannot remember doing so. I was very fond of Carey who was blonde and certainly one of the loveliest girls I knew, but I am not sure she enjoyed these parties any more than I did. We made a sort of team, sharing the same sense of humour and a tendency to behave rather wildly, which singled us out from the other debs and drew us together.

Most of the coming-out balls were held in London but others took place in the country and we would spend the weekend with grown-up friends or relations. Several young people would be invited to stay and a formal dinner would be given before the dance. One weekend I was invited to stay with Bernard and Lavinia Norfolk (the Duke and Duchess of Norfolk) at Arundel Castle in Sussex. Some of our party were determined to visit their respective beaux who were staying about seventy miles away for another ball at Mereworth Castle in Kent. A group of about five decided to make the trip and although I wasn't particularly enthusiastic, I volunteered to join them as I thought I might bump into Dommie Elliot, a friend of mine whom I rather fancied. We ordered a taxi to drive us there and bring us back but we had no idea that it was so far and we did not arrive back at Arundel until eight or nine the following morning. A terrible fuss was made. At first I got a huge ticking off from Lavinia Norfolk, then I was sent for by Rachel Davidson, Bernard Norfolk's sister who lived at nearby High-field House, where our old governess Melle was employed to look after her two children, Duncan and Harriet. Finally over tea Melle gave me the most humiliating rocket of all.

Unchastened, I realised, just as I had done at school, that as a way of overcoming my shyness and lack of confidence I could make an impact and get myself noticed by behaving in a rather boisterous and outlandish way. I would throw slightly risqué stories into the conversation which I had heard from Daddy but didn't begin to understand. At one grand dinner party I repeated an obviously exaggerated account of some exiled Poles who were taking refuge during the war in Edinburgh, who had been apocryphally reported as having a wild tendency to bite off women's nipples. 'Did you know that there are 3000 Scottish ladies walking around titless?' I enquired loudly of my table during an unfortunate lull in the general conversation. For a moment the entire room fell into a stunned silence, followed by an enormous uproar of laughter. Five minutes later a waiter brought over a folded piece of paper from another table on which were written the words 'God is watching you'. The actor Douglas Fairbanks Junior was an old friend of my parents from Mount Stewart days and, having heard the story and the shrieks of laughter coming from my table, felt that he should keep an avuncular eye out for me. From that moment onwards he was always known to me as 'God'.

Much of the season passed in a blur. My view was then, as it still is now, that if I have to do something, I might as well get on with it and make the most of it. Looking at the huge list of parties that was published in *Tatler & Bystander*, many of which I dragged myself to, I only remember a few. Among those that stood out were Caroline Child-Villiers's ball, which was held at the Spanish embassy in Belgrave Square, where strolling Spanish minstrels played their banjos for us; the party given for Mary Roche, future aunt to Diana, Princess of Wales, as well as the one held for my cousin Clarissa Chaplin, whose mother Alvilde subsequently became an internationally famous gardener and married the writer Jim Lees Milne. One of Daddy's best men friends was Bobby Kirkwood and his daughter Caroline came out the same year as me. The Kirkwoods were considered rather exotic as they lived in Jamaica and the presence of the suntanned and sexy Caroline among our pale English-rose skins meant that she was always surrounded by admiring young men. Her dance was the most spectacular of the whole season for me, not for its grandeur but because of the terrific jazz band who played that night.

The fundamental purpose behind the elaborate and extravagant ritual of the Season was of course to find a husband but romance did not blossom that summer for me. The 1950s were shot through with a Puritanism that made it unthinkable that anyone should 'go the whole way' and every innocent kiss was analysed at length the following morning. Divorcees were not allowed into the Royal Enclosure at Ascot and amazingly the legacy of stuffiness in aristocratic circles, albeit hypocritical, persisted until the 1970s when the news of my own pregnancy by Jimmy Goldsmith while still married to Mark Birley hit the headlines.

Most of the Deb's Delights were a few years older than me and among them were Dominic Elliot, who often accompanied Princess Margaret, Dominic Elwes and Julian Plowden, who both had a reputation as bad boys and were turned away when they tried to gatecrash my own party. David Metcalfe was a familiar figure, as were the Manners brothers, Johnnie and Roger, and their elder brother Charles Rutland (Duke of Rutland). We also often saw Charlie (one-time husband of Margaret, Duchess of Argyll) and Bobby Sweeney, although they were much older and well out of my age group. Many of the married aristocracy were invited including the Somersets and the Blandfords (now the Duke and Duchess of Marlborough). Shaun Plunket would be at most of the balls, as would Patrick, who was by then equerry to the Queen.

But at last I started to emerge slowly from a cloud of insecurity and towards the end of the year my romantic prospects began to look up when Johnnie Spencer kissed me. Johnnie had been engaged to Carey's sister Anne, who was lodging for the Season with Lady Fermoy, the mother of Frances Roche. When Anne introduced her fiancé to her landlady's daughter, who was then only fifteen, she was not to know that Johnnie and Frances would become husband and wife within two years and later the parents of Lady Diana Spencer. That autumn I had another kiss, this time with Johnnie Manners (Lord John

Manners) rather daringly while in the back of a car that was being driven at the time by Mark Birley.

I also started going with my friends to one or two nightclubs, occasionally to the Astor and more often to the Four Hundred, the Annabel's of its day. Once I went to the Astor with a man who will remain nameless who bored me so much that although we had already ordered dinner, as soon as he left for a moment to go to the loo, I bolted.

Despite all this gaiety, I only really began to enjoy myself socially when I was twenty-six, seven years after my marriage to Mark, and I was immensely relieved when the Season was over. It does not exist any longer, thank God, in the same form and it has, as Geordie Greig the current editor of *Tatler* recently explained to me, 'moved away from being a rigid social structure where class mattered and it is now as much about money and social mobility and simply having a good time'. I would have hated to have put either of my daughters through the old process. In fact, I am sure they would both have refused to have anything to do with it.

On 2 June 1953, nearly eighteen months after the death of her father, the Queen was officially crowned although the planning of such an enormous event had started a whole year earlier. To my father's pride Jane was invited to be one of the Queen's maids of honour along with five other girls, all roughly the same age and all of them the only or eldest daughters of senior peers. The other maids of honour were my best friend Carey's elder sister Lady Anne Coke, Lady Jane Willoughby, Lady Mary Baillie-Hamilton, Lady Rosemary Spencer Churchill (who was engaged at the time and had to postpone her wedding in order to preserve her status as 'maid') and Lady Moyra Hamilton. Their principal duty was to carry the Queen's twenty-yard-long train of purple velvet. They had to be matched in height so that the symmetry of the processional crocodile in the Abbey was perfect. Jane was paired with Mary

Baillie-Hamilton, and they were positioned in the front row behind the Queen. Anne was to walk with Jane Willoughby and Moyra and Rosie, being the tallest, were to take up their positions at the back.

For years after the coronation, in the Pathé news review that used to precede films in the cinemas and more recently during the 2002 Jubilee celebrations, the pictures of the six girls standing next to the Queen on the balcony would be shown again and again. It was always easy to pick out Jane, partly because she was in the front next to the Queen and also because to my mind she was by far the prettiest.

I am not entirely certain why these particular six girls were chosen but Jane felt her name might have been suggested by Patrick Plunket. Everyone in my family was very excited at the idea of Jane being part of this unique event and for Jane, aged only twenty, it was tremendously exhilarating to be taking part in such a momentous and historic occasion. There were endless photographs of her in the paper, and countless dress rehearsals and dress fittings with the royal couturier Norman Hartnell, and everyone made a big fuss of her. I, of course, had the inevitable and familiar mixed feelings of pride and jealousy. Alastair and I were not invited to the Abbey for the actual ceremony but we were given tickets for the dress rehearsal a few days before, which was almost as thrilling as the actual event and I still have my entry ticket in a drawer at Ormeley.

On the big day itself we watched from special stands near the Abbey in the pouring rain, cheering the coaches as they passed. Daddy knew exactly where he would be sitting in the Abbey, splendid in his crimson and ermine robes, and a somewhat apprehensive Jane felt greatly reassured when during the service she managed to spot him in the congregation of 7500 people and saw him give her a big wink. After the ceremony itself and before recessing out of the Cathedral, the Queen and her maids withdrew for a moment into a little anteroom where the Archbishop of Canterbury, Dr Fisher, produced a pocket flask from beneath his magnificent robes and handed round little nips of brandy to warm them all up.

A year earlier Jane had been invited by Princess Margaret to stay at Balmoral, and vividly remembers sitting in the back of a car with the Princess and the Queen's equerry Peter Townsend, and noticing an unmistakable intimacy between the two of them as they shared a secret joke. On returning home she told Mummy that she thought she had detected something special between the couple but my mother told her not to be ridiculous. Townsend was much older than the Princess and Mummy dismissed Jane's romantic suspicions by reminding her that not only was Townsend married but that all equerries have to be nice to princesses.

The second thing Jane remembers about that visit was that she had forgotten to pack more than one pair of pants and couldn't imagine asking the Princess if she could borrow some, so she spent every evening washing her only pair and praying they would dry on the towel rail overnight.

After the coronation Jane was invited to stay at Windsor for Ascot Races, which threw her into a panic because everyone was expected to take a lady's maid with them and Jane did not have one. At that time Mrs Kausin, the Latvian lady who had originally come to help out in the kitchen at the Brown House, was still working for us. She was known affectionately by us as Kausin Kunz, which we thought was Latvian for Mrs. In lieu of a lady's maid Kausin Kunz was asked to accompany Jane to Windsor and although this time Jane could be sure that more than one pair of pants would be packed, she could not be responsible for the unexpected racial prejudice that emerged from below stairs. When Mrs Kausin brought in her breakfast tray in the morning Jane was alarmed to see her looking red-eyed and miserable. Sobbing, she confided in Jane that the other very grand servants downstairs had turned on her, suggesting she should go back to Latvia where she belonged. Jane was appalled, but was helpless to do anything about Mrs Kausin's distress.

The news of Mrs Kausin's ill treatment by the staff at Windsor did not, on the other hand, particularly move me as by now Kausin Kunz had turned into a spy and detective, and like a stalking ghost would patrol the top floor of 101 Park Street where Jane and I slept, hoping to catch me borrowing some of Jane's clothes.

My admiration of my elder sister knew no bounds and the nearest I could get to looking like her was to wear her clothes. Despite the difference in our shoe sizes, for hers were two sizes smaller than mine, I would cram my feet into a pair of her black very high-heeled evening shoes, like one of Cinderella's stepsisters, thus guaranteeing for myself an evening of utter agony with my toes scrunched into balls. No wonder my feet have never recovered and are misshapen to this day. Mrs Kausin grew increasingly adept at catching me and finally locked Jane's cupboard, putting an end to any more borrowing. (Anticipating the lock, however, I had cunningly managed to get a couple of her dresses copied even though I knew they did not look quite the same on me as they had on Jane.)

And then, for the first time, I fell in love.

Mark Birley was the least likely person on my list of eligible young men to become my boyfriend because everyone else was in love with him and he was the best-looking young man around. Our romance began at the Queens ice-skating rink in Bayswater. Occasionally a party of my friends and I would go there in the evening but I was quite hopeless at skating and spent most of the time flat on my back on the ice. Mark Birley was equally uncoordinated and hopeless, and we would both cling to the side of the rink making tentative little gliding movements which inevitably led to us crashing on to the ice. Mark always maintains that as I fell over for the umpteenth time he picked me up by one of my bosoms and after that we spent as much time as we could together, which was not easy because of my commitments to Wynyard and Daddy.

Daddy's drinking was becoming more and more serious and the burden on Jane was enormous. He had reached the point when he was drunk by breakfast and one day at Park Street, thoroughly exasperated by his behaviour, Jane went into his room and asked him why he was drinking so much and putting us through such hell and he answered, 'Because I want to die.'

Daddy had never contemplated a life without my mother and we began to realise that he was incapable of existing without her. He had worshipped her and knew she would not tolerate drunkenness. He had drunk excessively as a young man, but during their engagement in the summer of 1931 and already aware of her disapproval he wrote, 'I felt so ashamed of myself last week getting drunk and going to the 43 Club. I must say you were very sweet about it. Why I don't know. It was such a childish thing to do.' But only ten days after this remorseful letter he writes, 'I have been summoned for not driving with due care in Wiltshire though I have no recollection of the incident.'

Barely a week before their marriage he tries to reassure her: 'One is always three parts tight but I have gone teetotal.'

After their wedding he managed to keep his drinking under control and while I was growing up, I was always rather surprised that he drank orange juice, just like us, and at school Parents' Days he would never join the other fathers with their glasses of sherry. In fact, during those years I never once saw him touch an alcoholic drink.

But when parted from Mummy during the war, he would sometimes lapse and Jane remembers him being drunk on leave and in terrible moods in his study. I found a letter written on board ship from 1941 in which he apologises to Mummy for the shame he felt after one such occasion: 'As you must have noticed, I have been drinking far too much lately. It is very contemptible and I hope this voyage will cut it right down. I have been beastly to you, but I never meant to be. I am just too selfish.'

Devastated by her death and without her restraining influence, he saw no reason not to drink as much as he wished, becoming very bitter towards his mother and sisters for the way they had once treated Mummy.

He had always been attractive to women and after Mummy's death he was not short of admirers, among them Maureen, Marchioness of Dufferin and Ava and Lady Ancaster, whose visits to Wynyard he would alternate. Occasionally, possibly on purpose as he rather enjoyed the drama of that sort of situation, he would get the timing wrong and invite them both together.

He became very fond indeed of Valerie Hobson, the movie star and actress, and for a short time, because we all loved her, we hoped that she might inherit Mummy's role and stop him from drinking. Having starred in more than forty films, she famously gave a wonderful performance in 1949 in the greatest of the Ealing comedies, *Kind Hearts and Coronets* with Sir Alec Guinness. She was very good to us children and we remained close to her until her death in 1998 at the age of eighty-one.

When Valerie was starring as Anna in *The King and I*, with Herbert Lom playing the king, Daddy took a box in the theatre almost every night of the week. Sometimes he would persuade me to go with him and we would sit side by side as he hummed the tunes, getting them all wrong. We longed for her to marry Daddy but although she cared for him and for us as a family, in 1954, a few months after my own wedding, she fell in love with and married Jack Profumo. Throughout Profumo's affair with Christine Keeler and the resulting political scandal she remained loyal to her husband, declaring 'Love is the important thing. I have been happy to have had it.' And knowing them as well as I did, I can state without hesitation that they never stopped loving each other.

On hearing the news of Valerie's engagement Daddy was furious and, getting very drunk, sent Robert the butler round to her flat to demand the return of all the presents he had given her although the only presents I can remember him giving her were a string of Palethorpe sausages so I hope she did not have to return those as well. Later Daddy would acknowledge that she had made the right choice, comparing himself unfavourably with Jack Profumo, a young up-and-coming politician, as 'a moribund marquess stuck in the North'.

Although sometimes Jane and I now laugh, remembering some of the more embarrassing acts Daddy committed when drunk, the terrifying mood swings were not funny as anyone who has lived with an alcoholic will know. One moment he would be almost maudlin and the next he would fly into a rage. While my mother was alive I never saw my parents have a row once because Daddy's drinking was so rarely an issue. My parents had always maintained their extremely close relationship and (according to Neil Chaplin) despite Mummy's illness they shared a bed until a few weeks before her death, which in an era of separate bedrooms, with husbands tending to pay their wives irregular nocturnal visits, I found quite surprising.

There were still occasional periods of sobriety in his last years when he was capable of being extremely funny but these moods were short-lived as any alcohol-induced emotion whether of rage, affection or humour would become exaggerated with the drink and he would lose control.

It is sad to see the dignity of someone you love and respect slip away and Daddy became unrecognisable as the father who had played those magical games with us, who had read to us, loved us and chastised us. We saw instead a shambolic figure, shuffling in and out of his bedroom at Wynyard, forgetting that he was still in his pyjamas. Sometimes he would act in a suggestive way towards any female who happened to be around, usually in a harmless nudge-nudge, wink-wink kind of way, but occasionally in a manner that was thoroughly inappropriate.

One afternoon, after a Wynyard cricket match, Daddy, who had begun the morning quite sober, started some serious tippling and as the afternoon wore on he began making advances towards the girlfriend of the local Conservative Party agent, Mr Galloway. At first he put his hand up her skirt. She removed it, pretending she hadn't noticed and then he did it again. Mr Galloway was not sure whether to ignore the behaviour of the local Marquess, the ex Member for County Durham, or to hit him. While Jane and I tried to defuse the situation Daddy pulled Mr Galloway's girlfriend on to his knee and bounced her up and down while saying to us, 'This lady's a bit of all right.' It seemed an eternity before Mr Galloway and his girlfriend managed to extricate themselves and escape.

Amazingly, Daddy was still being asked to make speeches at public events but it was becoming impossible to gauge whether he would be drunk or sober on the day and several dreadful incidents took place when he was drunk on a platform. On one occasion he was due to propose a friend of Jane's, Tom Egerton, as a prospective Member of Parliament for one of the northern constituencies. Jane and I felt we had kept Daddy reasonably sober during the day but as he stood on the platform swaying slightly he broke into a self-pitying ramble, lamenting lost opportunities for happiness, complaining that life had dealt him some bad blows and that he found little solace in his children. He then fell over backwards and had to be carted out of the hall. For us this was embarrassing rather than hurtful because Jane and I knew not only that he would forget what he had said but had he been sober he would never have said such wounding things in the first place.

★

At around this time my appendix, which had been grumbling away for months, was removed. I had heard horror stories of burst appendixes so I exaggerated my symptoms and ended up in the Westminster Hospital having it taken out by none other than Mummy's surgeon, Sir Stanford Kade. Having never had an operation or anaesthetic before, apart from the removal of my tonsils and adenoids when I was too young to remember, I was very apprehensive and although Daddy made lots of jokes about leaving the hospital feet first, I think he was worried too.

However, emerging from the anaesthetic, which was much heavier in those days, I opened my eyes with difficulty and saw Daddy coming through the door with Sasha, his 'friend' from the Bag o'Nails pub in Shepherd Market in Mayfair. He had a foolish grin on his face and at the sight of them both I turned my head and was violently sick over the side of the hospital bed.

By now I was seeing Mark Birley on a regular basis and had found the courage to introduce him to Daddy. At first Daddy was rather impressed by Mark who, having excellent manners, was very patient with him, listening to the same stories over and over again and laughing at the same jokes. He also liked the idea of Mark working at the J. Walter Thompson advertising agency because he was particularly fond of a series of advertisements the agency had made for Horlicks, the hot drink, for which Mark had done some of the drawings. The advertisements involved a variety of domestic situations where things were always going wrong but were magically put right by Horlicks, invariably ending with the caption 'Later, thanks to Horlicks'. 'Later, thanks to Horlicks' became a family catchphrase which we would always use when something went well.

Daddy drove a Humber car, which he used for journeys up and down to Wynyard, but he also had a rather sporty little Hillman Minx, which he drove when he was in London and as he was spending more and more time at Wynyard, for a time he lent Mark the little car. One evening at a dinner party I was seated at the end of a long table near Brookie (later Lord Warwick) who turned to his neighbour, a journalist and great friend of mine called Alastair Forbes, and asked who I was. Without hesitation Allie replied, 'She's the daughter of the owner of Birley's car.' I had known Allie since I was a schoolgirl and he was another of those many men who suffered but endured unrequited love for my sister. He wrote a political column for the *Sunday Despatch* which involved travelling all over the world and I would receive endless long-distance calls from him which were intended for Jane but as she was often out or refused to take them, Allie and I would chat for hours. His telephone bill must have been horrendous.

Mark and I would occasionally be invited to stay in the country for the weekend by the Hambledons as Kate, the sister of Harry Hambledon (Viscount Hambledon), was a friend of mine. Although Mark and I were what was known as 'going steady', suitably decorous behaviour was generally expected of us and we were always given bedrooms as far apart as possible. On the first evening Mark crept into my room to say goodnight and we were engaged in a passionate embrace when the door opened and in walked Harry's and Kate's mother, Patricia Hambledon (Patricia, Viscountess Hambledon). Luckily Mark was fully clothed lying on my bed but nevertheless Lady Hambledon was icily furious and ordered Mark back to his room. I spent a miserable night wondering how on earth I was going to be able to face her the next morning and whether she would ring my father. I decided to get up really early and make my apologies to her at breakfast before anyone else was up. She was sweet but firm, telling me that she would never tolerate that kind of behaviour in her house and that she hoped I would not do it again. By lunchtime the whole house party was sniggering over the incident.

Soon afterwards Mark and I were caught together in the

Londonderry coronation coach, which was permanently parked in the huge hall at Wynyard among the marble statues. One weekend Mark and I were exploring the hall when we heard voices. Miss Bertie, who had been the principal of the teachers' training college at Wynyard during the war, was giving some of her pupils a tour of the house. Mark and I had climbed into the coach, not with amorous intentions but in order to hide from Miss Bertie, who was a monumental bore. To our horror, we heard voices coming nearer and nearer, and suddenly I felt a tugging at the coach door which I struggled to hold shut from inside. When it was finally wrenched open, a dozen startled faces stared in amazement at the undignified sight of Mark and me crouching together on the brown leather seat.

It was fortunate for me that Mark appeared to be unshockable, taking most of my father's antics in his stride and continuing to listen patiently to all his stories. But even Mark was taken aback during his first Christmas at Wynyard. Jane and I had spent most of Christmas Eve decorating the huge tree which stood in the drawing room and laying the wrapped presents beneath it. Early on Christmas morning while the rest of us were still asleep Mark got up and wandered downstairs for breakfast alone. Going into the drawing room, he was astonished to see that during the night the brightly coloured glass balls hanging from branches of the tree had been added to by long looping garlands of French letters. Luckily, with Jane's and my help we managed to remove them all in time for the arrival of the Reverend and Mrs Worsley who were popping in for their annual pre-Christmas lunch drink. I thought that Daddy might have forgotten his deeds of the night before or at least appear to show a little remorse but I could not have been more wrong as instead he was rather annoyed that we had removed the offending condoms and grumbled away telling us what spoilsports we were.

In view of this escapade it is perhaps hardly surprising

that Mark remained quite calm when one evening Daddy persuaded the local vet's daughter to remove her clothes and dance naked on the dining-room table while he drank champagne from one of her shoes, held impassively by Robert the butler.

Soon after Christmas, Daddy started to be a little less cordial to Mark. Maybe he felt we were getting too serious, that I was too young and that Mark was not settled enough, but I think the more likely reason for his coldness was that he foresaw a time when he would lose my company at Wynyard, a deprivation he feared, not because, as Jane and Alastair would claim, I was his favourite child, but because I was the one who made him laugh.

SEVEN

Marriage to Mark

Daddy's disapproval of Mark intensified, and without giving any reasons he began to forbid me seeing him at Park Street. One day, overcoming the fear of a confrontation, I went into Daddy's study at Wynyard where as usual he was sitting at his desk, writing interminable letters of complaint, either to the Bishop of Durham, Michael Ramsay or to the Prime Minister, Winston Churchill. These letters were mostly rambling litanies about local government issues with which he had become obsessed but very few were ever posted and after his death Jane found dozens of them, stacked in the drawers of his desk.

That evening, nervously I sat facing him asking why he would not let me see Mark. At first I thought I might have chosen the right moment as Daddy seemed to be in one of his rare sober moods, but as I repeated the question there was no response and he continued writing his letter in silence. Eventually, after a long pause and without looking at me, he replied, 'Because his father was a bounder and his mother a whore.' This assessment was both monstrously untrue and unfair. Oswald Birley had been one of the most respected society portrait painters of the century and Rhoda was a well-known if somewhat bohemian hostess. My voice was unsteady, but as I objected that these were not valid or truthful reasons for forbidding me to see Mark, Daddy did not even look up from his desk and I left the room in tears.

I was very angry and knew that I had to get away from

Wynyard immediately, even though it would be difficult because George the chauffeur had been banned from driving me to the station, which was fifteen miles away. Surreptitiously I managed to call a taxi from the business telephone in Miss Bertie's old office hoping I would be in time to catch the last train to London.

As I waited on the station platform I was terrified I would be caught by Daddy, only relaxing once the train had moved off. I arrived at Park Street at night to find our housekeeper, Mrs Ruddy, too frightened to let me in as she had already been telephoned from Wynyard to be told I could not stay there, but being a true romantic of the Mills and Boon type, she relented and pretended not to notice when Mark joined me later. Only after I was married to Mark did I fully realise how kind Mrs Ruddy had been and how she had put her job on the line for me.

After the drama of my flight from Wynyard, Mark only came to Park Street when Daddy was away and although we were both careful not to mention Mark, Daddy and I were soon back on good terms and our unpleasant conversation in the study at Wynyard was forgotten.

I had recently started working for Meals on Wheels, which I thoroughly enjoyed as I loved meeting all the elderly people and listening to their grumblings about the revolting food. However, delivery girl for Meals on Wheels was not the occupation Daddy had in mind for his daughter and he told me bluntly that if I wanted to stay in London I must get a proper job, otherwise he would insist that I return to Wynyard to study estate management.

The second alternative was quite out of the question, as I did not want to leave Mark, so I decided to try to get into journalism. I wrote to Frank Owen, the editor of the *Daily Mail*, and asked to be considered for any work at all on the paper. To my amazement he gave me an interview and offered me a position which, although it would probably have involved making the tea, filled me with excitement. But other circumstances intervened and I never took the job.

Not surprisingly, Mark found me very unworldly because apart from one brief summer in Paris and a few years at boarding school I had been cocooned at Wynyard for most of my life. Mark and I *had* talked about marriage, but our conversations had been rather jokey, if full of plans about the things we would like to do together and the places we would like to go to. I found myself torn as although I knew that I wanted to spend the rest of my life with Mark I also hated the idea of leaving the familiar safety of home. I wanted both worlds. Soon, however, one thing led to another and Mark and I forced Daddy to agree to our marriage.

At exactly the same time, and along with the rest of the nation, we had been following the newspaper accounts of Jimmy Goldsmith's dramatic love story with the nineteen-year-old Isabel Patino and been thrilled by their elopement in January 1954. Because I was also only nineteen, I found the fairy tale particularly romantic and prayed that Isabel's father would not catch them. Two months after my marriage to Mark, when I read in the newspapers about Isabel's death in childbirth, I felt I shared an intense emotional bond with her and the tragedy affected me deeply. I remember looking at the harrowing pictures of a grief-stricken Jimmy and feeling desperately sorry for him.

In 1954 the law forbade marriage without parental consent for anyone under the age of twenty-one and I think Mark and I married partly in defiance because in truth we fell far more deeply in love with each other after we married. In retrospect we both went into the commitment fairly ignorant of what we were doing and I am sure Mark considered backing out in the face of the opposition he met from my family. He was given a particularly tough interrogation by Uncle Simon who, acting as the formidable head of the Combe family, was worried that

Mark was not yet professionally settled and also expressed his strong disapproval of my marriage at such a young age. While Mark had an awful time with my relations, I was shown nothing but kindness and encouragement from his family, particularly his mother Rhoda, Maxine his sister and Rhoda's best friend Maria Harrison.

In preparation for the wedding my godmother Patsy Ward and I set off to buy numerous nightdresses for my trousseau but the lead-up to the rather hasty ceremony was filled with moments of panic and chaos.

On the morning of the wedding, while getting myself ready, I realised that I had no face powder so I crept into Jane's room to borrow some from her. Understandably, Jane was rather tired with all the arrangements as it was she who really made it possible for us to get married at all, acting as negotiator between Mark and me and Daddy. Fed up with my incurable habit of borrowing all her possessions, she told me to get lost. In years to come Mrs Ruddy would tell me how amused she was to overhear me plead with my sister, 'Oh come on, Jane, what's a bit of powder on a day like this?'

To add to the last-minute confusion, Mark had forgotten to buy a wedding ring and Jane was sent flying off to the Burlington Arcade where she managed to find one, second hand, for £2.10s. and I remember her handing it over to Mark saying, 'Don't forget to pay me back.' (Jimmy also forgot to buy a ring when I married him in 1978 and I'm afraid I used the same one, simply removing it for a moment and then replacing it on the same finger.)

The night before marrying Mark, while being forced by Patsy to have a manicure and pedicure by a French manicurist who used to do my mother, I received a barrage of calls from Daddy whose tone ranged from abusive to sentimental, but by the morning he had calmed down, realising the marriage was already a fait accompli.

If you were going to get married in a register office in the

1950s, Caxton Hall in Westminster was the place to choose. Many famous people, and couples marrying for the second time round, have married there including the Prime Minister Anthony Eden, and Paul and Linda McCartney, but it was most unusual for girls from my background not to get married in church.

When we arrived at the Hall I was amazed to see an enormous crowd of onlookers as well as masses of photographers. The previous day about two dozen newspapers ranging from the national press, including *The Times*, the *Daily Telegraph* and the *Daily Mail*, to local papers as far apart as Brighton and Dundee, had carried stories about the impending wedding. About 300 people, mostly women, had crowded around the steps of the hall, eager to catch a glimpse of the bride. They were somewhat baffled when Valerie Hobson arrived, in a chic floral dress and, mistaken momentarily for the bride, she received a huge cheer.

Instead, the real bride was wearing what the papers called 'a clerical grey spring suit' with a very tight-fitting waisted jacket that emphasised how slim I was. I wore black gloves and was carrying a smart shiny black handbag with a spray of camellias in my buttonhole. I had a little red hat, which sat on the back of my head with a short net veil and I was wearing my favourite two-strand necklace and a pair of sapphire and diamond earrings that had belonged to my mother. It was certainly an unconventional outfit for the daughter of a marquess to get married in.

Mark arrived a few minutes after me with his best friend Douglas Wilson. Mark and Douglas shared a flat in Eaton Place where they were looked after by Bunda, a four-foot-high Indian Jeeves. Although Douglas had officially been invited to be Mark's best man, there was a strange mix-up and somehow Bunda took the role instead. According to one newspaper report Mark 'bounded up the steps of Caxton Hall two at a time wearing a navy-blue suit and a red carnation'. I have never spotted Mark bounding up anything before or after, but maybe they mistook Bunda for the groom.

Inside the hall our respective families were waiting. Jane, Alastair, the Plunket brothers and the Combe relations were all there with Mark's mother Rhoda, Maria Harrison and Mark's glamorous sister Maxine although I don't think any of the Londonderry aunts or even Mama came.

Mark, Daddy and I were shown into the front row facing James Dumsday Holiday, the wonderfully named Chief Superintendent Registrar, who was to conduct the ceremony. He had been at Caxton Hall for years and had officiated at many famous weddings. After Mr Holiday had welcomed us with his customary opening words, I glanced behind to see Jane and Valerie alone among the rather grim-looking congregation struggling to give me encouraging smiles. They might just as well have been at my funeral.

I knew Mark had been given a lot of names at his christening but I never knew quite how many. They were: Marcus Oswald Hornby Lecky Birley, while I was just plain Annabel Vane-Tempest-Stewart. Mr Holiday began the ceremony by asking, 'Do you, Marcus Oswald Hornby *Leaky* [sic] Birley take Annabel Vane-Tempest-Stewart to be your. . .'

There was a pause during which you could have heard a pin drop followed by an explosion of laughter from Daddy, echoed by a ripple of nervous hilarity from behind us and complete hysterics from Mark and me.

We continued to shake as Mr Holiday tried again. As he paused for us to repeat the words after him there was at first total silence, since Mark and I did not trust ourselves to speak a word for fear of laughing. I could hear Valerie, Jane and Alastair out of control behind me. Mr Holiday slowly removed his spectacles and looked at us very sternly. 'Even if you don't take this seriously, we do,' he said. Mark and I made a monumental effort to pull ourselves together.

This time, on his third attempt, and by now aware of the

reason he was having such an effect on our composure, Mr Holiday wisely left out the Lecky altogether, and triumphantly pronounced us man and wife.

The entire ceremony had taken just fifteen minutes and we emerged into the London sunshine to the cheering of the crowds and the strange experience of facing a bank of cameras from the press. The *Daily Despatch* from Manchester indicated their disappointment that there had not been more of a show, headlining their report FOR A MARQUESS'S DAUGHTER – NO ORANGE BLOSSOM. Sensing a missed opportunity and clearly feeling rather short-changed, their reporter observed, 'It could have been the society wedding of the year, but instead they chose a simple quiet civic ceremony, with no top hats, no satin, and no orange blossom.'

After the service we went back to Park Street for a family reception. The Plunket brothers gave me a beautiful gold bee with diamond eyes, which I still have, and I remember watching Daddy and Rhoda having a very civilised and, unusually for him, sober conversation in the corner of the dining room. Mark's sister Maxine, who was twelve years older than me, chic, beautiful, very worldly and the epitome of everything I would love to have been at the time, gave me a pep talk about what a strain Mark was under and how I must look after him on the honeymoon. Poor Mark. I am sure that had he been able, he would willingly have taken a rocket to the furthest place he could find.

When the time came for us to leave for the airport I had a moment of sheer panic, wondering what I was doing and what, indeed, I had just done, suddenly realising that my life was going to change irrevocably. I put my arms round Daddy and hugged him, holding him very tightly. As tears started rolling down my cheeks he, never liking open displays of emotion, patted me on the back saying, 'Come on, come on' and gently guided me into the waiting taxi.

The plan was to leave immediately for the airport, to catch

a plane to Paris and to spend the honeymoon night in splendour at the Lotti Hotel, paid for with the large cheque that Tony Lambton had very generously given us for the honeymoon. But on the way to the airport we called in at Mark's flat, taking with us a very overwrought and tipsy Patsy Ward. Ever since my mother's death and the start of Daddy's drinking my godmother had been a staunch defender of us three children, but the cumulative strain leading up to that day finally became too much for her and by the time she reached the flat she was already absolutely paralytic.

Patsy, Douglas and Mark continued to drink a great deal more champagne and by the time we finally arrived at the airport we had missed the flight. We got there eight minutes after boarding had finished and Mark was furious as he could see the plane sitting on the tarmac. 'This is outrageous,' he shouted as he stormed up and down the departure lounge, but the officials refused to budge. Such was the notoriety of our wedding that the press had followed us to the airport and reported that I sat in a corner looking very embarrassed, eating a currant cake and drinking orange squash while begging Mark not to make such a fuss.

Eventually we caught the next plane and arrived at the Lotti Hotel where we were shown to the bridal suite. I was exhausted but Mark was anxious to have dinner at one of his favourite restaurants and the only thing I can remember about that dinner is Mark knocking over a chair. Back at the hotel he suggested I unpack while he went to the bar for a nightcap. I changed into one of Patsy's well-chosen nightgowns and waited for him. I waited and waited but there was no sign of Mark. Eventually I rang down to the concierge and asked, '*Où est Monsieur Birley?*'

'*Ah Madame,*' he answered, '*il est allé au Circle.*'

Le Circle was a well-known gambling club and for the first and last time in my life I showed a lack of judgement about how to treat a serious gambler. In the years I spent as the wife of two committed gamblers, I learned that you never interrupt a man who is running a winning bank. Mark, whose nerves had got the better of him, had gone round the corner to Le Circle. He was playing chemin de fer and was indeed running a winning bank.

Without thinking, I asked the concierge to go and tell my husband that his wife was extremely unwell. I was damned if I was going to spend my wedding night waiting for Mark to finish gambling. This was a mistake. I cannot imagine what the two concierges must have thought as they frogmarched the reluctant bridegroom up the stairs to the bridal suite but Mark was so angry that he called me every name under the sun and even went so far as to ring Douglas Wilson to tell him what a spoilsport I was. The wedding night was a fiasco.

Thankfully, by the following morning Mark could not remember much about the night before and as we boarded the train to Garmisch in Germany, I remained very quiet as I knew he must have a dreadful headache.

For the rest of the honeymoon my new husband was adorable and after a few days in Garmisch we went to Kitzbühel in Austria to ski. The memory of my graceless attempts at staggering up and down those slopes and my hopeless efforts to learn to ski put me off the sport for life. But it was on those slippery slopes that we started to get to know each other properly.

We had never been away on our own before and we soon discovered that we were soulmates. Recently Mark said that getting married to me was the most important thing that ever happened to him and that we were the true loves of each other's lives. Although years later I certainly fell in love with Jimmy Goldsmith, for me the heady intensity and special quality of that first love will always remain irreplaceable.

We spent the last days of our honeymoon staying with Mark's sister Maxine in Paris. She was living with the celebrated film director Louis Malle, later famous for countless wonderful movies, among them *Atlantic City* and *My Dinner with André*. Maxine was then a very talented dress designer and rather liked modelling her clothes on me. She would make me try them on in the apartment and I nearly died of embarrassment when she insisted on pulling the top of my dress down, trying to show Louis Malle what 'an amazing bosom' she thought I had.

Eventually we had to return to England and although I was longing to see my family again, I was not looking forward to having to face reality. We had no idea where we were going to live as neither of us had any money of our own and the honeymoon had eaten up all of Tony Lambton's generous gift. More worryingly, I had never cooked and I was dreading the prospect of making Mark's first breakfast.

EIGHT

Married Life

For the first few months of our marriage Mark and I rented a little house off Montpelier Square and it was here that I first met John Aspinall. Nicknamed by Jimmy Goldsmith's brother Teddy and later known to us all as Aspers, he was famous for two wildly contrasting passions. The first was his love and, in his case it should be said, talent for gambling. From his undergraduate days at Oxford, he was determined eventually to set up a casino that would rival in elegance and reputation the gambling venues of the eighteenth century. Aspers's second passion was for animals, in particular mammals, for whom he had an affinity almost unrivalled in documented relationships between man and beast. Both his casino, the Clermont in Berkeley Square, and his two zoos at Howletts and Port Lympne brought him fame and notoriety. However, the worlds were not unconnected as one paid for the other. The income from his gambling pursuits provided the funds which fed and housed hundreds of animals, many of which he saved from ultimate extinction. His biographer Brian Masters says Aspers was a maverick from his earliest days who was 'destined to fashion his own rules and develop an amused disdain for orthodox expectations'. When Aspers died in 2000 at the age of seventy-four, his friends and colleagues published a book celebrating his life with contributions from us all, and I wrote the following piece:

I cannot recall why he came to see us in our house in Chelsea, or who introduced him, but I do remember the evening and John Aspinall very vividly. In latter years he described our meeting: 'There I stood, a blond Nordic god, and Annabel, who was rather beautiful herself in those days, was spell-bound.'

He took to calling me Wasabel, and whatever age I happened to be, he would automatically add ten years, as part of his habitual teasing of me. That first evening, although I did not perceive Aspers as a god, I did find him quite extraordinary, and unlike anyone I had ever met. He told me a story called 'The Pearl', which went on for two hours. He was an incredible raconteur, to the end of his days, although most of his stories were grossly exaggerated, adding to the amusement of his audience.

I knew him from the beginning, with his first baby tiger, his first Capuchin monkey and, later, his first gorillas, as well as from the time he found and began restoring Howletts.

I remember the famous gorilla walks, and his first wolf cub, Noushka. When I first met her, she was allowed to sleep in the house because she had fallen into a wasps' nest and was badly stung. She made herself a den under the stairs, but rarely stayed there. That weekend, she attached herself to me, and would wander up to my bedroom, stealthily stealing as many objects as took her fancy: my book or my bag, with the occasional forage into the bathroom when I was having a bath, pinching my sponge and my slippers. She was the most enchanting animal I have ever encountered, far sweeter than any dog. Later, she was to become the matriarch of a large tribe of wolves kept at Port Lympne.

Mark and I were lucky enough to be taken by Aspers on wonderful holidays including several memorable yachting trips around the Mediterranean and the Greek islands. The Aspinall hospitality extended sometimes to my whole family when Alastair and Nico as well as Jane were invited to join us on the boat. On one of those holidays in Greece I met

Jimmy Goldsmith's brother Teddy for the first time who was not only eventually to become my brother-in-law but also a great friend of Alastair's. In Teddy's then wife Gill I immediately recognised a kindred spirit, sharing much in common with her, not least three children who were the same sort of ages as her own three, Dido, Clio and Alexander. She became and remains one of my greatest friends.

Aspers would tell everyone that I refused to explore the Mediterranean, preferring instead to sunbathe on deck, but however addicted to the sun I might be, sightseeing with Aspers as a guide was irresistible as he made it such fun. On one occasion, disembarking in Gallipoli in Turkey, we piled into a restaurant where, encouraged by me, Aspers broke into a loud rendition of his favourite song, 'Marta, Rambling Rose of the Wild Woods'. He became so carried away by his singing and our applause that he continued to sing it on the balcony of the restaurant and we were all arrested by the local police.

Even when he became ill with cancer, Aspers never lost his sense of humour, nor the pleasure he took in his daily visits to his animals. With his face swathed in bandages, he would clamber over the gorilla enclosures, feeding and talking to them, helped by his wife Sally and his children. Sally nursed him devotedly, hardly ever leaving his side. He hated spending any time in hospital, despite his many visitors and the home-cooked meals Sally would bring in for him; nor were the hospitals particularly sad to see him leave.

On one occasion Aspers begged the nurses not to wake him up at the mandatory six in the morning time to take his pulse and temperature but after the third such awakening, Aspers told the nurse that if she woke him up again, he would throw her out of the window. To demonstrate this, he got out of bed and opened it wide. When Sally arrived, her arms laden with his lunch, she was met by the matron with these words: 'Lady Sally, I feel that Mr Aspinall would make a speedier recovery at home.' Sally removed him that day.

With Sally, Aspers not only found a soulmate, but someone who shared his love of wild animals – as indeed had both his previous wives. One evening I arrived for dinner at Lyall Street to be told by Aspers that Sally might not be able to join us; she would, he said, be too busy upstairs with the 'baby'. Somewhat baffled, I went upstairs and found her in the bedroom with a tiny baby gorilla in an incubator and a paediatric nurse from University College Hospital.

Alas, Aspers has gone and I do not expect to meet anyone like him again. Most people will remember him for his enormous contribution to wildlife, and in particular gorillas, and I too will remember him for these things. However, I will also remember him as a loyal friend and one of the most amusing men I have ever met.

During our stay in the Knightsbridge house, Mark embarked on a lifelong passion for dogs. As a wedding present Jane had given us a smooth-haired miniature black-and-tan dachshund, who was a replica of Tony Lambton's dog Fly, and when we collected our present from the breeder in Oxted we both fell instantly in love with him. Noodle was a highly intelligent little dog and his breeder had impressed on us that he must be taught to sleep in his own basket at night, preferably in the kitchen, and be house-trained on newspaper. Noodle broke both these rules from the word go and slept tucked up between us, deep down inside the bed and he proved very difficult to house-train, as we had no garden, only a small backyard. As soon as he was big enough to jump off the bed he would rush out on to the top landing and do his first pee of the day, followed by a shit in the small sitting room. Although I persevered and he did improve a little, he never quite succeeded in learning much more than the rudiments of house-training.

He loved us so much that he could not bear us to go out without him and would howl until the neighbours complained, so we always took him with us to sleep in the car. He lived to a good age, saw us through three house moves and had an unerring sense of direction. When we were living at Pelham Cottage in South Kensington he managed to make his way back to our previous house in Halsey Street and became very keen on a dachshund bitch I had given to a large German lady called Mrs Godfrey, who used to help us out in the evenings. Her husband, a bad-tempered one-legged milkman, was so angry when he discovered that their dog was pregnant by Noodle that he threatened to break Mark's legs should she die giving birth. In any event she produced three puppies whom, with a flash of originality, Mrs Godfrey named Jane, Annabel and Alastair.

Mark's mother Rhoda lived near Seaford in Sussex in one of the prettiest houses I have ever known, Charleston Manor, where she had created a beautiful garden backing on to the Sussex Downs. Although she was very kind to me and I think she genuinely loved me, there was no feeling of warmth between her and Mark. Mark described their relationship in an interview he gave years later with Naim Attallah as not so much strained but 'more the absence of any relationship'. To her credit she was very keen on my taking an interest in everything artistic, including music and the ballet. I think we got on better in her later years because there was nothing left to disagree or argue over. An absence of affection, that was the point. Her encouragement of his artistic interests, however, were to have a significant effect on Mark's adult life when he started to create his beautiful clubs and restaurants but any love or affection that Mark had received as a child had come from Rhoda's maid Jackie, who brought him up and to whom he was devoted. Although Mark was extremely fond of his father, Oswald Birley was fifty when Mark was born and so was inevitably a remote figure, often seeming more like a grandfather to Mark. They did, however, find a reassuring unity in their feelings towards Rhoda, from whose constant arguments Oswald was always seeking refuge, longing to be left alone to paint.

Mark and I would drive down to Charleston for most week-ends, happy to escape from London and to enjoy the luxury of delicious food mostly cooked by Rhoda herself. Rhoda was Irish and had married Oswald Birley in 1921 when she was a young girl, twenty years his junior. Oswald was not only famous for painting all the grandest people of his day, including the leading members of the royal family, among them George V and VI, the Queen Mother and the present Queen, but also Prime Ministers Baldwin, Chamberlain, Attlee and finally Churchill, with whom he became so friendly that he asked Oswald to give him painting lessons.

Oswald was born in New Zealand in a town called St Asaph, coincidentally the same name as the fictional school Daddy had invented for Alastair's childhood games. As well as painting, Oswald and Rhoda were both enormously interested in the theatre and ballet, and had many friends in all these worlds. Together they established a sort of glamorous countryside salon at Charleston, where guests included Sibyl Colefax, Rudyard Kipling and Harold Nicolson. They frequently held concerts in their lovely garden, and when the Russian Ballet came to perform on their visits to England their leading dancers, among them Danilova and Nijinsky, would sit for their portraits by Oswald. After Rhoda's death I was delighted to be given the chance to buy his portrait of Nijinsky's daughter, which hangs in the drawing room at Ormeley.

During the summer holidays following our marriage, Rhoda had rented Charleston to a great friend of hers called Maria Harrison. Maria Harrison was Latvian, small, blonde and deeply affectionate and loving. She was also wonderful looking as is quite evident in a copy of a painting I have that Augustus John did of her. Her background remains a complete mystery to her many friends and no one seems to know when she arrived to live in England, but in 1939 she married an English stockbroker called Mike Harrison and they had two children, Nicolette and Benjy. Maria used to say Rhoda had '*la beauté du diable*', which was a good description of Rhoda's dramatic appearance, and between them these women exerted a powerful and impressionable influence on my young life. I was so close to Maria that I came to regard her as my surrogate mother.

Maria had known Mark since he was a boy and she immediately adopted us as a young couple, insisting we come down to Charleston for the first weekend of the holidays. When Mark and I arrived on a beautiful summer evening we found that Maria and Rhoda (who was also a guest for the weekend in her own house) were running a charity fair in the garden. Wandering around, I spotted a young blond boy playing among the stallholders who were dotted around the lawn. He was Maria's son Benjy, who must have been ten or eleven, and beside him was a beautiful young girl with long blonde hair. 'Darling, that's my daughter Nico,' Maria explained, 'come and meet her,' introducing me to the girl who, despite the age difference, became my closest friend until her death in 1993.

That first weekend there were, as was usual at Charleston, several other guests staying – among them the actor Michael Denison and his wife Dulcie Gray, and the playwright and film writer Wolf Mankowitz as well as Nico's best friend Tracy Pellissier. Tracy's mother was the actress and famous socialite Penelope Dudley-Ward – the daughter of Frieda, an intimate friend of the Duke of Windsor – who, after divorcing Tracy's father, had married Carol Reed, the film producer. Carol and Pempy, as she was known, were Maria's and Mike's greatest friends and they spent all their holidays together.

Mark and I shared the pretty guest cottage next to the main house with Nico, Tracy and Benjy. Years later Nico told me that they were all mesmerised by Mark's and my romance and used to listen outside our bedroom to hear if we were 'doing it'. Although not quite fourteen, she was extraordinarily mature for her age, while I was still a particularly childlike nineteen-year-old. Bored by the older guests, I managed to escape while they were having coffee in the main house to spend most evenings playing games and having midnight feasts in the woods or up on the South Downs with Nico, Tracy and Benjy. Cookums, their increasingly exasperated housekeeper, reported back to Maria that I was a very bad influence, but this only made Maria laugh and she continued to invite Mark and me to stay nearly every weekend.

By the end of that summer, Mark and I had run out of money but Rhoda owned a terraced house beside her own in St John's Wood, which she had divided into three flats and she allowed Mark and me to live rent free in the apartment on the top floor. It was tiny, consisting of a small bedroom with a large bed, a little sitting room, a pocket-sized kitchen and a bathroom. I considered it my first real home and although it was so small I loved it. I was too young to worry about the future although I am sure Mark did. He would travel each morning to J. Walter Thompson in Berkeley Square, sometimes taking the bus, if I needed the car and I look back on that year as one of the happiest Mark and I spent together.

We were both very untidy and needed a daily to come in occasionally to do a bit of cleaning and washing. Mrs Trindle, the daily at Park Street, told me about one of her neighbours, a Mrs White, who lived in Borrowdale Road, Wandsworth. Mrs Trindle explained, 'She's not much to look at but you should see her house; it's so clean you could eat your dinner off her floor.'

After Nico and Maria, Mrs White was the third person I was fortunate enough to meet that year who would become hugely important in my life. The first thing I noticed about her was the perpetual cross expression on her face, and her down-turned mouth, but despite her appearance she was a hard-working woman who became as devoted to me and the children as we were to her, and she remained with us until she retired in the early 1980s. Life had not been kind to Mrs White. Her mother had been both heartless and domineering, and she had never met her father, and I wondered if the stigma of illegitimacy was behind the harsh treatment her mother showed her.

Mrs White had married Reg White, a sailor, during the war and they had one daughter called Joyce, who in turn had twins called Ian and Elaine, whom Mrs White adored. Although she had her moments and I managed to make her roar with laughter, fundamentally she was not a happy woman. At first she was very unforthcoming about her personal life but as I grew to know her better I began to learn about her past and to admire her. In spite of her mother's behaviour, she was a dutiful daughter, not only allowing her mother to live with her, but returning home every day at noon from her morning work at Pelham Cottage in order to cook her lunch.

When I was married to Jimmy and living in Richmond she still came to Ormeley Lodge to look after Zac and Jemima on their own nanny Mimi's day off. All my children adored her and Robin still recalls looking forward to Thursdays at Pelham Cottage with *no Nanny Wendy* (the Birley children's Irish nanny). Instead, Mrs White would provide him with extra sweets and Popeye on the television in the evening. He remembers his delight at seeing that familiar cross face waiting outside Hill House School to collect him, a packet of Smarties in her coat pocket and India Jane beside her in the pushchair. After Mrs White's retirement I bought her a little flat in Mortlake where she lived with Reg, who was not only the most hen-pecked but also had to have been the most frustrated husband in the world. Mrs White had a total aversion to sex and poor Reg had not been allowed to have what she termed 'his way' for years, giving 'my polyps' as the reason for the termination of their sex life.

She was definitely aware that Mark and I had, at some point, slept together as even she could not persuade herself that my three children were a result of immaculate conception, but she preferred to believe, and I did not disillusion her, that Mark, like all men, had to have 'his way'.

She used to divide my girlfriends into 'them that did and them that didn't', meaning those who were a bit flighty and those who weren't. Needless to say she usually got it wrong. Miss X would be described as 'she's one that don't' but little did Mrs White (or 'Wags' as she was known to us) realise that Miss X did and rather a lot at that.

Alas she knew me well, too well, and when in the mid 1960s the routine of my life altered slightly, Mrs White noticed at once. At first she said nothing as I tried to continue to behave normally, taking the children to school, spending a great deal of time with them at home and still preferring early nights with dinner in front of the TV, sometimes inviting Mrs White (whose mother had finally died) to join me. Although Mark and I were still living together, by then we were effectively leading separate lives and Mark, for whom fidelity was never a top priority, had always had several girlfriends on the go dating from the early years of our married life.

On the rare evenings that I did go out it was mostly to Annabel's but when I began to spend the occasional entire night away from home, Mrs White was too intuitive not to realise something had changed. I was desperate to keep the truth from her, but I knew it would not be long before she discovered that I was having an affair with Jimmy Goldsmith.

Mrs White often arrived for work looking bad-tempered so one particular morning I did not find anything ominous about her scowling face, although as usual I tried to avoid her until her bad mood blew over. As my very first employee, she was very possessive and the moods were usually connected with her dislike of Nanny Wendy, or for that matter her jealousy of anyone else in the house who worked for me and to whom I was close. However, that morning she managed to grab me by the arm outside the children's bathroom and swung me inside

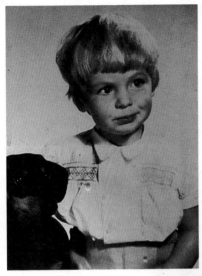

Above left: Rupert, my first child, aged eighteen months, with Noodle.

Above right: India Jane, my first daughter.

Right: Geoffrey Keating with my two eldest sons, Rupert and Robin. We decided to call Robin after daddy. Geoffrey was one of Mark's and my closest friends and often dropped in to visit us at Pelham Cottage.

Clockwise from top left

My sister-in-law and best friend, Nico, wearing the Londonderry tiara, on her way to a ball in London.

My cousin Patrick Plunket, who served as the Queen's Equerry for twenty-seven years. I thought he was simply the best company in the world and I saw a great deal of him.

My cousin Dominic Elwes and John Aspinall, known to us all as Aspers.

Aspers was famous for two wildly contrasting passions. The first was his love and talent for gambling, the second passion was for animals, in particular mammals, for whom he had an affinity almost unrivalled in documented relationships between man and beast.

In the garden at Pelham Cottage with India Jane and my nieces Sophia and Cosima.

With Jimmy in 1978 at Teddy's daughter Dido's wedding. Our romance had begun on the night he picked me up in Annabel's in 1964.

Jimmy and me arriving at Bow Street magistrates court for the *Private Eye* libel trial in 1976, publicly facing the press for the first time in our relationship.

Holidays

Top left: The Birley children in the small fishing boat that we rented on holiday in Porto Ercole, with Libero the boatman.

Top right: Nico with her second husband, Georgie Fame and their two sons, Tristan and James.

Above: In Las Vegas with Mark and Liz Brocklehurst, during the early days of my relationship with Jimmy.

Top: On holiday in Mexico in 1973. Lord Lucan was among the guests at Jimmy's rented villa. We would all have lunch at a hotel on the beach, seated at a long wooden table. In 1975, the *Sunday Times Magazine* printed a large picture of Lucan and myself, taken in Mexico. It was nothing more than a typical holiday snap, but the way it had been cropped suggested an intimate relationship between us.

Above: Victoria Getty also joined us on holiday in Mexico. She was one of the most beautiful and witty girls I knew.

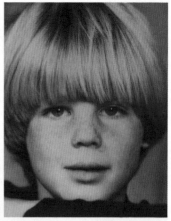

My second family

Top left: On 30 January 1974, my first child by Jimmy was born. We named her Jemima, the female equivalent of James, which means 'little dove' in Hebrew, although I cannot think of a less dove-like person than Jemima.

Top right: Zacharias, known as Zac, was born on 20 January 1975, making him and Jemima twins for ten days in the year.

Above: Benjamin, my youngest son, was born on 28 October 1980.

Top: Jimmy with Margaret Thatcher at the launch of *NOW* magazine in 1987.

Above: Jimmy in Barbados at Easter 1981 with all his children: (*from left to right*) Isabel, Zac, Manes, Jemima, Jimmy holding Ben, Alix.

Top: Ormeley Lodge.

Above: In the garden at Ormeley, with Ben, Zac, India Jane and Jemima.

saying, "Ere, I want a word with you. You been carryin' on. I never thought you'd do that. I always thought you was a lady.'

As I gazed at her in horror, trying to gather my wits, she continued, 'No, it's no good tryin' to get out of it, my lady, I know I done wrong but I read one of them letters you tore up and put in the basket.'

While I tried desperately to remember what I had put in the letter, knowing it must have been one of those you write to your lover, pouring out your heart and then deciding not to send, I realised she must have read enough to be sure of her facts. It was vital somehow to put her in the wrong because life with Mrs White knowing I was 'carrying on' would have been intolerable. Drawing myself up and forgetting my grammar I said, 'You done *what?*'

'I know I done wrong, I shouldn't have read the letter but I had to know,' she replied.

'You done very wrong,' I told her and proceeded to make her feel so guilty about reading the letter that I changed the footing.

By then I knew very well that unless I made Mrs White an accomplice life would be impossible, so I sat her down on my bed and explained that Mr G (her name for Jimmy) was really more of a platonic friend who helped me out financially and occasionally liked to take me out in the evening. Of course sometimes he had to have his way, I acknowledged, but that was men for you and to keep him happy I had to submit.

At my explanation she cheered up and we had a woman-to-woman chat about how strange it was that men had to have sex, bemoaning our lot as the women who had to put up with it. From that day onwards Mrs White became my eager collaborator. Whenever I was watching television with India Jane and Cosima, my niece, she would answer the telephone and then come into my room and hiss loudly and con-spiratorially, 'It's Mr G on the phone. I said it's Mr G! He's waiting for you.'

The girls were nonplussed, as at that stage they did not know Jimmy as anything but a friend and could not understand why he was referred to as Mr G.

In November 1954, many years before I involved Mrs White in the conspiracy over Mr G, I began to feel rather unwell and found getting Mark's breakfast in the morning a nauseating experience. Pregnancy was the last thought on my mind, but the first on Mrs White's. 'I'm afraid that you've fallen,' she told me with relish. After a visit to Dr Hannay, our family doctor, my pregnancy was confirmed, much to both Mark's and my consternation. There was no way we could have a baby living in the cramped conditions of Rhoda's little flat. But Daddy, despite his deteriorating health, became rather excited about the idea of the baby and although I was not yet twenty-one, he persuaded the trustees that we had to be given enough money to buy a house. Nowadays Halsey Street in Chelsea is a much sought after address, but in 1954 the houses sold for under £4000. We bought number 9, a narrow terraced house on three floors with a small garden at the back, which was mostly taken up by a bomb shelter.

In the late spring of 1955, when I was several months pregnant, Billy Graham the evangelist and preacher arrived in London with his wife Ruth and a vast entourage of disciples. He took over the Crystal Palace and thousands of people went to hear him address the crowd in his mesmeric and compelling style. My sister Jane became not only a fervent follower, attending several of his meetings, but she also became very friendly with both Billy Graham and Ruth. She had met them the preceding winter when she was staying in Jamaica with her godmother Adele Astaire, Fred Astaire's sister and occasional dancing partner. Jane was obsessed by Billy Graham's preaching and describes herself as being swept up by a spirit that was verging on religious fanaticism, a force that compelled her to keep going to these extraordinary evangelical meetings.

Although I was highly sceptical of it all in advance, one evening she managed to persuade me to go with her and I was completely won over, and when Jane introduced me to Billy and Ruth I became an instant convert. Billy Graham was a true orator and held his audience spellbound as his resounding voice rang out exhorting us to give up our evil ways and accept Christ. The experience was almost hypnotic and the audience was enthralled as he talked without pausing for about an hour. Nearing the end he asked those of us who wanted to accept Christ to leave our seats and stand before him, and we all obediently moved towards him, many people with tears streaming down their cheeks.

I was determined to return with Mark, who reluctantly agreed and on that night Billy Graham was particularly fervent, and his voice rose and fell dramatically as he urged us to change our lives and accept Christ. I glanced nervously at Mark from time to time but he seemed to be listening intently although at the end as we rose to stand I heard him muttering beside me that it was time to go home.

On being ushered out of the vast hall we saw two signs. One pointed towards the counselling room and the other to the bar. Mark was making swiftly for the bar when a smiling counsellor took his arm, said sweetly 'This way, brother' and guided him in the other direction to the room where the counsellors were waiting for us. Mark could not think of a single question to ask Billy's acolytes about religion so instead he asked about McCarthyism. He was not irreligious – indeed, quite the opposite as he had always believed in God (as did most of Billy Graham's audience) – but he objected to being told to accept Christ when he was already a believer.

On the way home Mark and I gave a lift home to a young couple who were part of the Graham entourage. They were newlyweds and expecting their first child. They told us that they had recorded their marriage vows and often played them back, and asked us whether we had done the same. I exchanged glances with Mark and we both got the most appalling giggles, not daring to admit that not only had we married in a register office but that recording part of our vows would have had to include Mr Holiday issuing his final warning: 'Even if you don't take this seriously, I do.'

My friendship with both the Grahams, and particularly with Ruth, continued outside the meeting halls. She was a delightful woman and knowing Daddy was very unwell had asked whether she could meet him, so Jane invited Ruth and me to lunch at Park Street. Daddy was in bed suffering from pleurisy and we rather hoped we could persuade Ruth that he was not well enough to receive visitors as we never knew how Daddy would behave or what he would say and we did not want to embarrass her. Halfway through lunch, to Jane's and my horror, Robert the butler came in to announce that Daddy would very much like to meet Mrs Graham. Jane and I tried to dissuade Ruth from going up to his bedroom, claiming that Daddy was not really strong enough to meet visitors, but she insisted. So up we went and there was Daddy, sitting up in bed, almost fully recovered from his bout of pleurisy but definitely the worse for drink. He kept referring to Jane and me as 'dames'. 'Just take a look at those dames; they could do with a bit of salvation,' I heard him say, giving Ruth a conspiratorial sideways look. Fortunately his innuendos were lost on Ruth who insisted on giving him a bible signed by Billy but Daddy indicated that he had some far more interesting books in his bedside table that he would like to show her. I suspected that he meant dirty books and as soon as we were able we ushered Ruth Graham out of the room. We could hear Daddy calling out, 'Hey lady, come back' as we went down the stairs but Ruth was oblivious, pronouncing Daddy to be a charming man.

I was amused to find this incident recalled in the recently published unexpurgated diaries of Cecil Beaton, although his story that Daddy actually invited Ruth Graham to get into bed with him, much as Daddy may have been tempted to do so, is not, I'm afraid, accurate.

My pregnancy seemed to last for ever as at first I was under-weight and very spotty, and then I developed swollen legs and a balloon for a stomach. On 20 August Rupert was born at the private nursing home, 27 Welbeck Street, after a gruelling twenty-four-hour labour. Mrs White had taken me into the nursing home the day before, muttering ominously about the pain I was about to experience but Rupert was not born until the following morning. I was shut in my room and told to sleep but I remember screaming and screaming as the nurses held me down, and in the morning I went into post-natal shock. At some point I opened my eyes and saw Jane, Mark and Mrs Smith (who had known me all my life as she had been the cook at Park Street when I was born) all gazing down at me lying in my bed and at that moment I believe they all thought I was going to die. I stayed in 27 Welbeck Street for over two weeks and although I loved Rupert and was very proud of him, what I remember most about my stay at Welbeck Street was missing Noodle, so when I spent the next few weeks recuperating at Wynyard with Rupert and Sister Abel, the maternity nurse, Noodle came straight up to join us.

Meanwhile Mark had overseen the interior decorating of Halsey Street and when we all eventually arrived home, I remember Mrs Ruddy, the housekeeper from Park Street who had been helping to get the house ready, along with Mrs White, whispering to me, 'Mr Birley has taken so much trouble; you must tell him how much you like it.' And she was right. Mark had transformed a very ordinary little house into a mini paradise.

Luckily for me Rupert was an angelic baby because after Sister Abel taught me all she knew, she left me on my own. Although I had the occasional temporary nanny, in those days nannies were terribly spoilt and expected their meals to be brought to them on trays and to be waited on hand and foot. None of them would agree to stay permanently because they loathed the steep narrow stairs. With a baby in the house and no live-in help it became difficult to go out in the evenings, which Mark loved to do particularly in view of my lack of cooking skills.

One evening some friends of Mark's invited us to their house for a delicious dinner made by their German cook, Frieda, whom they described as a treasure. I was therefore rather surprised when a few weeks later the same couple rang us up and offered us their 'treasure' for reasons that seemed plausible at the time. I was ecstatic because Frieda was inexpensive, loved dogs and babies, and nothing was too much trouble for her. She was almost too good to be true and seemed to be the answer to all my prayers. So Frieda moved in and for a while it was heaven. She even managed to ingratiate herself with Mrs White – not an easy task as Mrs White loathed all foreigners on principle and the saying 'Wogs begin at Calais' might well have been written specifically for her.

Three months later I was seriously considering strangling Frieda, shooting the couple who had so generously introduced her to us, or simply running away. Frieda was an alcoholic. She drank a sickly concoction called VP Wine and she became more and more cunning at finding places to hide the bottles, sometimes rather ingeniously down at the bottom of Rupert's pram, and Mark and I invented a new game called 'Hunt the Bottle'. Frieda still managed to cook like a dream but only on the rare occasions when she was sober.

One day Mark decided to invite a rather smart young couple to dinner. He was anxious to impress them as the husband had been offensively patronising to Mark when he was a boy. They were an infuriatingly perfect couple, with a smoothly run house and a very smart nanny who ruled the nursery. I really wanted the dinner to be a success for Mark's sake, so I tried to keep Frieda within view all day. She was going to make a delicious soup followed by chicken paprika with noodles – her great speciality. I observed her closely until the evening and as everything seemed miraculously calm I found the time to dash upstairs to have a quick bath and change, and returned to the kitchen to find Frieda still looking quite normal as the couple arrived and we went in to dinner.

A few minutes later Frieda carried in the soup with an ingratiating smile on her face and my heart sank. I knew instantly that she had been drinking. However, the soup was delicious and we were looking forward to the famous chicken paprika. Minutes passed, Mark was getting restless, I was getting desperate and the couple were exchanging odd looks. Suddenly the door opened very slowly and Frieda appeared, sidling into the room with a drunken grin on her face bearing the paprika chicken at a most peculiar angle. Slowly the whole dish began to tilt and the next moment the entire paprika chicken was spread over the carpet. As Mark and I gazed in horror, Frieda sank to her knees muttering in German, picked up the serving spoon and began ladling it all back on to the plate. Meanwhile Noodle, not slow to take advantage where food was concerned, stood in the middle of the mess licking it up. Undeterred, Frieda staggered to her feet and was about to offer the scooped-up chicken to the guests when Mark, his foot itching to kick her up the bottom, ushered her out of the room and into the kitchen.

I could hear his furious hushed voice and Frieda whining, 'Vot for sir so angry with Frieda?' We did have many more hair-raising incidents with Frieda over the next two years as it was impossible to find her another job, but eventually she was offered suitable employment with a household of Catholic priests who drank even more than she did.

In the early autumn Daddy returned to Wynyard for the last time with his nurse, Bernie O'Neill. As a result of the colossal amount of alcohol he had consumed over the last four years most of his organs had begun to fail, including his heart. His condition worsened and after a week at Wynyard he was taken straight down to the London Hospital in the East End. We visited him daily and sometimes he would rally and joke with us but at other times he would appear almost comatose. Shortly after his arrival there, his doctor explained very bluntly to us that it was only a matter of time and it was amazing that he was still alive.

Although I knew the doctor was telling me the truth, I found it hard to accept. It seemed as unlikely that someone could die from drinking too much as that they might of a blistered mouth. We spent as much time as we could at his hospital bedside and I remember one heartbreaking moment when he confused Jane with Patrick Plunket, stroking her hand saying, 'Patrick, you must take care of them for me.' The tears rolled down Jane's cheeks as he spoke.

Sometimes we could make him laugh with silly jokes, at other times we would be summoned urgently in the middle of the night, only for him to recover. The strain on all of us was immense and I could not help sobbing to Mark that I wished Daddy would die soon, aware that Rupert would never know his grandfather and thinking that if only he could have stopped drinking earlier what fun they would have had together. Loving children as he did, I thought a grandchild would have given him a reason to live. However, in the final days Mama and his sisters visited him to demonstrate that despite their disagreements they still loved him and *this* made me happy. As the end came we all gathered round the bedside where Daddy was propped up on his pillows in an oxygen tent. Alastair was so distressed that he paced up and down the corridor wearing a long black overcoat, later confiding to me the depth of bitterness he had felt towards Daddy at the time of Mummy's death explaining how he believed that he had abandoned us, and how he despised and hated him for his drunkenness. We took Daddy's body back to Wynyard where he himself had arranged for the Bishop of Durham, Michael Ramsay, again to conduct a service up in the wild garden.

And once more there were moments of black farce at a Wynyard funeral. As the Bishop scattered the ashes over Mummy's grave, a gust of wind caught some, blowing them over his dazzling white hair and up his nose. Afterwards, at the funeral lunch, Mama's false teeth tumbled right out of her mouth and under the table, where the dogs fought over them in an unseemly scrap.

Daddy had started life with such advantages. He was the godchild of Edward VII, and had been baptised in the Chapel Royal at St James's Palace. He had been born into one of the most distinguished aristocratic families in the land and he had been blessed with a remarkable gift for oratory, a beautiful wife and loving children. And all these gifts were snuffed out in the rainswept garden at Wynyard, the place he had been happiest. His death at the age of fifty-three had been so pointless.

For us, losing both parents within four years was almost unbearable. I had loved Daddy very much, even through the bad times, and although I was no longer a teenager and happily married with a child of my own I still felt terribly lost and vulnerable.

NINE

Spreading Wings

For ten years I had lived under the sometimes restrictive shadow of two ill parents but much as I regretted their early deaths, with their loss I began gradually to enjoy the easing of responsibility and to find an independence that allowed me to live a little more adventurously.

Nominally and emotionally I grew to consider my cousin Patrick Plunket as the head of the family. I had known him since the time we had spent together during the very early days of my childhood, at Mount Stewart after the appalling tragedy of the death of his parents in an aeroplane crash. As I grew up I began to think of him as one of my closest and most respected friends. I spent a great deal of time at Patrick's house, The Mount in West Malling in Kent. Weekends there were great fun as the house was always full of guests occupied in putting on plays and watching home movies, and playing charades. For some time I had been mad about Shaun, the youngest and the closest to me in age of the three brothers and one day sitting in his room I asked him why we were being so closely observed by Patrick. Looking slightly sheepish himself, he told me to ask Patrick. When Patrick finally told me the story about Papa and his affair with Fannie Ward, I was both amazed and thrilled, although it did not prevent me from being keen on Shaun, and we are still great friends. I do not know why the truth of our cousinship was withheld from us for so long, as it seemed rather ridiculous to keep the secrecy going three generations after the event.

Patrick had been on active service with the Irish Guards in Italy and Belgium, where he was wounded and shipped back to England. After the war he was based in Palestine and on his return to London, the Colonel of the Regiment was asked on behalf of George VI to find out whether Patrick would be interested in becoming an equerry. Patrick gave a polite but firm refusal, but some correspondence followed between the Colonel, Patrick and Buckingham Palace, resulting in Patrick being persuaded in 1948 to join the royal household. He accepted because the offer was not only an honour but would only be for a limited period. He stayed in this temporary job for twenty-seven years.

With an immense capacity for fun, combined with instinctive good manners, he quickly became an extremely popular figure at court, and particularly friendly with the young Princess Elizabeth, who was only three years his junior. Indeed, I think she may have grown to regard him as an elder brother. When she became Queen, she invited him to stay on, his experience with her father fortuitously providing her with her own equerry who could give her continuity in her challenging and sudden transition to head of state. Staying with us at Wynyard one weekend shortly after taking up the job at Buckingham Palace, Patrick was playing the piano in the drawing room, with an adoring young Alastair for his audience. Confused but aware of his cousin's grand new job, Alastair asked, 'Are you a Court Plunkey?' which made Patrick laugh so much that he became incapable of playing another note.

In the early summer of 1956 Mark and I were invited to a large reception at Londonderry House. The Queen and Prince Philip were expected to attend, and Patrick was very keen that Mark and I should be there. On the evening of the party we joined hundreds of people who were milling around the great ballroom until Patrick grabbed me. 'There you are,' he said. 'Come and meet the Queen.'

I confessed to fright at being tongue-tied but Patrick, who by this time was Deputy Master of the Household, was insistent and we crossed the room to where the Queen was standing. As Patrick introduced me, a suitable conversational topic occurred to me. With Mark standing beside me, and knowing that she loved dogs, I said, 'Ma'am, we have a very small dachshund called Noodle whom we love and who is very spoilt and sleeps every night in our bed.'

After she had answered me in her usual polite way it was Mark's turn. Quite clearly he had not been listening to a word I had said. 'Ma'am, we have a very small dachshund called Noodle who is very spoilt and sleeps every night in our bed. . .' he began as the Queen, used to nerves in those meeting her for the first time, simply nodded and smiled. Other than exchanging a few words at my coming-out ball, I had only ever seen photographs or television news pictures of her and I was quite taken aback by her beauty. She was small and delicate, with the loveliest skin, and her smile lit up her face. She looked so young and it was very easy to see not only why Patrick loved and admired her so much, but also why he felt a need to protect her.

In his masterly biography of the Queen, Ben Pimlott says that the relationship between the Queen and Patrick was 'intimate and fond' and 'contained a kind of camp normality which people admired, envied and were amused by', observing that their rapport depended on Patrick's 'particular blend of wisdom, dry humour, friendliness, conservatism and selfless loyalty' which fitted her needs well.

Apart from the unique Plunket sense of humour, Patrick had incredible taste, a gift like none other for organising the most wonderful parties. He was responsible for choosing presents for the royal family's distinguished visitors and the designer of astonishing and dramatic flower arrangements for the great state banquets.

I thought he was simply the best company in the world and

I saw a great deal of him. He was quite capable of joining me in absurdly childish behaviour. Once, when staying with Rhoda at Charleston, we went together to a party at the Brighton Pavilion. The party was very dull and we were bored stiff as well as urgently in need of the loo. We searched the entire Pavilion but with no luck until eventually, helpless with laughter, we were both forced to pee into a pair of priceless china bowls, speculating how long it would be before the bowls were discovered.

He was completely in love with Pelham Cottage, the little white Regency house standing in its own half-acre garden in South Kensington that I had discovered in 1958 and into which Mark and I had moved from Halsey Street in 1959. He would occasionally come down from the Palace to have lunch with me and it was there that John Ward, the distinguished portrait painter, began to do a water-colour of him. Patrick was very ill by then but although in terrible pain he refused to take painkillers. Eventually John Ward was forced to cut short his sittings and I would drive Patrick, who was doubled up with agony, back to his grace and favour house in St James's Palace. As his condition worsened he was taken into the Sister Agnes nursing home in Harley Street where I visited him as much as I could, but towards the end he told me that he longed to get out of bed, afraid he would become too weak to walk. He would trail off a sentence by saying, 'As long as one hasn't got some dreadful incurable disease.' As I tried to reassure him, I was struck how firmly the mind remains in denial even when facing a terminal illness. On leaving the nursing home one day I ran into Shaun and the doctors, and stressed to them all how important it was that Patrick continued to believe he was going to get better. He must have successfully convinced himself that this was the case because recently Shaun told me that Patrick actually left his bed in the hospital ten days before he died and, with the help of morphine, he dressed in full white tie and was driven to Buckingham Palace to fulfil his traditional duty of introducing all the guests to the Queen at an important reception. He returned to the hospital in the early hours of the morning and was deeply moved to find a special note of thanks from the Queen already on his breakfast tray.

His funeral was held in the tiny white Chapel at St James's Palace (where most recently the Queen Mother's coffin was placed before the lying in state at Westminster) with only his relations and the entire royal family present.

The service was heartbreakingly lovely. Patrick had a passionate love of classical music and the singing of the choristers, chosen for the exquisite purity of their young voices, soared up to the roof of the lovely chapel, reminding me of nightingales. I tried not to cry as Jane and I had vowed to each other that we would not, but glancing sideways I caught a look of deep sadness on the Queen's face. Not only had she lost one of her closest friends aged only fifty-one but someone who was almost irreplaceable within the royal household. After the funeral we all went back for tea at Patrick's new apartment at St James's Palace, which overlooked the chapel. He had only recently moved in and with his usual flair had made it beautiful.

A very grand memorial service was held at the Guards' Chapel a few weeks later, conducted by Bishop Anselm Genders, and Prince Philip read the lesson. The chapel was so full there were people standing on the steps outside.

One of the Queen's ladies-in-waiting has recently said that the death of Patrick was the greatest tragedy of the Queen's life as he was the only person who could talk to her on equal terms. With Patrick's death much of the gaiety of life at court vanished.

He was concerned about me and my future because by the time he died in 1975 I already had two children by Jimmy (Jemima and Zac) and Patrick thought my life was becoming alarmingly confused. He had always felt that Pelham Cottage was my refuge and in his hospital bed he had begged me not to sell it. Not wanting to worry him, I assured him that I would try to keep it but I did not have the heart to tell him that Jimmy and I were already looking for a bigger house for our respective large families.

In the summer of 1956 Mark took me to the South of France on my first proper holiday abroad. We drove there in our car and stayed in a little seaside hotel near Antibes. This was my first visit to the Mediterranean, and the hot sun and the warm sea seemed like a delicious dream.

I remembered my mother telling me how she loved swimming in the Mediterranean and that holiday marked the beginning of a lifelong worship of the sun. Despite all today's warnings, unheard of in those days, I have to admit that one glimpse of the palest English sun sees me prostrate in its rays. Nico was even more obsessed with getting a suntan than I was and throughout the 1960s she, Jane and I, desperate for warmth after a long cold winter, would fly off to sunny places like Majorca or southern Italy, where we would find a small cheap hotel and bask there like lizards for a week.

On 4 November 1956 Mark and I went to a grand dinner at the Dorchester Hotel in London and on our way home, switching on the car radio, we heard the impassioned voice of the deposed Hungarian Premier Imre Nagy appealing to the West. Under Nagy's direction the people of Hungary had taken to the streets to protest against the crippling Soviet communist regime and campaign of terror that had been imposed on them after the Second World War by Joseph Stalin.

At exactly the same time Britain was in the middle of the Suez Crisis, and a month earlier the English and the French had begun their bombing. The Western world, having already fought two wars in the last fifty years, was reluctant to become involved in a further war, which carried with it a nuclear threat. The future of thousands of desperate Hungarians fleeing their country was in danger of being ignored. Flooding over the

Hungarian border into Austria were 200,000 men, women and children who had begun their escape. They had nowhere to go and there were no resources to help them, and that night something in the dignified but urgent voice of Nagy touched Mark and me profoundly. 'Today it is Hungary,' we heard Nagy say, 'and tomorrow, or the day after tomorrow, it will be the turn of other countries, because the imperialism of Moscow does not know borders and is only trying to play for time.' Mark and I looked at each other and drove home in silence.

The next morning Mark resigned from his job at J. Walter Thompson, sold the car and bought a dark blue Hillman van which we had painted with a huge red cross on the side. I rang up the Save the Children office in Vienna and discovered they were anxious to encourage volunteers to come out to help, so Mark and I spent that week in London collecting as many clothes, particularly for children, as we could. Everybody we knew started sending contributions round to Halsey Street and, leaving Rupert in the tender care of Maria Harrison's nanny Mabel, we set off for Vienna a few days later in the van, which was crammed with nappies, food and anything that we could fit in that might bring some help to the refugees. The journey took about two and a half days and having found a little bed and breakfast we went straight to the Save the Children headquarters in the heart of the city.

I was taken to a warehouse where the central collecting point for all the charitable donations was based. The clothes would come shooting down a large shaft into a huge basement where my job was to sort them out into different piles of vests, pants, sweaters and trousers according to size and age.

Douglas Wilson, Mark's best friend, worked for the Institute of Directors and with their help he organised a fleet of Dakotas from the Silver City Charters to bring food and clothing out to us three times a week. They claimed that they could fly over anything we asked for within two days and as there was a tremendous shortage of towels I asked Douglas on a rather bad telephone connection to pass on this request for more supplies. He must have misheard me as two days later when I was standing at the bottom of the shaft talking to Mark who had come to take me out for a break he saw a huge consignment of Kotex heading straight at me. Just in time, he whisked me out of the way and Mark has often reminded me since how he saved me from being crushed to an ignoble death by an avalanche of sanitary towels.

My ultimate goal was to reach the little frontier town of Andau and the small bridge over which the flood of refugees were crossing into Austria. During the exodus the Austrians did not turn back a single refugee from the border, making it clear that they regarded them as heroes. As the town was heavily guarded, the refugees would escape at night in silence, to lessen the risk of being shot by Russian guards and in order to keep them quiet their parents drugged the children with sleeping pills, sometimes in their anxiety accidentally overdoing the doses, leaving the Red Cross to revive them.

After a couple of weeks of basement life I was at last taken down to the frontier. I could hear the guns clearly and in one unfortunate incident my sister Jane (who was out there helping with another organisation) and I were photographed with some Russian soldiers who had allowed us for a moment to hold their guns. When I got home I discovered that the photograph had appeared in the *Daily Express* with a story that implied Jane and I were on some frivolous mission in Austria. I was furious, as my work there was extremely important to me but it was too late to object.

The proud Hungarians arrived in Austria exhausted by mistreatment and abuse at the hands of the Russians, but with their dignity and principles intact. As they reached safety, families were divided up, with the women and children being taken into the schoolhouse while the men were sent to another building. We volunteers would give them blankets and mattresses to lie on, and something to eat and inexhaustible quantities of lemon tea to drink. I also survived those exhausting nights on that refreshing tea. I became so tired that I used to lie down to sleep for an hour still wearing my jeans, oblivious to the deafening noise of the children all around me.

We would work all night and at dawn we would drive back to Vienna and sleep in the daytime. Occasionally if we woke up early enough we would spoil ourselves with a delicious breakfast of Sachertorte and Viennese pastries. During those weeks on the Hungary–Austria border I met an extraordinary and wonderful mixture of people. The average age of the refugees was only twenty-three and they were mostly well educated (there were 500 students and 32 professors from one university alone). There were also musicians and athletes, actors and engineers, many of them very colourful and romantic with wonderful clothes and they would sing songs from their homeland through the night. The American novelist James Michener was on the Austrian side of the border during the exodus, watching the Hungarian flight, and from his experience he wrote his famous book *The Bridge at Andau*.

Many of the refugees would tell me their life stories and secretly I began to feel a tremendous appreciation for my own life in an unthreatened country.

On occasions the work involved heartbreak as some of the families became divided from each other on the journey over and the women used to weep for fear of never finding their husbands. One day Mark and I befriended a little boy aged about ten or eleven and although neither could understand the other he attached himself to us and followed us everywhere. I had no idea what had happened to his parents, as he seemed to have come over entirely on his own. We gave him chocolate cake and took him back to our bed and breakfast, where we had another bed put in our room for him. He was a very solemn little boy and every time he passed a church he crossed himself. Mark and I briefly considered trying to adopt him and take him back to England with us, but happily he was eventually reunited with his own parents.

Although I had managed to hitch several lifts on Douglas's Dakotas back to London to see Rupert, who was only one year old, after a while I began to miss him dreadfully and so we decided to go home. Just before Christmas, on the night before we left, we went to a wonderful performance of *Tosca* with some friends of Maria Harrison, unconcerned that we were going to the grandest of all opera houses wearing trousers and sweaters, which were the only clothes we had. We donated our blue van to Patrick, one of the other volunteers, as we had no need for it in England but one night on his way back from the border to Vienna, a journey that Mark and I had done dozens of times ourselves, Patrick fell asleep at the wheel crashing the van and writing it off and breaking nearly every bone in his body.

On my return I was happy to be back with my baby and the whole Hungarian adventure began to feel slightly surreal. I am not sure if we had ever been in real danger and I didn't feel terribly heroic but I found it quite difficult to settle back into the routine of my life in England. I was somewhat disillusioned that after risking so much many of the refugees actually returned to Hungary, although thousands did indeed find new homes in Canada, America, Germany, France and England. The Soviets swiftly crushed the revolution and Nagy, arrested only hours after making that powerful radio appeal, was himself hanged.

By the end of the summer of 1957 I was feeling sick and once again had the unmistakable symptoms of pregnancy. Unlike today, there were no little magic sticks that gave you the result straight away and instead you had to go and give a urine test to your GP and he would ring you a day later with the news. I am not quite sure why I bothered to do the test at all as Mrs

White had already told me, dolefully, that I had 'fallen again' and as usual she was right. I had had such a horrid experience giving birth to Rupert that I rather dreaded going through the whole thing again. Also, Mark was annoyed with me because he had not really wanted any more children and we both worried about how we would fit another child into number 9 Halsey Street. I changed my gynaecologist and on Dr Hannay's advice went to Roger DeVere at the Westminster Hospital, who was known by the nurses as Divine DeVere. He was kind and reassuring, and was to deliver my next four children, and we became great friends. My pregnancy with Robin seemed to last for an eternity and my stomach felt even bigger than it had been with Rupert. The baby was late and I kept having false alarms until finally he was induced on 19 February 1958. As my pains increased I was pushed shrieking down the corridor on a trolley on my way to the labour ward. The Sister in charge of my trolley was so exasperated by the noise I was making that she told me to shut up in case I frightened all the other expectant mothers. This time, however, the whole process was much quicker and the baby and I were wheeled back to my hospital room. I fell asleep, only to be woken by Mark tapping my shoulder. 'Darling, you must wake up,' he said. 'There must have been a mistake. I think you've been given the wrong baby – this one is simply hideous.' I opened my eyes and saw this bright red wrinkled little face lying next to me. As he was three weeks overdue he did look rather odd. He was such a big baby that he became known very unfairly as the Westminster Monster. He seemed so vulnerable that I felt instant love for him. We decided to call him Robin after Daddy. His brother Rupert, an angelic little boy, never showed him any jealousy and became very protective of him, and they formed an instant and lifelong bond.

Robin's christening took place in London at that lovely church, St Paul's Knightsbridge, and my grandmother, Mama, and Aunt Mairi were there, as well as Nico Harrison and my sister Jane who were godparents. Nico had become very much part of my life since our first meeting at Charleston in 1954. I tried several times to get her and Alastair together without success until the summer of 1957 when she was sixteen and I invited them both to stay in the little cottage I had rented for the summer at Littlehampton. They did not appear to be particularly interested in each other and spent the day giggling in a rather irritating way, and I was more than relieved to drive them back to London on Sunday evening. But unknown to me they began seeing each other from that day and by the time Robin was born they were engaged.

With two children, I realised that Mark and I would have to consider moving somewhere bigger. When I told Maria Harrison that we were looking, she told me she knew of a lovely little house off Pelham Street with a large garden but she thought it might be too small. She and Mike lived in Argyle House in the King's Road, which was exactly like a beautiful country rectory with wonderful panelled rooms leading on to a large garden. Mark and I often had Sunday lunch there and it was the house that Mark most coveted in London. Without ringing up the agents I sneaked off, determined to find Pelham Cottage, even if it only meant looking at it from the outside. I wandered up Pelham Street until I spotted a little lane with two pillars on either side on which were written Pelham Cottage and Park House. I crept down the lane rather furtively and I could see a gate marked Park House at the end and a black garden gate on the right, which I assumed must be Pelham Cottage. I was about to climb up the fence beside it like a cat burglar when something made me turn the handle and to my amazement it opened. I found myself in a garden with the most enchanting little white Regency cottage on two floors facing it. Aware that I was trespassing but unable to resist exploring further, I walked into the middle of the garden and was transfixed.

★

Park House and Pelham Cottage had been a farmhouse in the nineteenth century when Kensington was a village and at some point, probably later in the century, it had been divided into two houses. It was so spectacular that I raced out into the street to the nearest telephone box and rang Mark to tell him I had found the equivalent of Argyle House, but even better, and that he must come and look immediately. I don't think he really believed me but the moment he saw it he loved it as much as I did.

The garden surrounded the house entirely and was particularly huge because next to the property there was a neglected bombsite where bushes and trees had grown up, giving the extraordinary impression of a little orchard in the very heart of Kensington. The estate agents Cluttons leased that part of the garden to me until the late 1960s when sadly a big block of flats was built over it.

Pelham Cottage had fewer rooms than number 9 Halsey Street but we managed to get planning permission to build a nursery and night nursery over the drawing room with the help of the architect Philip Jebb. Mark took over the decorating and we moved in with Rupert and Robin in March 1959. Some time that year, searching for a permanent nanny, I interviewed a young Irish girl called Wendy Jacob and she came to look after the Birley children until they grew up. Wendy stayed in my life until her death in 1978. She was not only our nanny but over the years she became my confidante. To be fortunate enough to have a nanny you both love and trust is a blessing, and I have been privileged in having two. As well as Wendy I also had my lovely North Country nanny Mavis Young (but never known as anything other than Mimi) who had worked for Nico and Alastair but came over to me to look after my Goldsmith bunch and stayed until they all grew up. She has never really left as she still comes down to stay with me whenever she can, and all my friends love her and she is virtually a second mother to my children.

On 16 May 1958 Alastair and Nico married at Mike's and Maria's country house in Netherhampton. Although Mama's health was bad and she had only just under a year to live, she bravely came to the wedding with the aunts. This fortitude was typical of Mama who at her final Christmas gave a grand dinner at Londonderry House in celebration of her own eightieth birthday, with Harold Macmillan as her guest of honour. Nico looked lovely at the wedding in her white satin full-skirted Hartnell gown, five great bows at the back stretching from her waist to the floor, and her blonde hair held in place by the Londonderry tiara. The wedding photographs, which were taken by Maria's great friend Cecil Beaton, show the touchingly young age of the bride and groom as Nico was barely seventeen and Alastair was not yet twenty-one.

We settled into Pelham Cottage in 1959 with the two boys and Noodle, and while Mark started decorating, our neighbour at Park House, Lanning Roper, gave us advice on the garden. Lanning was the most famous landscape gardener of the day. He was involved in the planning of many of England's most beautiful gardens, including Scotney Castle, Wisley, the home of the Royal Horticultural Society, and in 1981 he was commissioned by Prince Charles to help with the designs for Highgrove. We were very lucky with our neighbours because after Lanning and his wife Primrose left, they sold the house to Maxwell Joseph, the head of Grand Metropolitan, and his wife Eileen. In the twenty-odd years we spent at Pelham Cottage, builders were an ever present part of our life because Mark, being a perfectionist, was never satisfied. It became a joke among our friends that whenever Mark wanted to add a further bit of extravaganza to the house he would breezily suggest that maybe Nico, Jane and I should go on another holiday. On my return I would inevitably find that work had already started on a new project. Despite these disruptions Pelham Cottage was a truly magical place; the gate was always open and friends would simply turn up and drop in.

One of Mark's and my closest friends, and a constant dropper-in, was Geoffrey Keating. There has never before or since been anyone remotely resembling Geoffrey. Eccentric is not the right word to describe him – maybe outrageous would be a better one. Geoffrey had a heroic war record and was promoted to Commanding Officer of the Devonshire Regiment in the Eighth Army during World War Two, having earlier worked as an outstanding war photographer. His patriotic photographs of Monty in the desert handing out cigarettes to the troops had managed to transform the rather stiff and uncharismatic image of the General into one of national hero back home. His work, along with that of the other war correspondents and cameramen like Alan Moorehead, Christopher Buckley, Chester Wilmot and Alexander Clifford, was credited with presenting the British Army's achievements in battle to the world. Geoffrey's closest colleagues during the war were General Sir Freddie de Guingand, Montgomery's Chief of Staff, and the distinguished television journalist Alan Whicker who, while director of the army film and photo section of the Devonshire Regiment, served under Geoffrey's command. Whicker and Keating were virtual prisoners in the German siege at Anzio and had agreed that if the Germans broke through they would make a run for Rome dressed in the tattered gardening clothes that they had found in an old shed, although this contingency plan proved unnecessary as eventually the Fifth Army arrived from southern Italy bringing liberation.

Geoffrey's war tales, in particular the story of his own, possibly apocryphal, moment of triumph, when he liberated the Italian residents of Montecassino from the Germans single-handed, became legendary. He was an Irishman who invariably managed to infuriate and then charm one out of a bad mood. I met some fascinating people through Geoffrey, some of whom like Alan Whicker remain lifelong friends. Among others were S. J. Perelman who wrote two of the Marx Brothers' scripts, and even Groucho Marx himself who turned out to be just as funny in real life as he was in his films. Whenever I was cross with Geoffrey he would come up with some ridiculous saying which never failed to make me laugh. 'There may be *non-non* on your lips but there is always *oui-oui* in your eyes,' he would say to me.

On another occasion when getting impatient in a restaurant in France the waiter, trying to calm him down said, '*Tout de suite, monsieur, tout de suite.*' Geoffrey replied, 'The *toute*-r the *suite*-r.'

Once Geoffrey rang Mark very early one morning asking him to come round straight away on a matter of the utmost urgency. Worried, Mark rushed over to Geoffrey's flat in Three Kings Yard only to find Geoffrey sitting up in bed roaring with laughter while four naked girls were peering beneath it, searching for his false teeth.

Alan Whicker confesses in his autobiography *Within Whicker's World* that he wishes airlines would reserve one section at the back of the aeroplane for families, rather than have them jumbled up with adults flying alone who long for some peace. He explained the thinking behind his solution: 'All the kids can romp and scream together, their parents can exchange horror stories – and the rest of us can read the magazines or settle down to work. The airlines could promote flying nannies as a new facility supplied regardless of expense.' He continues to describe with envy how Geoffrey Keating had devised an infallible method of ensuring he got a railway carriage to himself, even during the rush hour: 'He took a window seat early and removed his false teeth, leaving the few remaining home-grown stumps dotted here and there between drawn lips. When travellers approached his carriage, he grinned at them fiendishly. It was out of Hammer Horror. People went white. The adjoining compartments were always packed.'

Never neglecting his wartime talent for taking pictures,

Geoffrey would whip out his camera at the slightest opportunity and take natural unposed photographs. I have hundreds that he took of the children, which hang on my bathroom walls, and some poignant ones of Mark and Nico and me on holiday. By the 1970s he had bought up several of the houses around and was beginning to have great success in the property business as well as becoming head of public relations at British Petroleum.

By 1960 I began to feel broody again although I hardly dared tell Mark. I yearned to have a little girl but I felt in my bones that I would only have boys. Nanny Wendy had set her heart on my having a daughter because she had always preferred little girls. By the summer I had 'fallen again' and the baby was expected in January 1961. This time, because I was not worrying about moving house or searching for the ideal nanny, the pregnancy was very relaxed. It was marred only by an incident at Christmas when my Spanish au pair went mad and tried to stab me with a bread knife. Pilar was a sweet, gentle girl who did a bit of cooking and housekeeping and lived in. She had been with us for almost a year when I noticed in the weeks preceding Christmas that she had become a bit vague and erratic. The tree had as usual gone up a few weeks before, decorated by Wendy and me. Presents were stacked underneath and stocking presents hidden away.

Our Christmas tree was always over-lit with hundreds of little bulbs and I used to worry that the lights would fuse on the actual day. Pilar had been acting very oddly on Christmas Eve but nevertheless I placed her stocking and a small pile of presents in her room before I went to bed. The boys were awake at the crack of dawn, opening their stockings and shrieking with delight, joined by Mark who would start nudging his stocking with his foot in the early hours of the morning. I went down to switch on the Christmas tree lights and light the fire in the sitting room, and found to my amazement Pilar pushing the

Hoover furiously around the tree, managing to break the lights. I removed the Hoover from her hand and she returned to the kitchen mumbling. I followed her a bit later and tried to put my arm round her and find out what was wrong. Suddenly she gave a mad laugh and, saying 'I going to kill you,' she grabbed the bread knife and lunged at me, as I tried to escape round the kitchen table. I managed to run up the backstairs into my bedroom, leaving her brandishing the knife. Mark was sitting up in bed rummaging in his stocking and looking like an excited little boy. 'Pilar is trying to kill me,' I sobbed. 'She has gone quite mad.' We rang Dr Hannay who came straight round and went to talk to Pilar in her room, and I left her munching a huge bun while talking to him. She had in fact gone completely round the bend, maybe because of a love affair, and was carted away shrieking to a psychiatric ward in St Stephen's Hospital.

My first daughter was born on 14 January 1961. She was an outstandingly pretty baby with enormous blue eyes and dark hair. I called her Jane after my sister and Romaine after my mother, and Mark loved the name India so she became India Jane Birley. Nanny Wendy was in seventh heaven and I now felt the family was complete. If anyone had told me then that I would have three more children over a decade later I would have laughed at the very idea.

As the summer holidays approached the fashionable thing to do with your children in those days was to rent a house on the sea at resorts like Frinton, or to book rooms in a hotel and send your nanny and the children down to the seaside to be with all the other nannies and children. I did not want to spend the holidays away from my children so I used to take houses at Middleton-on-Sea near Bognor. We would spend most of the week down there and Mark would come down for the weekend, usually with some friends to play backgammon. The first house I rented was called something like Sea Wind or Sea Spray and was quite hideous but the garden was practically on the beach and the children loved it. Mrs Godfrey, the owner of the dachshund that Noodle had fallen in love with, came down to cook for us, bringing with her the three puppies, Jane, Annabel and Alastair.

Those summers were very jolly and not only can I still hear the rattle of the dice against the background noise of the waves breaking on the shingles but I also remember with some amazement how men as sophisticated as Claus von Bülow, Tony Lambton, Mark Brocklehurst and Mark Birley were perfectly happy playing backgammon and drinking Pimm's and lemonade in that very ordinary little house.

TEN

Holidays

Over the last two years nostalgia has once again driven me to rent a little house by the English seaside. I have found a charming cottage in West Wittering in Sussex, which I can reach from Ormeley within the hour. The house is right on the beach and I have spent many happy summer weekends there with my niece Sophia, her three daughters Hermione, Allegra and little Maude, and the grandchildren.

Throughout my adult life I have been fortunate enough to have spent innumerable wonderful holidays all over the world and the combination of a love of the sun and of spending long hours in beautiful places with people I care about has been, and remains, one of the joys of my life.

My first visit to the Mediterranean in 1956 in that modest little hotel in Antibes with Mark was the beginning of a lifelong love affair with the South of France. In the summer of 1960 when I was pregnant with India Jane, John Aspinall and his first wife Jane rented a yacht and invited Mark and me to go sailing with them there for a week. Aspers had met Jane in the late 1950s through an old friend, Charlie Sweeney, who used to rent a famous grouse moor near Tomintoul, the highest village in the Scottish highlands on the northern slope of the Cairngorms and he always invited lots of our old friends to stay up there including my sister, Billy Dudley my godfather, and Peter Ward his brother. At one of these shoots, guests could not help noticing a very beautiful, tall, black-haired girl among the beaters. Her name was Jane Gordon-Hastings and her family lived locally. As he got to know her, Charlie Sweeney encouraged her to leave Scotland and come to London to try her hand at modelling. One afternoon Aspers was having tea at Fortnum and Mason in Piccadilly when a breathtaking girl walked by his table. In those days the store would employ beautiful models to show off the clothes from their fashion department in order to encourage the restaurant customers to buy them. That day Jane Gordon-Hastings was modelling an outfit billed as 'The Spirit of Park Lane' and on seeing her Aspers was smitten, and he and Jane were married soon after. Although she was a little aloof, and some people considered her rather haughty and unapproachable, I liked her very much and got to know her quite well during the numerous holidays Mark and I spent with them.

In 1960 I had never been on a yacht before and I loved every minute of it. However, Aspers was not happy with the crew and found them lacking in manners. The yacht was skippered by Captain Pewter, a real old sea dog and among other members of the crew there was a rather effeminate steward who kept muttering under his breath as he minced round the table serving lunch. This annoyed Aspers so much that he eventually lost his temper and threw the steward overboard.

Another year Aspers took us on safari in Kenya, where we camped at the foot of Mount Kilimanjaro. Leaving the camp before sunrise to look for the animals, we had many hair-raising adventures, including the unforgettable experience of riding in a jeep that was being chased by an enraged rhino.

One summer Mark and I rented a lovely old mill house near Mougins, belonging to Francis Egerton, then managing director of Malletts, the fine arts dealers, which we liked so much that we persuaded Nico to rent it with us for the months of July and August. Nico had several guests to stay, among them Robin Douglas-Home and Simon Keswick. Simon and I spent a great deal of our time on the beach, covered in baby oil and competing with each other for the deepest tan.

That summer Nico was pregnant with Cosima, her second daughter. Although Nico and I were incredibly close, I had failed to notice that she was having an affair with Robin Douglas-Home. Robin, while not good-looking in the classical sense, had a wonderful gift for making everyone laugh. At the time of his and Nico's affair he was married to Sandra Paul, the model, who is now the wife of the Leader of the Conservative Party, Michael Howard. I always felt Robin was a mass of wasted talent as he was both academic and musical, and he could have succeeded in almost anything he chose to do. Instead, he expended too much well-documented energy in pursuing famous beauties including Princess Margaret and Princess Marguerite of Sweden, and I remember seeing him near the end of his life when he was employed by the Clermont as the club's piano player. I still have some of his letters, which are among the wittiest and most beautifully written I have ever received. Sadly, he took his own life in 1968 at the age of thirty-six. In retrospect I wonder how I could have been so blind to Nico's and Robin's romantic situation, but as she and Alastair had married when they were little more than children I was not surprised that over the years they began slowly drifting apart.

I first took Rupert and Robin abroad when they were six and four sending India Jane, who was only a baby, to Ireland with Nanny Wendy as we felt Majorca would have been too hot for her. I rented a villa in Formentor and Alastair and Nico came too with their daughter Sophia aged three.

The villa was built high up on the rocks looking down on the sea and had a large sea-water pool. The warmth of the water and the sun entranced the boys, and they spent all day in the pool wearing armbands and rubber rings. I can remember Sophia shrieking with terror when she was lowered into the pool as the boys splashed her mercilessly. After Nico and Alastair left, we were joined first by my sister Jane and later by

Nico's brother Benjy. Having two small children and no nanny gave me the perfect excuse to avoid a social life although we did occasionally go for drinks at the house of Whitney Straight, the chairman of Rolls-Royce, and his wife Daphne, and also to visit a marvellous couple called June and Vane Ivanovich. He was not only a famous Yugoslavian shipping magnate, but also a passionate deep-sea diver and in his youth had been an Olympian athlete. That Majorcan holiday established the beginning of our annual custom of spending most of the month of August in the Mediterranean while the rest of the children's holidays were spent at Wynyard with Alastair and Nico. Wynyard was a place away from city life that became the haven for my children that it had been for me at that age. After Pelham Cottage, it was the place they loved most in the world and with the customary flair that she had inherited from her mother Nico had completely redecorated it, converting two of the wings with the help of David Hicks. Alastair was particularly brilliant with my boys and used to delight them by showing wonderful old black-and-white vampire and Frankenstein movies.

As they grew older the children formed a little gang and did everything together. Rupert and Robin, as the eldest, were a very bad influence on the girls – Sophia, who was one year younger than Robin, and Cosima, two years younger than her sister and the same age as India Jane. They drove all the nannies, Mabel and later Mimi and Nanny Wendy, mad. Lucy Fox, the daughter of Tracy Pellissier, Nico's best friend, became Sophia's closest friend. As a drama student Tracy had met and married the young actor Edward Fox, who was then playing in rep but who went on to become one of our best-loved actors, famous for his starring roles in *The Day of the Jackal* and as the Duke of Windsor in *Edward and Mrs Simpson*. Lucy was a leading member of the gang and remains very much part of our family, as does Kathryn Ireland, Cosi's and Jane's best friend. Mimi, who had taken over from Mabel in

1975, told me that the boys would make Sophia and Lucy take off their clothes and race madly round the tea table 'to annoy the nannies', and she would advise Wendy in her northern accent, 'Don't take a blind bit of notice of them!'

Towards the end of the holiday the whole gang would descend on Pelham Cottage, making me laugh with the stories of all the naughty things they had done.

Three years after Cosima's birth, in 1964, I was at home watching *Top of the Pops* on television and was so struck with the good looks of the young man whose record had reached the number one slot that I immediately rang Nico to tell her to switch on the programme. She was just in time to catch the end of Georgie Fame singing 'Yeh, Yeh!' and she was star-struck. A few years later Georgie and his group, the Blue Flames, were playing concerts in a double bill with the Supremes in the northern provinces, and Alastair invited them all over to Wynyard, and it was there that the romance between Nico and Georgie began.

After Nico and Alastair were divorced in 1971 she and Georgie got married, spending their honeymoon with Jimmy and me in Jamaica. On their return they went to live at Maperton in Somerset and Cosima, who was at St Paul's Girls School in London with India Jane, came to live with me at Pelham Cottage.

Meanwhile Alastair had fallen in love with the wonderful ballet dancer Doreen Wells, whom he married at about the same time. Both marriages produced two sons. Nico and Georgie became the parents of Tristan and James, both of whom are my godchildren, and Frederick and Reginald were born to Alastair and Doreen, but despite such marital upheaval Nico and Alastair somehow remained the best of friends.

I was well aware that in the last few years of her life Nico had been suffering from clinical depression, brought on in part by the misery of watching her adored and vibrant mother Maria begin to sink into senile dementia. At the same time her boys were growing up and leaving home, and to the profound sadness of all of us who loved her, possibly as a result of this sense of abandonment, she finally took her own life in 1993. Behind her she left Georgie, her family, including her four children and me, all struggling to accept the loss of a much loved wife, an adored mother and an irreplaceable best friend. The only – and great – consolation for me in her death was her legacy of her children. I think of Tristan and James almost like sons and because I had such an active role in their upbringing Cosima and Sophia have always been two extra daughters to me, and I am just as close to them now and see them as often as I can.

Sophia has, happily for me, become my frequent travelling companion in much the same way as her mother was for so many years. We share a love of adventure and of the sun, and the Londonderry sense of humour. She married Johnnie Pilkington and had two beautiful daughters, Allegra and Hermione, and a few years later met Jean Pierre Martel with whom she had another daughter (another great-niece for me), the delectable Maude.

In the summer of 1962 Mark rented a house in the South of France with Mark Brocklehurst. The two Marks would go out together after dinner to the local nightclubs, rarely accompanied by me as I didn't drink and liked my early nights. One morning I woke enraged to see Mark staggering into the bedroom at four-thirty. I was about to ask him where the hell he had been when I spotted a tiny brown dog under his arm. Mark had found it in a nightclub and had bought it from the club owner. He stumbled into bed, collapsing under the mosquito net with the puppy still in his arms, which promptly squatted down and did a turd between us. Furious, I leapt out of bed and went to sleep in the next door room. In the morning I crept back into our bedroom and there, curled up together, were Mark and the little dog who, on seeing me, uttered a protective little growl as she lay wrapped round Mark's head. I loved her from that moment onwards. She was a brown miniature dachshund and we called her Midge. She was a sweet and intelligent dog but we knew that if we were to keep her we would be faced with the huge problem of getting her back to England without putting her into quarantine kennels. The quarantine laws were very strict and you would then have incurred a heavy fine for breaking them, but nowadays you might even be given a prison sentence. We decided that Mark would smuggle Midge back in his airline bag after the local vet had given her the anti-rabies shots and some sedatives for the aeroplane. There was a night flight, which left at one o'clock in the morning, which we thought would give Mark a chance of sneaking her successfully past the sleepy customs officers. After he had left, with Midge sound asleep in his bag, Mark Brocklehurst and I stayed up until dawn worrying. At six-thirty Mark rang to tell us that he and Midge were safely home at Pelham Cottage. Mark's mouth had been so dry as he walked through the customs hall that when the customs officer asked him if he had anything to declare, his description of his new shirts was quite unintelligible. That was the only time I have ever been involved in dog smuggling, but a few years later I did bring Rupert's hamster out to join him on one of our holidays in Porto Ercole in Italy, safely tucked in my handbag.

One year we rented the explorer Freya Stark's villa in San Zenone in Italy. It was remote and beautiful, with an enormous garden and a tiny pool, far too small to accommodate all the children but no one minded as we had such fun. Cosima and India Jane fell in love with a donkey called Roma so I 'rented' her for the summer from the local dustman. Unfortunately Roma was a disaster as she managed to eat the whole garden including Freya Stark's beautiful roses. Mark and Liz Brocklehurst came out to stay with me there and I found out that Mark was even more terrified of wasps than I was. Somewhere hidden in the woods around the swimming pool was a nest of very militant hornets and occasionally they would dive-bomb us as we were getting into the pool. On one occasion I was talking to Michael Stewart, a diplomat and friend of Freya Stark's, who lived within walking distance on the other side of the woods. Mark Brocklehurst, who always dressed very elegantly whatever the occasion, strolled up to the pool wearing a silk shirt and linen trousers carrying a glass of white wine. I introduced him to Michael Stewart and as they were about to shake hands Mark let out a piercing shriek and fell, still holding the wineglass, head first into the pool as a hornet dived at his head. The Stewarts, accustomed to the swarms of hornets, were quite bemused by his behaviour. During that summer I seemed to be equally under attack and spent most of my time leaping into the pool and crouching under the water. San Zenone is not far from Venice and we would often go over there for the day. I was predictably spellbound by my first sight of its beauty, enchanted by the blue-and-white-striped-shirted gondoliers, by the faded painted elegance of the *palazzi* and the grandeur of St Mark's Square.

Another holiday was spent at Gassin in the hills above St Tropez. Nico and I drove from London in her Alfa Romeo with Rupert in the back of the car, and the rest of the children and Nanny Wendy joined us two days later. The children loved Gassin as the house was surrounded by forests where the boys found tiny wild tortoises and brought three of them back to London in their luggage. For years they lived very happily in the garden at Pelham Cottage and Methuselah, the oldest, came with us when we moved to Richmond although one day he escaped on to the golf course never to return.

In 1965 I took the children to Porto Ercole on the Italian coast and it became one of my favourite holiday places. By then I had been having an affair with Jimmy Goldsmith for two years but I had strict rules about holidays, half-terms, and school outings. The children always came first, a priority that Jimmy understood as he already had two children of his own. Isabel, Jimmy's eldest daughter, whose mother Isabel Patino had died so tragically in childbirth, became part of my life when she was nine. Only a year older than Rupert, she grew up with my own children and we have always remained close. Manes, Jimmy's eldest son, decided in his teens that he wanted to be near his father in England and came to live with us at Ormeley. I grew to know Alix, the youngest, when she too reached her teenage years. Jimmy's expectations for holidays varied somewhat from mine in those days. He would take sumptuous villas in different parts of the Mediterranean for July and August, and his chauffeur Cliff Howes would drive out ahead of him in the Daimler ready to meet Jimmy at the airport. That year the boys, their friends, Nanny Wendy and I all flew to Rome on the same plane as Jimmy. Jimmy and his friend Hugh Smyth travelled first class and we travelled economy. On arrival at Rome airport I collected my hired car, a very small Fiat Cinquecento which I discovered to my horror had no roof-rack, and Robin watched wistfully as Jimmy and Hugh got into the spacious air-conditioned Daimler and were whisked away by Cliff Howes while I struggled alone to fix on a roof-rack, sticking some suitcases on the top, shoving one in the tiny boot, and managing to squeeze four children and Nanny Wendy into the car. It was boiling hot and the children's knees were underneath their chins, and as we drove off Robin remembers me snapping at them, 'Right, I don't want to hear one word of complaint from any of you.'

Many affluent Italians had summer villas in Porto Ercole, a fashionable little fishing port which they chose for its undeniable charm, with its brightly coloured fishing boats moored in the harbour and the small painted houses which circled the edge of the water. Most of the Italians had their villas in the hills above the town; however, in my usual haphazard fashion

I had left finding a holiday house until the last moment when there was nothing suitable available and so I ended up renting my friend Geoffrey Keating's flat, which was right in the centre of the port on top of the Yacht Club marina. Although there is no doubt the flat had appeal, it was not really suitable for a family of my size. My two boys, and Nick Hildyard, one of Rupert's friends, all squashed into a makeshift dormitory in the semi-converted storeroom on the ground floor while I, India Jane, Nanny Wendy and any other guests slept upstairs. To start with the boys thought it all rather a lark but unfortunately the small lavatory next to their bedroom was used by anyone who cared to drop in from the port and consequently the smell became increasingly worse.

My son Robin remembers that the flat was over a fishmonger's but while it may have smelt like a fishmonger's I know I am not mistaken in my certainty that it was in fact over the Yacht Club, because on one unforgettable day, the very day of the Yacht Club's annual dinner, the plumbing packed up. The small plumber who arrived to attempt to fix things was voluble and excited, and tried to explain exactly what the problem was. My Italian must have been worse than I thought as I failed to understand that he was warning me on no account to flush the loos or turn on the taps for twenty-four hours. When the first loo was mistakenly flushed the entire contents of the plumbing waste of Geoffrey's flat descended through the floor into the Yacht Club's kitchen, emptying itself on to the preparations for their big night. Although Mark was most amused when I wrote to him to describe this incident, the Yacht Club's owner was not and only after much cajoling from Geoffrey plus a generous handout was he finally appeased.

At Geoffrey's suggestion we rented a small local fishing boat and we would chug very slowly out of the port, anchoring twenty minutes later, opposite the beach. The children and Nanny Wendy would wade in and Nico and I would sunbathe on the boat, jumping into the water when it got too hot or when we were invaded by wasps. At the first buzz, without stopping to retrieve our bikini tops, we would leap shrieking half naked into the sea as Mario, the elderly boatman, would sit in the boat, smirking at our antics. Nico was convinced that he kept a bag of very ripe apricots hidden in the stern to attract the wasps, thus forcing us to dive for cover for his entertainment. At lunchtime we would gather up the children and chug back home again.

In June that year my sister Jane had married Max Rayne, a great friend of Jimmy's who had introduced them. Max was one of the best-known and most widely admired businessmen and philanthropists of his generation, whose myriad interests and charitable support ranged from the London Festival Ballet and the National Theatre to St Thomas's and Guy's Hospitals. Max was one of the most generous men I have ever met and I never knew him to refuse a request for help. Encouraged by both Jimmy and me, Jane and Max fell in love and, until he sadly died in 2003, remained happily married with four children, Natasha my god-daughter, Nicky, Tammy and Alexander the youngest, who is three months older than Jemima. Their wedding had taken place in New York and that August they had chartered a yacht to cruise around the Italian coast, and I had made them promise that they would come to Porto Ercole some time during their honeymoon and see the children and me, but none of us had ever really expected them to rent such an impressively large boat. Robin has described to me how he felt as the honeymooners sailed into the port.

I must have been about seven years old when I was spending the August holiday in Porto Ercole, a name that usually spells style and a certain swishness. Our flat, though, was above the fishmonger's, noisy, smelly and distinctly squalid. I was washing my hair that morning when Mum called out, 'Quick, Robs, come and see the boat sailing into port – I think it's

Max and Jane.' Rubbing the soap from my eyes, I walked on to the balcony. She pointed to a boat sailing into the port; huge, white and gleaming, it was so large it was anchored half in and half out of the harbour. 'That's Uncle Max's boat?' I asked. She nodded. My grip on the rails tightening, my eyes misting, I felt a sudden explosion of love for my Uncle Max.

A tender was sent to pick us up, Jane and Max having seen our frantic waving, and as we cruised past the rather decrepit fishing boat that normally chugged us out each morning to the beach for a daily grilling in the sun I felt deeply content. Turning my gaze to the colossus in the water, I thought only of making the best possible impression on my new Uncle Max.

Climbing on board, my feet sank into the thickest white carpet I have ever known, my excitement mounting – Rupert was as usual detached and cool. Onassis-like Max appeared in one of the doorways, smiling, kind and generous. I noticed Rupert tucking a birthday tenner into his pocket. We set sail and lunch was spent in a reverie, crew gliding here and there, and then it was time to return home. From then on my relationship with Max went from strength to strength.

We had many friends in Porto Ercole, among them Giaconda Cicogna who had been married to and had two children by Bluey Mavroleon but was now married to Beno Cicogna, and they and her two enchanting little blond boys, Luca and Gianfranco, lived in a marvellous villa in the hills. Her oldest son Carlos Mavroleon was one of Robin's best friends from Eton, an adorable black-haired urchin with an unerring ability to think up the most devilish escapades for him and Robin to indulge in. Once they had the brilliant idea of having their own barbecue on the hills and started a fire, which they could not put out. This could have been a real disaster as it is almost impossible to stop a fire from gaining control in that heat, but by some miracle we managed to beat it under control. Robin was punished by being sent to his room without any dinner, although I did catch India Jane and Cosima trying to sneak spaghetti through his bedroom window.

Geoffrey later acquired two or three more little flats in the square behind the port and, unable to resist the lure of Porto Ercole despite the accommodation drawbacks, I went back again but this time I rented two of the little flats in the square as well, so it was more civilised. Along with the usual gang of children I took Simon Elliot with me. Simon's parents, Bill and Rosemary Elliot, were close friends of Mike and Maria Harrison, and Nico and Simon had known each other in their prams. Bill Elliot had been ADC to both King George VI and the Queen. He was also Air Chief Marshal until he retired in 1954. I met Simon through Nico and Alastair, and from that meeting he became and remains one of my closest friends.

Having Simon on holiday with me was the equivalent of having a girlfriend, but better, as we could go out to nightclubs together. Although it would seem quite natural to have a platonic friendship with someone of the opposite sex in England, the idea was unthinkable in Italy, even though it was the 1960s. Undeterred by this, on his first night I took Simon, who was single at the time, to the large popular outdoor nightclub in Porto Ercole. I had heard that there were some rather pretty Belgian girls staying in a villa in the hills and thought they might come down to the club. While we were having a few sambuccas and casing the joint an Italian friend of mine wandered over. She was very sexy and fiery, and when I told her of my quest to find girls for Simon she winked at me and whispered 'Don't bother' as she swept Simon on to the dance floor. As his holiday romance began the Italians, assuming my beau had decamped with another woman, gave me commiserating looks. They would have been incredulous to know that our greatest moment of intimacy came when both the plumbing and the electricity failed and, sharing one small candle for light and half a bidet of water, Simon shaved his face while I shaved my legs.

Later Nico joined us and we grown-ups spent most of the time cruising round the coast followed by a flotilla of small children in a second fishing boat. Once Geoffrey was rash enough to lend us his speedboat, which we managed to sink in a particularly rough sea much to his fury. Jimmy, who had come over from his own smart villa to see me, as he did from time to time, was sitting with all the children in their fishing boat crouching in the stern, being pounded by waves. He was livid at my irresponsible behaviour in taking children out in such bad weather.

When Simon developed appalling earache and became rather bad-tempered Nico and I drove him into Orbetello to the hospital. Never have I seen such squalor in the abattoir that was masquerading as an operating theatre. There was blood on the floor from the last operation and Nico and I wept with despairing laughter at the horror of it all. I could not help thinking *Please God, don't let anything serious happen to me in Porto Ercole if this is where I'll end up.* But worse was to come when the young Italian doctor swept into the room wearing a grubby white coat, but looking very attractive. He walked over to the basin and filled it with water. My hopes were raised as I thought at least he was going to wash his hands, only to have them dashed as, having very carefully washed and rinsed them, he then proceeded to run them through this hair several times, gazing at himself in the mirror before sauntering over to attend to Simon's ear. Holidays with Simon as a bachelor turned into holidays with Simon as a husband after he married Annabel Shand, sister of Mark and Camilla (now Parker-Bowles) in 1972. Annabel and I became great friends and nowadays it is almost unthinkable to have summer holidays at my farm Torre de Tramores in Spain without the entire Elliot clan comprising Simon and Annabel and their children Ben, Alice and Katy (who are roughly the same age as my Goldsmith children,

Jemima, Zac and Ben-Ben) being present for some part of it.

My final holiday in Porto Ercole was spent not in Geoffrey's flat but in a pretty rented mountainside villa. Geoffrey's wife Susie had begged me to look after her cat, which was heavily pregnant. But I knew that Geoffrey did not like cats and did not want Susie's cat in his flat and I also knew that the owner's housekeeper would certainly not have wanted them in her house either. Porto Ercole was full of the starving animals and the children and I were already in trouble for feeding them under the table at the trattoria next to Geoffrey's flat. But we could not bear to leave the mother to fend for herself and bring up six kittens after the pampered life she had enjoyed with Susie and now with us. So when she had delivered her kittens in the middle of Geoffrey's bed I scooped up the whole family and hid them in a cupboard in the villa. However, it was not long before the housekeeper discovered their hiding place and complained. Reluctantly we took them down to the port and left them near the part of the dock where the fishermen counted and sorted their fish, hoping we were giving the cats their best chance of survival, but we never saw them again.

After Jemima and Zac were born our holiday homes became more luxurious because by then Jimmy was footing the bill. In 1976 I took a very pretty villa on the beach just outside St Tropez. Nicky Haslam, the gregarious and talented interior decorator and writer, and an old friend of Nico's and mine, offered to drive Nico and her children down from England and I flew out with Jemima and Zac, India Jane and Mimi and Henrietta Konig, daughter of Nina Campbell, the wonderful decorator who had helped me to do up Ormeley, and her nanny Jessie. As the house couldn't take the whole family we had rented a small yacht (although not quite in the same class as Max Rayne's Porto Ercole ship) for Rupert and Robin, Rupert's friend Piers Gibson and Robin's friend Hugh Fairfax. The boat was owned and sailed by a couple called Ray and

Beryl who had previously run a pub in London but had sold up in order to buy the boat. Their idea was to charter it during the summer months and have their own holidays on it in some warm spot in the winter.

The yacht was anchored round the corner from St Tropez in the harbour of St Maxime and the boys went backwards and forwards to the yacht in the Boston Whaler whenever they could prise it away from Nicky Haslam who liked nothing better than racing across the sea to St Tropez. At the beginning there was a really jolly atmosphere about the holiday as it consisted of all the right ingredients for a good time, including endless days of sunshine, children of all ages, Nicky who was as amusing as ever, and delicious food. But one morning as I was sunbathing on the beach with Nico and the little ones, I saw Piers Gibson arriving at great speed in the Boston Whaler looking very worried. Barely able to catch his breath, he told me to come quickly, explaining that Rupert had heard an awful thud on the deck above his head and had gone up to find that Ray, the captain, had had a heart attack and was already dead. Nico and I went out to the yacht immediately on the Boston Whaler where we found a very shocked Beryl and four equally shocked boys who between them had managed to lug Ray's body downstairs into the sitting room, but as the temperature was already hitting the high eighties I knew it was imperative to get the body off the boat as soon as possible. Rupert and Piers managed to find a doctor and contacted the police but waiting for the endless formalities and bureaucracy, we were told that neither St Maxime, nor the adjoining port of St Raphael, was prepared to accept the body, let alone bury it.

I could not think what to do but as usual when faced with a problem my instinct was to ring Jimmy in London as he always came up with the right solution. Back on shore, I rang his office to be told that he was in a very important meeting at Rothschild's and on no account was he to be disturbed. Having obtained the Rothschild number with difficulty and realising I was making a terrible mistake, I nevertheless rang the number and begged to speak to him. At Rothschild's they also told me he had left strict instructions that no calls were to be put through, but I was desperate and with a hysterical note creeping into my voice insisted on speaking to him. Very reluctantly the secretary connected me.

Jimmy answered with a furious growl, 'OH WHAT?'

I explained the situation quickly and told him that I did not know what to do with the captain's body.

Whereupon Jimmy lost his temper. 'Oh for God's sake, what the fuck can I do about the captain's body?'

'But Jimmy,' I wailed, 'what are we going to do with the body?'

'I don't give a damn what you do with the body – throw it overboard,' he yelled and slammed down the phone.

For a moment, half laughing and half despairing, I considered whether Jimmy might be right and perhaps it would be easier to attempt a burial at sea. I had visions of the boys and me wrapping the poor captain in one of the boat's horrid nylon sheets that both Rupert and Robin had so complained about, and lowering him into the sea murmuring, 'We commit thy body to the deep.'

However, by the time I returned to the boat Rupert and Piers had everything under control. St Maxime had finally agreed that Ray could be laid overnight in their chapel of rest, and the next day the boys and I escorted Beryl to the funeral, and Ray was buried in the little cemetery there.

I look back on most of these holidays with my children and my friends as magical.

ELEVEN

Annabel's

I do not remember the exact moment that Mark decided to call his nightclub after me. I suppose there must have been discussions, but although I have never particularly liked the name myself, Mark thought it was a good one for a club and I agree with him. Now I look back on his decision with pride and consider it the most tremendous compliment he could ever have paid me. Having a nightclub named after you is much better than being immortalised as a rose which, unlike Annabel's, does not necessarily survive very long.

At the beginning of the sixties the fashionable world was turning its attention to London. The capital, emerging from under the great grey hangover of the Second World War, which had continued to linger through the fifties, had started to dazzle with a new and magnetic colour. London was at last beginning to swing. Twiggy, an ultra thin London teenager with spiky eyelashes, was modelling the indecently short skirts that Mary Quant was designing; Vidal Sassoon was giving us his bouncy pageboy haircuts; and we all started driving minis and taking the Pill. But above all it was the new music that symbolised the revolution that was taking place. The spirit of Elvis had crossed the Atlantic and here the Beatles were beginning to top the popular music charts. Everything seemed geared to the cele-bration of youth and, still in our twenties, my friends and I were intoxicated by it all.

In London the Four Hundred in Leicester Square was the only nightclub we really knew and we had all conducted our early romances there. Without any real competition, we were certain it would never close. A group of live musicians would play songs like 'Love is Like a Violin' and Cole Porter medleys, and then, in a small concession to the new popular music, a beat group would take over after midnight. There was no discotheque and the *Daily Express* described the discreet establishment as a place where 'A Duke could be devilish and a Marquess could manage a misdemeanour' and get away with it. But people were tiring of the Four Hundred and were ready for a sophisticated place that reflected the youthful spirit of the new decade, and the more upmarket end of Flower Power. Without immediately realising it, the perfect opportunity for Mark to develop his entrepreneurial gift had arrived.

Mark was never going to be happy as an employee. He is far too independent and creative, and I knew he was a mass of talent waiting to burst out. His mother Rhoda used to describe how he had shown signs of enterprise from the age of ten when, during the war, someone told him how quickly rabbits breed and he set about selling fresh rabbit meat to the ration-restricted locals. Unfortunately, in his haste he bought two males by mistake so the project was rather short-lived.

Mark was unquestionably his artistic father's son, and his energy was prodigious. I had seen the enviable decorative flair with which he transformed Halsey Street and Pelham Cottage, and he could draw beautifully, a gift that he passed on to his three children as both Rupert and Robin won the arts prize at school every single year, and India Jane became a distinguished artist.

Having left his job at J. Walter Thompson to go to Hungary, on our return Mark had started his own advertising agency, which for a while he enjoyed, but soon he was invited to launch and run the London branch of the French designer Hermès and from the small shop at the corner of Piccadilly Arcade and Jermyn Street he supplied his customers with the ultimate in impeccable taste from France. There were suitcases, luxurious leather handbags and briefcases, ties, scarves, all priced at exorbitant rates. But Hermès was not quite enough of a challenge for Mark and he longed to have his own project to throw his energy into.

In 1961 Aspers had found an empty building where, with the legalising of gambling, he could fulfil his own long-held ambition to open a gambling establishment. Number 44 Berkeley Square in Mayfair was a beautiful Georgian house that had been neglected for several years and was verging on the derelict. Aspers had decided to open his club, which he called the Clermont, on the upstairs floors and suggested Mark might like to lease the basement, a small but beautifully vaulted disused cellar. The proposition immediately appealed to Mark, who had been thinking for some time of opening a simple piano bar rather like the one at the Carlyle Hotel in New York. After seeing the building, but having no money himself, he went cap in hand to try to persuade people to invest. Several responded enthusiastically, although there was also a good deal of scepticism from others about the club's long-term prospects for success. My own trustees were the most wary of all and would not allow me to invest a single penny in it, which turned out to be the most short-sighted decision they ever made.

'The backers did it for a bit of a lark,' Mark recalls. 'It started out as a very unserious sort of idea, something that would be fun to do. I had no idea of making my living this way.'

Originally his plan was to establish a nightspot that would suit him and our friends on a relatively modest scale, but the project became increasingly ambitious and he was more and more absorbed by it, and I remember him striding round and round Pelham Cottage fizzing with excitement.

There was a tremendous amount of construction work to be done in that basement and the entire main room had to be dug from the ground, shovelling out 6000 tons of London clay. The dance floor was made from the old kitchen of the house and the garden was excavated to create more space. The whole building was then interconnected by a spiral staircase leading to Aspers's club upstairs, linking dancers to gamblers.

It took almost two years to get the place ready for opening and while he had some help with the design, all final decisions were ultimately taken by Mark. The decor of the club has continued to evolve over the years, but the appearance remains in essence very much the same as when it first opened. The discreet entrance has always been through the now famous anonymous blue and gold canopy down which a small staircase leads into a subterranean lobby. Unlike other clubs nowadays, there is still little visible sign of ostentatious security, other than the doorman. As you enter the club, to the right is the Ladies (which shall always be the province of beloved Mabel to me) and to the left is the Gents. Just off Mabel's domain is the staircase that once led to the Clermont but which was later shut off after Mark and Aspers had a serious disagreement. Down the corridor is the main sitting-out area, where the after-dinner crowd come to squash on to the cushion-stacked banquettes, and the comfortable feather-filled sofas. The first bar is to the left and the Buddha room is behind it, named after the large and magnificent wooden Indian figure that dominates one side of the room, one arm leaning magisterially on his knee. This room came slightly later, as did the bar, both added when Mark realised that the entrance way was getting too crowded and that there was not enough seating space. Up a small staircase to the right is the wall-to-wall bottle-lined private dining room. Rarely have I missed celebrating my birthday in that special room, invariably an occasion of great hilarity and consolation for the passing years.

Further on, through the aisle of shiny brass pillars, you reach the heart of the club. The main dining room, with the originally vaulted ceiling, its table lamps, red and green velvet chairs, and flower-patterned Limoges china, is arranged with the dance floor in the middle at the back and the second large bar running along one side. Near the dance floor are several secluded little tables. There are vases of fresh flowers everywhere, bunches of pale pink roses in the loos and log fires burn in each room. It feels more like a series of luxurious private sitting rooms than a club. The walls are crammed with a potpourri of oil paintings, some valuable like the Landseer and Munnings, some which have caught Mark's eye in a junk shop, their common link simply a reflection of Mark's own idiosyncratic taste. His deep love for animals, in particular for dogs, is strongly represented. There is a charming study of Mabel by John Ward in which she is wearing her distinctive round glasses. There are drawings and cartoons, notably many by Bateman, Bakst designs for theatrical costumes and dozens of photographs.

In the centre of the dining room on the left-hand wall hangs a large conversation piece by John Ward showing more than two dozen founder members and some of the original staff including Louis, Sidney and Mark's secretary Perdita. I am sitting in the middle of all these suited men, the only woman in the painting apart from Perdy. John had painted our children and I had got to know him well. When Mark commissioned him to do the painting for the club he wanted him to catch the special atmosphere of the place and asked therefore that the sittings should take place in the club itself. I would meet John there in my ordinary clothes and nip into the loo, change into my portrait outfit, a hand-painted floaty Thea Porter dress, and quickly backcomb my then very long hair. The whole place was freezing cold and I would sit shivering on the sofa in my evening dress as John worked.

This is the cast in John's painting of the founder members as well as some of the staff: Nolly Zervudachy, Philip Jebb, Michael Brand, Sidney, Douglas Wilson, Anthony Berry, George Galitzine (Prince Galitzine), David Metcalfe, Peter Blond, Louis, Perdita, Daniel Prean, Peter Munster, Jeremy Tree, Tony Lambton, David Somerset, Azamat Guirey (Prince

Guirey), Mickey Suffolk (the Earl of Suffolk), John Beckwith Smith, Henry J. Heinz III, Houston Shaw-Stewart, William de Gelsey, James Hanson (Lord Hanson), David d'Ambrumenil, Harry Hambledon, Norman Parkinson, Mark and me.

Mark set out with the intention of limiting the membership to the 550 founders' friends and then to their friends. Membership cost twelve guineas a year and five guineas for the under twenty-fives, but it was eighteen months before we began to break even. Among the founder members were several dukes, a couple of princesses, many millionaires, dozens of lords, some distinguished Americans, a few entrepreneurs, our greatest friends, my brother and sister and a collection of life enhancers who help to make an evening swing.

That spring, just before the club opened, Mark and I were invited to a party that reminded us of the formal, yet equally wonderful days before the discotheque era had arrived. The party was in fact a ball at Windsor Castle that the Queen was giving for Princess Alexandra and Angus Ogilvy two days before their marriage on 22 April 1963. I was incredibly excited because it gave me a chance to wear the famous Londonderry jewels as even then people rarely gave parties to match the grandeur of the diamonds and nowadays they are kept for safety on tantalising display at the Victoria and Albert Museum. Some of these celebrated jewels, which have been described as 'almost barbaric in their splendour', had been in our family since the time when the Stewarts were simply country squires. After the Foreign Secretary Lord Castlereagh had earned the gratitude of many world monarchs for negotiating for Europe in the aftermath of the Napoleonic threat, he was showered with priceless gems including a waistband measuring three inches wide with 1225 diamonds, that was transformed into the famous Londonderry tiara.

Frances Anne, the heiress to the Seaham coal mines, adored jewellery and as well as inheriting a vast collection which included the two magnificent matching sets of emerald and diamond necklaces, brooches, earrings and hair ornaments, she fell in love with the Russian Emperor who celebrated their love by giving her a glorious collection of Siberian amethysts and pink topaz. Unfortunately, Frances Anne was very fat and on seeing her dressed from head to toe in diamonds Disraeli remarked, 'The jewellery looked like armour and she like a rhinoceros.'

My great-grandmother, Theresa, Marchioness of London-derry, had eagerly seized every opportunity she could to show off the magnificent collection and, referring to the grandest of the tiaras as 'the family fender', caused a sensation at the Devonshire House Ball during Queen Victoria's jubilee year in 1897 as people gasped at pearls the size of pears, the bodice of her dress 'a rivière of huge single stones', diamond clasps holding the train on her shoulders, diamonds sewn on the front of her dress, as one single glorious ruby 'blazed on her wrist'.

Wearing my hair up, the tiara firmly fixed to my head, I went to the Windsor Ball, but as the evening wore on I began to realise that all was not well with me. When my boys started school they caught the usual contagious diseases of mumps, chickenpox and measles, and would then come home and pass them on to India Jane. Not having gone to school until I was eleven, an age at which most children have already caught these things, I was as much at risk as India Jane but I simply never thought of myself as a target. I was therefore totally horrified one morning to find my face and body covered with large pustules. I had caught chickenpox from the boys. These diseases at an older age can really make one quite ill, not to speak of the increased number of spots, and you could not have put a pin between mine, which itched unbearably. I remember ringing Maria Harrison in floods of tears and telling her I was going to be scarred for life.

Two or three weeks before the ball the boys went down with mumps, followed almost immediately by measles, and having had mumps at Southover, when I missed my chance of being a bridesmaid at my cousin's wedding, I was not worried, completely forgetting that I had not had measles. At the royal party I remember beginning to feel rather odd around midnight and although I had worn the tiara before, that evening it felt more than usually heavy and was pressing on my head. By one o'clock I thought I was about to faint and I suddenly caught sight of myself in one of the mirrors. To my horror my face beneath the tiara was scarlet and covered with little red spots. I ran to find Mark and hissed at him that I had caught measles from the boys and I thought I was dying, and we fled home immediately. As I lay in bed with a roaring temperature for the next ten days I could not help wondering how many people I had unwittingly infected at the ball. I can tell you that measles as an adult is not a pleasant thing – I really was ill. I did not know Princess Alexandra well enough to tell her this story until years later when I was living at Ormeley and she became my neighbour at Thatched Lodge in Richmond Park. She has since become a great friend for whom I have huge admiration.

Fully recovered and spot free, we decided to launch the club in June by giving a party for our friends. Mark had worked so hard and suddenly all his dreams seemed to be coming true. By then the club had been in the words of one member, Caroline Graham, 'transformed from an underground shelter into a magnificent stage set'. It looked quite beautiful and I was determined that the party would be a success and a great tribute to Mark as the truth was that my role in the creation of Annabel's had been purely a passive one, although a writer called Barry Reed, in his novel *The Choice*, had tried to give me an imagined but more substantial part. As he had clearly never set foot inside the club he was under the mistaken impression that I was some sort of hostess of the night. Describing a fictional evening he wrote, 'They were escorted to an elevated table overlooking the glamorous patrons by Lady Annabel herself. She bowed courteously as she settled them into place,' continuing, 'Lady Annabel stopped by several times to assure impeccable service.' And during a delicate moment towards the end of dinner, he concluded, 'Lady Annabel appeared just in time to deflect further discussion. "Ah-hah." Symes rubbed his hands together. "The pastry cart."'

I had a new dress made especially for the opening party by Balmain, designing for myself the sort of thing I wanted and as I couldn't face travelling to the Paris salon for more than one fitting I sent my measurements to the dressmaker, Ginette Spanier, in France. When I flew over to Paris with Nico for the only fitting, wearing my usual torn knickers and dis-coloured bra, Miss Spanier was both amazed to see that I had no lacy underwear and annoyed that I had given her quite the wrong measurements and she had to measure me all over again. But in the end she made me a simple, beautifully cut, short white sleeveless dress that suited me and fitted me per-fectly and that I wore again and again.

The club had a seating capacity of only 225 people, so Mark and I tried to explain to our friends in advance that as space was limited we would be unable to invite everyone we knew. On the day the telephone rang incessantly, with people begging to bring friends or relations after dinner. I repeated again and again that because of the restrictions on space it simply was not possible to include them all but no one paid much attention, although when Aspers rang saying that an old friend of his, Jimmy Goldsmith, whom I had met at Aspers's house, was in town, I reluctantly agreed that Aspers could bring him along.

That night, as people started to pour down the basement steps from Berkeley Square, I began to realise that there was going to be a problem with overcrowding and by midnight Annabel's was rapidly beginning to resemble the Underground during the evening rush hour. There were so many people whom I had never seen before and so many faces I recognised but had been unable to ask. I was so exasperated by the gatecrashers that I inadvertently managed to insult both David Bruce, the American Ambassador, and the movie star Peter

O'Toole by telling them that there was no room for either of them. For at least an hour it was bedlam. I had visions of oxygen masks and people being trampled to death. I recall thinking that the evening was turning out to be a disaster and that all our real and invited friends would either leave, or go upstairs to the Clermont to avoid the unbearable crush. I was on the verge of panic and I remember spotting Mark literally chewing his nails. But by the early hours of the morning, miraculously the crowd began to melt away and the rest of the night was magical.

What sounded like a roll-call for the pillars of society arrived to celebrate the launch of the club that night. They included: the Devonshires, Robin Douglas-Home, the McKewans, the Brocklehursts, the Douglas Fairbankses, Whitney Straight, Stas and Lee Radziwill (Prince and Princess Radziwill), the Somersets, the Cazalets, Evelyn Rothschild, Billy Dudley, Drue Heinz, the Maharaja of Jaipur, Tony Lambton, Rupert Loewenstein (Prince Loewenstein), Paul Channon, Andrew Parker-Bowles, the Plunket brothers, Max and Jane Rayne, the Tennants, George Weidenfeld and many many others. By the end of the party at about four or five in the morning there were only two dancing couples left: Mark and me, and Jimmy Goldsmith and his girlfriend Sally Crichton Stuart, who after a tremendous falling out had become reconciled that evening on the Annabel's dance floor. Two days later, on the first night of official business, things went much more smoothly despite a musical hitch as although Mark has always employed the best disc jockeys in the world and the music at Annabel's has always been seamless, that night the proper DJ had not turned up and I remember going over myself to try to work out how to use the turntables.

By the summer of 1963, when the Beatles' song 'She Loves You' and 'My Boy Lollipop' by Milly were riding high in the charts, the cramped basement in Berkeley Square had been transformed into the club with the reputation for being the coolest, hippest, sexiest, most sophisticated and glamorous place in town. An American journalist enviously but admiringly observed that Annabel's had become 'the place where you find the prettiest girls in the greatest clothes. Their hair reaches down to their bottoms and their dresses reach up to them.'

Almost overnight Annabel's established itself as the place to go to eat, to drink, to dance, to meet friends, to see and to be seen. Everyone who was my generation and older went to Annabel's. In those days, if you walked in you would have known over half the people at the tables. I don't remember in the first ten years ever once seeing it even half empty. As well as the ever present founder members and their friends, and a little later many members of the British royal family including Prince Charles, Princess Anne, Princess Margaret and Princess Alexandra, one was just as likely to bump into Frank Sinatra, Aristotle Onassis, or King Constantine of Greece. Another regular, and also a great favourite with the waiters, was the comedian Tommy Cooper. He would breeze into the club in the evening, swiftly becoming very merry indeed and, having reduced the staff to gales of laughter, he would leave to go and do his stage show.

People often ask me what the secret of the great success of Annabel's has been for so many years. I can only say that it is Mark himself. From the very beginning, each night without fail, the ubiquitous owner has been there overseeing and attending to every detail, and regulars are accustomed to the sight of this extremely tall figure, with a presence that is difficult to ignore. He has an unmistakable elegance about him. He is always beautifully dressed, his suits made by Douglas Hayward, his shoes by the famous cobbler, Mr Cleverley. I remember how Mark, Claus von Bülow and Mark Brocklehurst had a constantly running competition to see who could have the smallest, shiniest and smartest Mr Cleverley shoes. The journalist and long-term friend and enthusiast of the club David Wynne Morgan wrote of him in *London Life* magazine,

'Mark's shoes have the shine that would make a guardsman despair, his impeccably cut suits are worn with an air of disdain, the very manner of his walk indicates the constant effort required to propel his six foot five inch frame.'

His appearance has caused many admiring comments over the years. The writer Candida Lycett Green confesses that she has 'long been a little in love with the patron, Mr Birley. Isn't everyone? It's something about his elusiveness; the way he looks so inexorably sad; the way his suits are so immaculately cut; the way his eye for a picture never falters and a certain wild bohemianism hovers in his closet.'

Caroline Graham (Knott as she was then), a great friend of Mark's and mine, had been Mark's extremely beautiful and eligible young assistant at Hermès and describes his 'Hermès pocket chain swinging from his right trouser pocket as he strides through the door his large distinctive eyes roaming, checking everything: the details perfect.'

An American journalist from *Town and Country* magazine questioned his qualifications for the role: 'Birley gives off such an aura of true Brit that he is the very last man you would expect to be a club owner and restaurateur. You'd never see his like in Las Vegas. He looks like a buyer not a seller.'

Mark himself insists that there is no magic formula to his success and, although he disputes it, I believe it is because he is a perfectionist. He attends to every detail in the club down to the perfect curl of the butter in the butter dishes on the dining-room tables and his standards never drop. I don't believe any other nightclub has ever been so meticulously watched over. Mark himself explained the reasoning behind his attention to detail in the revealing interview he gave to Naim Attallah in 1989:

It's not so much perfectionism I'm after in the way I run Annabel's, as the way I think things ought to be. I just want to get everything right in the way I think to be best. Of course it is a matter of going on and on for years and staying interested enough to try to improve things. It is still all a bit of a one-man band. Management is the simple reason why I remain reluctant to take Annabel's across the Atlantic. I couldn't very well stay in America for a year or so and leave everything here in London to get on with itself. It would never work out.

However, Mark realised from the beginning that he needed the right staff to back him up:

While Annabel's was being built, I was trying to gather a little team around me and even then I realised that the key person was going to be the manager. I knew I would be in every kind of trouble, as I didn't really know how to do it myself. I remember calling at the Mirabelle and saying to Louis, the manager there, 'I'm looking for a manager and if you can think of anyone you think might be suitable please let me know.' It was just at the time when the Mirabelle was being taken over and its staff were a bit unsettled. Louis said he might be interested himself and that was my lucky break because he has been with me ever since. Then Mabel whom I'd known at the old Wilton's came to run the Ladies room and George Hobart whom I'd known at Jules Bar was barman.

Mark's relationship with this solid team operated beautifully based on values that some might have found old-fashioned. He explains,

The fact that I insist on my staff always addressing me formally doesn't indicate a lack of friendliness or cama-raderie, it's just that I feel that a degree of formality should be maintained. I'm used to making my own decisions in my business without reference to anybody else. I'm not good on committees. One of my failings is a lack of patience. I'm used to taking my own decisions in my business without reference to anybody else. That rather autocratic way of running things has advantages and disadvantages but one of the main advantages is that it makes for speed and makes your employees happier I think. They like somebody who can say yes or no.

He manages to inspire deep and abiding loyalties among his staff. They not only love him but also respect him. He is always there to listen to them, to help them when they are ill or have worries but, at the same time, God help them if anything goes wrong. Every one of the senior staff who was there on the opening night was still there ten years later. Mark was also insistent on absolute discretion from his staff. 'I would not be very pleased if any of my staff went around blabbing. People here are vulnerable: Members of Parliament, businessmen and so on. Everybody does something silly at some time. A club should be a community of trust.'

One of the reasons that I love the club is the very close rapport I have established with the staff. Sadly, some of them have died or retired since those early days but Louis, Freddy, Mohamed, Ted, Joseph, Johnny Robinson and above all my beloved Mabel became lifelong friends. Arriving at Annabel's for dinner was rather like returning home from boarding school on an exeat; you could always be sure of a special greeting. My concept of the perfect start to an evening was to arrive early enough to have a really good chat with Mabel, which was a habit I kept up until her retirement. With a flurry of greetings to all the doormen, I would dash into the Ladies and hug her. After we had exchanged the usual compliments and many enquiries after the children, we would settle down to a little light-hearted gossip.

Mabel was a stickler for cleanliness, particularly in relation to the washing of hands after visiting the loo. She would make this as obvious as possible by filling the basin with warm water and standing next to it holding a towel. As the ladies emerged, not many were brave enough to slip past her but there were a few who did. Smugly washing and drying my own hands, I would watch out of the corner of my eye as the 'Great Unwashed' swept out of the room, leaving Mabel and me pursing our lips and shaking our heads over this lack of personal hygiene. I would also be given the week's list of those who 'had' and those who 'hadn't'.

Mabel desperately minded my not owning a fur coat. She could not understand that I genuinely hated wearing them (I was ahead of my time). Nevertheless she would lovingly remove my black shawl and reverently hang it among the priceless fur worn by most of the female clientele. At the same time she would point out a particularly rare specimen and to please her I would try it on. One evening as I slipped on an opulent ocelot, I did a little catwalk dance, swooping round the room and kicking up my legs, much to her delight. She was cackling away until I noticed a sudden silence and glancing in the mirror, I saw a very smart woman standing by the door glaring at me. She had returned to retrieve her lipstick that she had left in the ocelot's pocket. 'Lady Annabel was just admiring your coat,' said Mabel defensively.

Now this was difficult and I did not want to get her into trouble. 'Lovely coat, just like mine,' I murmured and handed it back to Mabel.

Despite being caught red-handed, we both laughed about that for years although the experience did not deter Mabel from slipping me into a floor-length sable the following week.

People seemed to lose their inhibitions when they came in to see her. One evening a young lady raced into the loo, pulled off her knickers in full view of Mabel, washed them in the basin, put them on again and dashed out, without a word.

Mabel retired with some reluctance when she was in her late eighties and Mark had been dreading the interview that would precede her departure. He was, of course, aware of her increasing frailty but felt it would be impolite to raise the subject before she did. When they finally met to discuss the taboo subject, they stared at each other across Mark's desk for some minutes in a silence which was finally broken by Mabel who simply said, 'It's time, isn't it?'

She died not many years later and would have loved her own funeral as we were all there and the atmosphere was full of love and warmth. We were a community gathered to say farewell to an old friend. But there were moments when she would have laughed. At the Mortlake Crematorium we had all crowded round the hearse, which appeared at the appointed hour. Noticing an enormous floral tribute which spelt out the word 'Dad', I realised we were at the wrong door. Directed to the correct chapel of rest, we were then confronted by an ornate hearse drawn by four black horses, wearing plumed head-dresses. This seemed more appropriate as Mabel was born in 1908 but the horses were accompanied by a number of people dressed in black leather and sunglasses who seemed unused to daylight. I could not believe that this turnout was for Mabel. And I was right. A rock group was saying goodbye to one of their own.

I still get an unmatchable thrill as I walk into Annabel's but now there is some sadness involved in my visits. I invariably think of Mabel and when I go into the Ladies I can almost hear her talking to me; and I still half expect Louis, now retired, to rush out and give me a big kiss although Mohamed, who to me will always be head barman, is still there. He came over to London as a young Moroccan to work for a friend of Mark's and went from there to become a commis waiter at Annabel's. He is one of the most loyal people in my life and has been coming to help me at home on Christmas day every year since the sixties.

Bernard, who became head waiter, was another of the original team who joined also from the Mirabelle shortly after Louis's arrival. In 1976 he left Annabel's, having been persuaded to help start up a restaurant in Bangkok and when

Mark was on a trip there two years later he was concerned to find Bernard in hospital. Mark says, 'He was sitting on the edge of his bed when I came into the room and turned round with an expression on his face as if he was in quarantine.' Clearly miserable, he asked Mark whether he would take him back. 'I had *la nostalgie* for Annabel's,' he said and a couple of months later he was back in his usual place in the dining room at the club.

Mark's standards of excellence did not initially extend to the gastronomic and in the beginning, underestimating the importance of food, he offered the catering contract to Jo Lyons. Happily they turned down the offer and the dining room has since gained a reputation for serving the finest food of any club in London. Candida Lycett Green describes the temptations she cannot resist: 'A collage of treats: succulent truffles, mango ice, Maryland crab cakes and smoked salmon sliced as thin as tissue paper served with perfect toast.' However, it is the puddings and in particular the bitter chocolate ice cream for which the chef is probably most famous. Jane Proctor, a former editor of *Tatler*, tried once to recreate this mouth-watering dish at home but has described how she found the challenge too great: 'The secret that has tantalised the chattering classes, the aristocracy, the meritocracy, and even the demimonde for decades is the mystery ingredient in Annabel's bitter chocolate ice cream. This recipe was more closely guarded than the formulation for Coca Cola.'

Dancing is one of the overriding reasons that brings people back again and again to Annabel's. Candida Lycett Green says she comes 'not to eat or to drink or to talk or to snog, but to dance'. Annabel's was the first elegant dining club to replace live music with a discotheque (although there have been occasional evenings with live music, most memorably for me the time when the Supremes came in person to perform). After the initial opening night hiccup, the dance floor became one of the hottest six-foot-square pieces of ground in London. To dance with a girl at Annabel's was soon considered the ultimate in romantic sophistication. All the young came to dance, but so did the older generation like the Sweeney brothers, who always danced better than anyone in the room.

The reputation Annabel's had for playing the newest and best dance records in town was reflected in the twice monthly column published in *Queen* magazine under the title 'Annabel's Top 20'. Mark found a series of extremely pretty girl disc jockeys of whom Sherry Clarke was the first. These girls could wield immense power over the mood of the floor, by slowing down or revving up one's emotions simply by the choice of a record, sometimes driving us into a frenzy of activity through the twist, or inducing a feeling of romance with a smoochy number. Rupert Soames was one of the few male disc jockeys in the early eighties. He had taken a great fancy to a girl who came into the club on a regular basis with a regular wimp. Whenever he thought they were getting too intimate on the dance floor he would play something jumpy and energetic like Lonnie Donegan's 'Rock Island Line' to break them up. And we would all long to have our musical requests granted. One member who had just been made a life peer would arrive with a different girl each week and always ask for 'My Sweet Lord'.

Mark is a genius at organising the most amazing extravaganzas in the club, which usually last a week. Among others we have had are the Brazilian week, the Philippine week and the New Orleans week. The best and most memorable for me, maybe because it was the first, was the Russian fortnight. Within the club he created a miniature Russian palace, a fantasy of the once glittering life of St Petersburg. The combination of the music, the top Russian dancers and singers, and the food, which included royal golden caviar and sturgeon aux champignons, contributed to some unforgettable evenings. The performers were so friendly and such fun that Mark and I invited them to Pelham Cottage for a grand finale.

★

Shunning publicity and embracing discretion, the club has nonetheless always been more newsworthy than any other in London. Romances have been initiated, engagements announced, marriages cancelled, deals struck, mergers made, and although excessively boisterous behaviour is usually peacefully defused by a quiet word in the ear of the member concerned the tabloids did once report that a man took his life after the directors had taken the rare step of punishing some transgression by revoking his membership. The male dress code, although hardly radical, has sometimes attracted more press attention than anything else. For almost forty years the dress rule of a dark suit and tie remained unchanged and inflexible, although this rule in itself was a departure from the previous general insistence in nightclubs for black tie. But Mark's code was unchangeable and inflexible for everyone with no exception. On 31 December 1967 the Beatle George Harrison arrived at the blue and gold canopy, intending to see in the New Year in style. With him were his wife, Pattie Boyd, his manager Brian Epstein and his friend, the rock star Eric Clapton. Heavily bearded, wearing a polo-necked sweater and a thick scarf, he was astonished to be refused entry by the doorman. Insulted at being offered a shirt and tie, club policy when the dress code is not being met, Mr Harrison reminded the doorman that in his opinion Annabel's needed the Beatles rather more than the Beatles needed Annabel's. 'I don't think this is the case nowadays or ever was in the past,' was the doorman's reply and the Harrison party saw in the New Year at the nearby Lyons Corner House.

Ten years later the tabloid newspapers were once again impressed by the steely nerve of the Annabel's doorman who barred entry to the Queen's second son, when Prince Andrew turned up in Berkeley Square expecting to be let in wearing an open-necked shirt and a pair of jeans.

Yet another decade later an infinitely more original flouting of the dress regulations was witnessed. On a summer evening in July 1986, a few days before the wedding of Sarah Ferguson to Prince Andrew, two uniformed and spectacularly attractive young policewomen in black stockings, tight-skirted suits and black-and-white chequered PWC hats appeared in the club. They flashed their warrant cards and the doorman ushered them in. But as they took their places on the high stools at the bar, at first people interpreted their undisguised amusement as the sign of a successful entry for a couple of stripograms. One had short brown hair, the other a longer black hairstyle and both were wearing glasses, but there was something familiar about these two giggling constables. Sipping orange juice, which had been bought for them by an intrigued member who was sitting nearby, having declined the offer of champagne by saying they never drank on duty, they remained at the bar, laughing and talking, before finishing their drinks and slipping out into the night. The following day on an official engagement in the country, the Princess of Wales could not help confessing to a local Gloucestershire policeman how, on Prince Andrew's stag night, she and Fergie had decided to have a bit of a night out themselves and had briefly joined his ranks. 'The wig was hot and uncomfortable, and my feet were killing me as the shoes were two sizes too small,' she told him but added, 'You have to have a laugh sometimes, don't you?'

When the dress code issue was once again making the news Mark wrote an explanatory piece in the *Spectator*. He had decided that because so many restaurants had allowed the suit and tie convention to lapse he too should really follow their lead and move with the times by abandoning the tie requirement. However, he was unprepared for the result, and explains,

I had overlooked the simple truth that the British have no tradition of casual clothes. We seem to have a uniform for everything: weddings, births, funerals, racing, shooting, hunting, fishing, dancing, dining in the city, attending concerts, tennis matches and so on. Consequently when we are invited to use our initiative, it is invariably a disaster. Sights of almost Gothic horror appeared nightly. The staff themselves, elegance personified, hated it; the older members hated it; the younger members hated it and practically all the women hated it. To hell with moving with the times.

Mark reinstated the dress code and elegance was restored. If nothing else, the experience had been an exercise that proved that in the dress code, as in so many aspects of the running and design and ethic of the club, Mark had got it perfectly right from the beginning.

Despite the odd difficult moment between doorman and customer on the steps outside in Berkeley Square there have been few really bad scenes inside the club and no big fights. Inevitably, there has been a lot of drunken behaviour. Geoffrey Keating used to sit at the bar as if he owned the place and he was never frightened of the consequences of his behaviour, drunk or sober. Whenever things got too much and after he had insulted whole parties of Arabs, we had developed a procedure for getting him out. One of the doormen used to walk him home through Berkeley Square and as he passed the J. Walter Thompson building he would stop, undo his flies and pee into the letterbox with great accuracy all over JWT's expensive doormat. After that he would be quite happy. He was like a lamb once he had been led home and although Mark used to have frightful rows with him he adored him.

Annabel's is a one-off, a club that has managed to endure and to remain successful and fashionable over forty years, with virtually no concession to passing fads. Fairly recently a discreet announcement stating that mobile telephones were not permitted for use in the club appeared on the members' notice board. Mark and his staff maintain an ever-constant commitment to the highest standards of excellence in all Annabel's has to offer as well as in the three further clubs Mark now owns, Mark's, Harry's Bar and most recently George's.

Caroline Graham feels that 'Mark has produced a flawless opening night every night for 40 years'. For eleven years he was assisted by his managing director, Gavin Rankin, who was of invaluable help to Mark and is a great friend to us both.

The clientele is unfailingly loyal and of the original membership there are still nearly 200 who continue to walk down the famous basement steps while applications to join have never been higher. Joan Juliet Buck, writing in the American journal *Women's Wear Daily*, was intrigued and frustrated by the qualifications required of a prospective member: 'You have to be born to it – or be awfully rich, clever and discreet.'

In the interview with Naim Attallah, Mark revealed his own theories for his success:

> If you asked a selection of people to define their ideal nightclub they would all answer with different specifications but probably none of them would answer truthfully because they will all have little secrets which they're not going to disclose. But I think I happen to know what some of those secrets are and Annabel's incorporates a few of them. Since I launched Annabel's quite a number of other clubs have sprung up and every time a new one comes along there's a fresh wave of excitement. I know perfectly well that a lot of people will go rushing off there but equally I'm pretty certain that they'll be back. I strongly believe that if you do your utmost to look after people properly they will remain loyal.

The club opened at a time when London was ready for a new and exciting place to go in the evenings, but the climate of the sixties cannot solely take the credit for its enduring popularity. Carnaby Street and its fashions were also indisputably part of the movement that contributed to those heady days but Carnaby Street is no longer around.

Candida Lycett Green identifies the magical ingredient as an insatiable appetite for glamour. 'Annabel's is glamorous. It always was. It's a grown-up glamour though. Posh to the hilt, discreet and private. Not the clickety-clackety, filo-faxy glamour which the urgently-need-to-be-seen Liz Hurley-ish crowd crave. Annabel's affords a sensual, clandestine kind of glamour.'

For me, the place has been an important part of my life for a long time. Although I am not instinctively a nightclub creature, preferring instead to be safely ensconced in my bed by ten in the evening (covered by blankets and at least six dogs) Annabel's remains the exception. My visits there are less frequent now, but I still love the place and I feel a warm sense of belonging and of being among friends and people I love. In September 2003 Mark and I hosted jointly two parties at the club for some of our greatest friends in celebration of the fortieth anniversary of the founding of the club. Both evenings were magical and unforgettable with Dame Edna Everage doing the hilarious cabaret on both nights.

I will always regard Annabel's as one of my homes.

TWELVE

Meeting Jimmy

My romance with Jimmy Goldsmith began on the night when he picked me up in Annabel's but I first met him in 1962 at Aspers's house in Lyall Street in London at one of Aspers's regular gambling evenings. I remember being amused and intrigued by a rather exotic-looking young man who was sitting on the floor playing backgammon while at the same time, out of the corner of his eye, he was warily watching a small tiger cub that was circling the table beside him. During that year I saw him again once or twice at Aspers's house and we had chatted, but afterwards I didn't give him another thought. He had always been presented to me as part of French café society and his world was made up of that European jet set which had nothing to do with my life.

After the tragedy of the death of his young wife Isabel Patino, the beautiful daughter of a Bolivian tin magnate, during childbirth in 1954, Jimmy had shut himself away completely from social life and had thrown himself into his work as a distraction from his grief. Having married so young myself, I had followed their dramatic romance rather closely, including the emotional rescue of the baby from her grandmother, the Duchess of Durcal. After a few years, during which time he had hovered on the edge of bankruptcy, Jimmy was beginning to emerge into public life. However, he was not then part of the London scene and to me he was simply a romantic figure from the newspapers.

In March 1964 Mark and I, and Jane and some friends were

lent a vast penthouse suite next to the Copacabana Hotel in Rio de Janeiro by a friend of Stas Radziwill. It was Carnival time and not having realised quite how hospitable the Brazilians were, or that they partied all night, we were plunged into a hectic whirl. To add to the drama of this exhilarating place, there was tremendous political tension as the right-wing President Jao Goulart had been thrown out days before our arrival in a military coup and there were mass demonstrations in the streets about his successor, Humberto Castelo Branco. We were forbidden to go out but Nicholas Cobbold, a friend of Mark's, and I disobeyed the ban and escaped to take some photographs of the demonstrators in the main square. I didn't drink much in those days but I remember the delicious Cuba Libre, a cocktail made from Coca Cola and rum, which added to the heady mix of those magical days. On my return home, delighted at the novelty of having a suntan in March and after three weeks without any school runs, I knew I was feeling and looking particularly well. Shortly after the holiday I was having dinner in Annabel's with a great friend of mine, Caroline Peake, when I recognised the tall man who came up to our table and asked me to dance. It was Jimmy Goldsmith. The next morning Aspers rang me, sounding very excited, saying that Jimmy was extraordinarily taken with me and could I come and have dinner with him and Jimmy at the Clermont that night. I have never been very good at late nights and in those days I had to get up very early with the children, so while sorely tempted by the invitation I refused.

A couple of days later I was invited to dinner by Stas and Lee Radziwill. Teddy and Bobby Kennedy were staying with them, and they asked if I would like to bring anyone with me. Mark was already doing something that evening and as Jimmy had telephoned me several times since the dancing night, I invited him as my date. He came round to Pelham Cottage to collect me and we had a wonderful dinner with the Kennedy brothers. Afterwards everyone except Bobby went on to

Annabel's and I remember shuffling round the floor clasped tightly in the arms of Teddy Kennedy.

Jimmy, however, was absolutely mesmerised by Lee, and after that night I didn't see him for a week. I don't think anything happened between him and Lee although Jimmy would have liked it to have done and at that stage, while I was flattered by Jimmy's attentions I wasn't annoyed. Nothing had yet happened between us and everybody was in love with Lee. As well as being the sister-in-law of the President of the United States, men were fascinated by her beauty.

Up to this point the thought of an affair with Jimmy had not crossed my mind. He was a married man and I also knew that he had been passionately in love with Sally Crichton Stuart and that they had had a tremendous on again, off again affair. They had split up, only to be reconciled at the opening party at Annabel's and although we weren't close I regarded Sally as a friend. I had known them break up and get back together again so often that I wanted to be absolutely sure this latest split was final. Mark and I were still great friends and technically still married, but by this time Annabel's was consuming his attention during every waking moment and his total involvement in the club together with my own absorption in the running of our childrens' lives had resulted, almost imperceptibly to ourselves, in a drifting apart.

That summer came and went, and Jimmy and I continued to see each other and have the occasional dinner. But I was wary of a situation that I saw was potentially dangerous. However, in September we went to a dinner party together and as we were leaving he asked me to join him in his suite at the Ritz where he lived when he was in London. I walked up the main front stairs, feeling thoroughly conspicuous under the impassive gaze of Victor the porter while Jimmy took the lift. I had been wearing a garment called a merry widow, which acted as suspenders, corset and strapless bra all in one. It was almost impossible to do up oneself and as I couldn't very well ask Jimmy to do it up for me when I eventually left to go home in the early hours of the morning, I shoved it into my evening bag and tucked the bag under my arm. Reaching the foyer of the Ritz, I fumbled for my car keys and realised that I must have left them upstairs in Jimmy's suite. In my confusion I dropped the merry widow, and it fell with a great clang of suspenders on to the marble floor in full view of the night porter. I knew that although I had to retrieve the keys, I couldn't face Jimmy being seen coming downstairs to give them to me, so, crimson with embarrassment I rang him from the porter's desk to warn him that I was on my way back upstairs to collect them.

Our affair began that night but at first we managed to keep our relationship a secret by continuing to meet in Jimmy's suite in the Ritz.

Before I was forced to confide the truth to Mrs White, I had often been looking for good alibis for my rare overnight absences, so I was delighted when a perfect excuse fell into my lap in the unlikely shape of the Pestalozzi Village. The internationally celebrated, humanitarian home in East Sussex, originally founded in Switzerland to care for displaced orphans and refugees from the Second World War, always held its annual fund-raising ball in London and in 1964 I was invited to be the Chairman. I would pretend to Mrs White that occasionally I was asked to pay a visit to the Pestalozzi Village in order to learn how it worked. Little did she know that the nearest I got to the Village was a weekly committee meeting in the Dorchester Hotel. I had never chaired a fund-raising ball before, so my efforts were pretty amateurish. However, I had managed to persuade Larry Adler to play his mouth organ for the cabaret and as the evening had gone so smoothly I was invited back to be Chairman again. The next year I felt we had scored a major coup by landing the well-known movie star Laurence Harvey to sing as the cabaret. He was very handsome and was particularly popular at the time, since he had just had a triumph on the London stage as King Arthur in the musical *Camelot*.

A good many of my loyal friends took tables at the ball although I knew some were determined to mob the whole evening up. After dinner the plan was that I would make my carefully written little speech, after which it would be time for the raffle, which Laurence Harvey had kindly agreed to draw. In spite of being slightly inebriated, Laurence delivered a faultless performance, composed of songs from *Camelot*, after which he wandered over to my table where to his delight he discovered a mutual friend of ours in Mark Watney. By the time the raffle was ready to be drawn, Watney and Laurence were becoming increasingly intoxicated, roaring with laughter and busy scribbling an alternative speech for me, filled with rude jokes and obscenities.

After dinner Laurence and I walked over to the stand where a couple of well-corseted, horsy-looking ladies were holding the drum waiting for the draw to begin. I gave my speech and announced that Laurence would now perform the draw. His hand lowered over the drum and out of the corner of my eye I spotted Watney approaching, and as Laurence pulled out the first ticket Watney snatched it from his hand. Reading from it aloud he called, 'Number 43. Mrs Twistleton-Smythe?' And without pausing, swiftly went on to declare, 'Absurd! No one can possibly have a name like that!' Tearing the ticket into shreds, he threw it on the ground. The horsy-faced women blanched in horror and I hastily took over the draw as Watney and Laurence took to the dance floor together in a wild fandango.

Later we all went on to Annabel's and on arrival I saw Laurence lying spread-eagled on the carpet near the entrance shouting, 'Where is Watney?'

Meanwhile Watney had grabbed the prettiest girl in the club and had lurched on to the dance floor singing little out-of-tune snatches from *Camelot*. I was not very surprised that I was never asked to chair the Pestalozzi Ball again.

The following January Jimmy and I went to Kenya for a ten-day holiday and on the way home he told me he regretted the trip because during those days alone together he had fallen in love with me. Neither of us had intended things to go as far as they did, or become quite so serious. At first I continued to think that his life and his world were not for me but his friends were so welcoming and as I started to be drawn in, soon we were together whenever he was in London. The relationship intensified through his possessiveness as he loathed the idea of me spending time with Mark and I continuously found myself in the curious position of making excuses to Jimmy for seeing my own husband. I, on the other hand, never questioned or minded the weekends he continued to spend in Paris with his wife Ginette and their children.

Jimmy was thirty when I met him and in those early days, despite his debonair, jaunty confidence, there was a vulnerability about him that I found immensely appealing. I also had enormous respect for a man who worked quite so hard and who was unfailingly at his office desk by 8.30 in the morning. Riches did not come easily to Jimmy as, like Mark, he had started with nothing and neither asked for nor was given any help from his father. Jimmy's mother was a French Catholic and his father a German Jew who became a member of the British Parliament, and Jimmy had displayed an inherited entrepreneurial spirit and an ambition to succeed in the business world almost from the day he left school.

In the beginning he was helped by his brother Teddy who asked him to take over the running of his fledgling company which was marketing a revolutionary new cure for rheumatism. The reputation of Adremad, a miracle cream, was almost entirely based on the famous effect it had made on the previously rheumatoid joints of a French racehorse, which recovered enough to come second in the Prix de l'Arc de Triomphe. After only two years, thanks to Jimmy's unique energy and his extraordinary financial skills, the company had expanded, was selling an impressive array of pharmaceutical products as well as controlling the French rights to Alka Seltzer, and was employing a hundred people. As part of the expansion Jimmy employed a young French secretary called Ginette Lery. Ginette was tireless in her work for Jimmy, building up his confidence with her unshakeable belief in his ability. Within five years Ginette had given birth to their son Manes.

By the time I met him he had had numerous successes as well as many setbacks during his ten years in business and was still struggling to break through to the level that his ambition was driving him. At one point he came close to a major break-through when he was involved in an innovative company that specialised in mother and baby products. But a dissatisfaction with his financial position as the slightly unequal partner led him to sell his shares in the shop chain that was to become Mothercare.

By 1964 he was having a great success with a new product called Milical, a slimming drink that worked by suppressing the appetite, which seemed to have captured the imagination of the pioneering slimming market. This drink was the basis on which Cavenham Foods was to be founded and from which true financial rewards were to come to Jimmy. Ginette was still vitally important to him during this time and in 1963 they had married and the following January had a daughter, Alix, a sister for Manes. He was beginning to establish his business interests in England and it was during that spring on a trip over to London that he spent an evening at Annabel's and invited me to dance. As his business interests developed and became more complicated, Jimmy realised that he needed more experienced banking help. In 1967 he met Gilberte Beaux, the daughter of a Corsican banker whose family had moved to France when Gilberte was only fifteen. Demonstrating a precocious talent, she rapidly made her way to the top of a banking career and was working at Union Financière de Paris during Jimmy's negotiations to take over part of the company. Realising immediately what an astute woman she was, he asked her to come and work for him. Through her own dedication and cool-headed efficiency she organised his disparate affairs for him and consolidated them into one company which they named Générale Occidentale.

Shortly after the beginning of Jimmy's partnership with Madame Beaux I met her at dinner at the Carlton Hotel in Cannes. Jimmy had talked so much about her that I wasn't sure whether to be jealous of her, but he assured me their relationship was based purely on business. He told me she was a remarkable woman, with the best mind he had ever encountered and she became the closest business associate of his working life. Faced with this paragon of all the intellectual virtues, I was rather apprehensive about meeting her. At first I found her brilliance intimidating and I remember how when in the middle of a very high-powered conversation about business in Russia she wanted my opinion, I was completely flummoxed and thought wrongly that she had asked me with the intention of making me look stupid. Little did I know that I would discover an affinity and closeness with this woman after that initial rather scary start. If I consulted her, she always managed to give me sound advice about Jimmy without betraying him. She crossed easily over the business boundary to become a family friend who often joined us all on our Barbadian holidays along with Jimmy's other business partners John Tigret and Thierry Clermont Tonerre and his wife Rosanne. Gilberte is Jemima's godmother, and remains a woman I adore and for whose wisdom I hold the utmost respect.

During Jimmy's negotiations with Générale Occidentale he took me to meet one of the leading business figures of the day, Armand Hammer, and his wife Frances. Jimmy was in the middle of a very important deal with Hammer and he urged me to be on my very best behaviour. Although Frances was charming, I was not particularly taken with Armand Hammer, who seemed a rather puffed-up little man and extremely pleased with himself. Nevertheless I did my best, perking up enormously when he announced that he was flying us in his private plane to see Disneyland in California. I was really excited about going to Disneyland because I had always longed to see it, although I realised it was a bit of a sacrifice on Jimmy's part as I knew Disneyland would certainly not be his cup of tea. When we arrived there were so many different rides to choose from that I would happily have spent all day trying them out, but Armand Hammer was insistent that the four of us should take a boat ride through the Pirates' Lagoon. I felt this was a rather tame choice – I had looked forward to being simultaneously terrified and excited by one of those really fast rides – but this expedition was strictly business and donning a falsely excited smile I climbed into a small boat, with Jimmy and Frances in the front and Armand Hammer and me in the back.

It was a boiling hot day and I was wearing a thin summer dress with no stockings. I felt a bit uneasy as I couldn't help noticing Hammer was doing a little bit of peering down my dress and kept putting his arm round me. Sailing along, I noticed that the Pirates' Lagoon had one or two long tunnels and as we entered the first one I felt Hammer's hand sliding up my leg. I quickly moved it away with a little laugh, pretending to exclaim at a couple of model pirates brandishing their cutlasses on the bank side. As we came out of the tunnel I gave Jimmy a nudge in the back because I could see in the distance a really long one approaching but he did not turn round and we duly entered the tunnel. By this time Hammer's arm was clamped to my shoulders, his hand trailing a fraction above my cleavage and to my horror he pulled me close and kissed me. At that moment we came out into the sunlight and I was relieved to see that we had reached the end of the lagoon. We all climbed out of the boat but I was so embarrassed I could not look at him, although he seemed quite composed.

Waiting until I got Jimmy alone, I told him what had happened and how I was *not* going to go on any more rides with Armand Hammer. Jimmy was quite dismissive and insisted I must have imagined the whole incident, but when Hammer started walking us briskly towards the Ghost Train I pleaded a headache, knowing exactly what would be in store for me in the darkness. I was furious with Jimmy but I realised that I must not risk jeopardising his deal and luckily he too wanted to return to the hotel. I could not help wondering whether Frances Hammer had any idea of what her husband was up to in the back seat because there was no doubt in my mind that I was not the first or the last female to be groped by him in the Pirates' Lagoon.

Some of the best moments in my early relationship with Jimmy curiously mirrored some of the happiest parts of the beginning of my marriage to Mark when we had lived in Rhoda's little flat in St John's Wood. Jimmy would wake up filled with energy, but after an immensely hard-working day he hardly ever wanted to go out to parties. One of the most lovable things about him was his cosiness. His favourite sort of evening was dinner in bed, preferably scrambled eggs and bacon, which I would make for him, with a cup of tea and sometimes yoghurt and apple purée. He also loved watching television in bed, occasionally leaping out to kick it if a politician or a political view annoyed him. There was a simplicity about him then and it was impossible to be bored by him as he had such an enormous capacity for life, and I think part of my attraction for him was that I was as irrepressibly enthusiastic as he was. He taught me how to have an open mind and how to see things from all perspectives, and I learned new things from him every day. Certainly he was passionately jealous and obsessive, but he was also generous, funny and kind.

He had a completely different sense of humour from our family. We have always laughed at lavatory jokes but he hadn't been brought up to find any of that sort of thing at all funny and I had to coax him a little before he could respond. Slowly, and with little choice, as the Londonderrys and the Birleys are unrelenting in this area, he started to laugh with us. He had a very fierce temper and if the fax machine or the television would not work, he would pick it up and hit it, and subsequently he was capable of throwing the whole thing out of the window. I remember an incident that occurred many years later while the children and I were staying at Jabali, Jimmy's magnificent pink palace, built high in the Mexican mountains beneath the tremendous volcano at Colima. On the second day I was on my way down to breakfast when I noticed some of the little Mexican maids in their pink uniforms sobbing into their handkerchiefs. Mystified, I wandered towards the dining room where I was met by a very excited Ben-Ben revelling in the drama as he explained, 'Daddy got into a frightful rage with the television set and he and I have thrown it over the mountainside,' adding, as his face clouded with disappointment, 'I hoped he would miss the video machine as I thought I could smuggle it back home and sell it to one of my friends at Eton, but he spotted it sticking out from underneath the chair where I had hidden it and made me throw it down the mountain as well.'

I later learned that Jimmy had been unable to sleep because of a noisy malfunctioning boiler and, in a fearful mood, had tried without success to get CNN on the television, whereupon he lost his temper and threw out the set. He also told everyone within earshot that he was closing Jabali for good and he was never going to set foot in it again. Knowing it would all blow over by the evening and used to seeing malfunctioning fax machines flying through the window, I wasn't fazed by this particular bit of destructive extravaganza but I saw Jimmy's son-in-law, Alix's husband Goffredo, looking very depressed and worried. Needless to say, back at the main house at Cuix-mala and following a rather good dinner, Jimmy had forgotten all about it. Whether he was angry either with you or a machine, his bad temper would always vanish quickly. I have never met anyone less moody or sulky.

However, he did have one rather disturbing preoccupation that no good humour could relieve him of. While most of us have phobias (mine is wasps) Jimmy's was rubber. He had an absolute horror of it. There was no question of having any flippers or masks round the swimming pool. He couldn't even bear anyone to touch rubber. Rubber bands were the worst manifestation of the phobia and he could be physically sick if he saw one. If anyone brought in his post bound by a rubber band there would be a shriek of horror, and you had to remove and dispose of it immediately, while you went to wash your hands. No one is quite sure what initiated this extreme reaction but a wonderful woman called Aya Robinson, who was a friend of Marcelle and who became a sort of adored nanny to Teddy and Jimmy, had her own theory.

When Jimmy and his brother Teddy were very young, their mother Marcelle, who loved her boys, returned one day from a trip to Paris with presents of very chic little rubber mack-intoshes. Aya told me that she saw Jimmy take one look at his mother's mackintosh and flatly refuse to wear it. Marcelle told him that it had cost a great deal of money and forced him to put it on, whereupon he was violently sick. Aya dated his hatred of rubber from then.

The very worst rubber band incident occurred when we were both going to Rio in the early 1970s. Our vast quantity of luggage had been put on to the plane and as we sat in our first-class seats, I was immensely excited at the prospect of returning to Brazil for another three weeks with Jimmy to show him the glories of the Carnival. Moments before take-off, Jimmy spotted an elastic band in the middle of the aisle. I had already seen it and was praying he wouldn't, but he did. At first he quite calmly asked the steward to remove it. Then he announced that he couldn't fly on that plane.

'Oh come on, Jimmy, it's only an elastic band,' I said, knowing I was already on shaky ground.

'No,' he said, 'I'm getting off.'

In an attempt to save my holiday I protested weakly, 'We can't get off because all our luggage is on board.'

'It's coming off too,' he said. All the luggage had to be unloaded and we got off the plane and went back to the Scribe Hotel to decide what to do next. I argued that Varig Airways had plenty of other planes, but Jimmy was implacable, concluding that if Varig had one stray elastic band they were bound to have others. In the end we went back to the airport to board an Air Portugal plane which was rubber band free and spent three weeks in the Penina Hotel in Faro. We never made it to Rio.

When Jimmy's business interests in Britain began to expand, he left the Ritz and bought a house in Chester Terrace in Regent's Park. As he had moved Ginette and the children over to London, for a year we rented a tiny annexe belonging to Claus von Bülow's large flat in Belgrave Square.

Claus was a long-standing friend of Mark's and mine, going back to the early 1950s. I had first met him at one of Aspers's weekly gambling games, a tall rather saturnine figure, the antithesis of the nickname we gave him in later years – Claus-ikins. He became a regular visitor at number 9 Halsey Street and later at Pelham Cottage, always accompanied by the most ravishing girls. In 1965 he fell in love with an American heiress, Sunny von Auersperg, who had two children by a previous marriage. A seemingly fairy-tale couple, they married a year later and came to live in London. Claus and Sunny subsequently moved to New York and I used to see them both when Jimmy and I would be there on business. After Zac and Jemima were born we all used to go to tea with Claus's and

Sunny's little blonde daughter Cosima and for long walks in Central Park.

Whenever I was in New York Claus would join me for lunch at the Carousel and I would fill him in on all the latest London gossip. By then he had turned from a carefree bachelor to a domestic animal and loved the idea of a home life with his wife and child. Nevertheless, some time in the late 1970s I noticed during these lunches that Claus seemed rather depressed. I knew that he truly loved Sunny and that marriage had been an important and life-changing event for him, but there was evidently something troubling him and although he was far too loyal to speak a word of criticism against her, I think he felt she had in some way rejected him.

When, in 1980, Sunny was discovered in an irreversible coma, Claus was accused of attempted murder. My entire family were flabbergasted for, knowing Claus as well as we did, we knew it was unthinkable that he would ever harm Sunny. Unfortunately he often made a somewhat sinister impression on people, which did little to improve his image during the trial, and there were abundant rumours flying around, including the most extreme allegation that he practised necrophilia, an apocryphal story that had ironically begun with one of Claus's own poor-taste jokes against himself and had been picked up and embellished by Aspers. Mark, Nico, Jane, Alastair and I offered to help Claus by supplying character testimonials and although he was initially found guilty, after his appeal he was rightly acquitted and his daughter Cosima as well as many friends have continued to stand by him.

Claus had a mad butler called Knights who was a homo-sexual and had a predilection for rough trade and a secret longing to be beaten up. On the rare night we managed to spend at the flat we would be woken by heavy snoring and find Knights fast asleep on the sofa, usually with a black eye. He would explain the injury by telling us he had fallen over in the Tube although we knew he had almost certainly returned from a thoroughly good beating up. Terrified of being caught in the main flat by Claus in such a condition, using his own latchkey he would creep back to our annexe and pass out on the sofa. After Claus married Sunny she needed the annexe for her German maid (the same maid who was to betray Claus so dreadfully in the trial), so Jimmy and I had to move out.

After that first trip to Kenya we started to go on holiday together often. We saw a lot of Max and Jane, and Jimmy would jokingly tell Jane, 'My job is to keep your sister tanned.' In the cold English winter, during the school term, we would go to Nassau, or Mexico or to Jamaica until Michael Manley took over and it became too dangerous.

But weekends, half-terms and school holidays were a sacrosanct time for my children and on Easter Monday in 1970 I was therefore alone with the children who were becoming rather bored and restless in London. I was racking my brains for amusing things to do to fill the few days before we were due to go up to spend the rest of the holidays at Wynyard and the children wanted more than anything to go down to Howletts, John Aspinall's private zoo in Kent, and spend the day playing with the baby gorillas and tigers. All the children loved Aspers and Rupert in particular enjoyed going into the cages to feed the animals.

Aspers's zoo had grown since its early days when he only had one small tiger and a spider monkey, both of which he kept in London. The zoo was now fully established with whole families of gorillas, many tigers and other species of wildlife. He was beginning his crusade to raise animals in as natural surroundings as possible with the intention of releasing them into the wild when they were ready. Strange as it might sound, I never questioned entering the animal cages with Aspers. I really trusted him and particularly loved going in there to take the younger gorillas for walks in the woods. The males were quite rough and had a habit of hiding behind trees before darting out and grabbing us by the arm or the hair. Jimmy, who was more cautious than I was when dealing with wildlife, taught me that the best way to avoid being grabbed was to carry a baby gorilla on your shoulders, as they would then leave you alone. There was no malice intended by the gorillas; they were simply enjoying a boisterous adolescent game. I also went into the cages with some of the younger tigers and occasionally we would take them for walks too.

Rupert had always had a particular affinity with animals and at home he had a pet chipmunk, which he would carry around on his shoulder. At Howletts, which he frequently visited on school outings, most of the animals seemed to sense his complete lack of fear as he moved freely among them. On this particular Easter Monday the children clamoured to be taken down to Howletts but I was worried. Mark and Aspers had fallen out badly over the use of a wine cellar at 44 Berkeley Square and I knew that he would not want me to take the children there. By this time, although we were officially separated, geographically we were next door to one another, as Mark was living in 24 Pelham Street with a garden that backed on to mine, making it easy for the children to go backwards and forwards between us. The children continued to nag me to take them to Howletts, their enthusiasm increased by Aspers telephoning and begging us all to come. So I told Mark a lie; not the first or the last, but a significant one in view of the events that unfolded later. I told him I was taking them to the New Forest to see the ponies and that we would be back that evening. On the train to Littlebourne I had a real sense of foreboding. What if one of them had a finger bitten or a scratch? What if Mark found out?

The children, wildly excited, were very noisy and boisterous on the train and I snapped at them more than once. I had an uneasy conscience and took it out on them. We were met at the station by Min Musker, who had become Aspers's second wife following his divorce from Jane, and after lunch we all went to see the animals. We started with the gorillas and went in and played with the little ones, watching through the bars as Aspers wrestled with the big male and I always found watching him play like a brother with this powerful creature an exciting sight.

Then Aspers took us into the enclosure of one of his younger female tigers. There were nine of us in there: Aspers and Min, Rupert and Robin, Aspers's two children by Jane – Damian and Amanda – Aspers's younger stepbrothers, James and Peter Osborne, and myself. I sensed that Robin was a bit nervous and although he did not say anything some protective instinct made me keep India Jane outside the cage. She was furious and begged to come in, but I was adamant. Maybe I had a premonition of danger. Although Aspers did not know it at the time the tigress, Zorra, was in the early stages of pregnancy and afterwards he came to believe that in her pregnant state she might have been bewildered by Robin's height (he was very tall for his age) as well as able to sense his fear.

I will never forget my disbelief as I saw the tigress suddenly turn towards Robin and, standing up on her hind legs, place her front paws on his shoulders. Within seconds she had pulled him down, and I screamed and pushed Rupert out of the cage. Numb with horror I saw the tigress take the whole of Robin's head into her mouth and start to claw him with her hind legs. Robin says that the pressure was amazing, like having your head clamped in a carpentry vice. Aspers and Min moved like lightning. Aspers forced the tiger's mouth open, badly cutting his hands on her teeth, and Min held her legs. By some miracle the tigress released her grip and James Osborne carried Robin, who astonishingly had not lost consciousness, out of the cage. I felt my legs giving way and thought I was going to faint, and knew I shouldn't. I remember hearing James Osborne saying to me, 'Oh God, I've seen all this before.' Apparently a couple of weeks earlier the girlfriend of one of their friends had stuck her arm through the cage and had it mauled by one of the tigers.

I thought Robin was dead and I could hear Rupert howling. Somehow we got Robin into Min's car and I held him in my arms while we raced to the nearest casualty department at Canterbury hospital. Cradling him, I could see that his jaw was being held on by a thread and there was just a hole where one side of his face had been. In the casualty department he was quickly carried away for the doctors to examine him. He was still conscious and I knew he was trying to tell me something but it was hard to understand him. He pointed to his mouth and it was then that I realised his brace was still inside his mouth. He was taken away for a nine-hour operation and I collapsed. I did not know how badly he was hurt – I did not even know if he was going to live. I paced up and down the room and I have never cried so much or for so long, nor have I ever felt such terrible guilt, guilt that I was to feel for the next two years, maybe more. I rightly saw it as totally my fault. I should not have allowed any of the children into the private enclosure.

In the early hours of the morning while I waited for the outcome of the operation Mark arrived. He was very, very angry. Not only had I lied to him but his son had nearly been killed. We went to see Robin in intensive care, his head and half his face encased in bandages. Although he was not conscious the doctors told me the operation had been successful. Inexplicably there was no room to stay at the hospital so I went back to Howletts and Nico and Alastair flew down from Wynyard. In the morning we went to the hospital where Nanny Wendy joined us. Robin was sitting up in bed, frightened and shocked, and I held him in my arms for most of the day. He stayed in hospital for several weeks before he was allowed home but his jaw was so badly damaged that he was unable to eat for months. It took all Nanny Wendy's ingenuity to think up suggestions for Don, the chef at Annabel's, to prepare different flavoured milk shakes or soups that might help to tempt Robin and we fed them to him through a straw. We went back to Canterbury hospital several times that summer. We had been extraordinarily lucky with the surgeon on duty on the day of the accident who was brilliant, and also that one of the country's best plastic surgeons had been working in the hospital that day too. Between them they had done an extraordinary job but privately they told me Robin would have to have many plastic surgery operations later on, although mercifully neither Robin nor I was aware at the time of quite how many there would be.

He had to wait until he was fifteen before the first and for a short time after his fifteenth birthday Robin, who had been so brave and resilient, became pretty depressed about everything. In a literal as well as emotional sense he began to turn his face to the wall. I felt desperately sorry for him but although it almost broke my heart I knew my own unhappiness would not help him to get better, so I steeled myself to tell him that he had two choices – either to give in to his depression, or to get up and confront it. Leaving him in his room, I wondered how I could have been so cruel, but a few minutes later he came into my bedroom with that wonderful smile and said, 'OK, Mum, I'll have a bash.' And that is exactly what he has done ever since. He left his prep school and went to Eton, where he was known as Tiger Birley, and although Robin never told me himself, I knew from Rupert that he was cruelly teased about his face. I have never to this day heard him utter one word of self-pity. Adversity such as this can go both ways; it can either destroy you or be the making of your character. In Robin's case, however high the price, it has made him into the person he is today. He is a fighter; he never gives up, works harder than anyone I know and is quite simply the kind of son any mother would wish for, but for years afterwards I could not look at a tiger, even on television.

★

During term-time when all three children were at school I was by now all but living with Jimmy. As both Jimmy and Mark were gamblers, gambling had been part of my life since the chemin de fer fiasco of Mark's and my wedding night. Jimmy had developed a keen interest in betting on anything that was available to an Eton schoolboy including cards, dogs and horses. During the very early days of his career when he was struggling to make ends meet, Jimmy went to the races at Longchamps in Paris with his brother Teddy. After asking Teddy to go to the Tote for him to put his money on one horse, the brothers stood together to watch the race. Both Goldsmiths had a tendency to chew things when they were nervous or excited and as they saw Jimmy's horse romping past the winning post Teddy, who was chewing Jimmy's Tote ticket, suddenly swallowed the whole thing and Jimmy did not speak to him for months.

But gambling never dominated either Mark's or Jimmy's life as obsessively as it does with those who develop an addictive problem. Most gamblers continue to try to recoup their losses while they are losing, which is invariably a disaster. I was never by nature a true gambler, as unlike Mark and Jimmy I knew when to stop.

Until 1960 gambling was illegal in Britain, and even in France you had to be twenty-one before you were allowed into a casino. The nearest legal casino was at Le Touquet, in Normandy, in northern France, which was a very easy hop for the weekend by plane from England. The first couple of times Mark took me I was under age and had to wait outside in the restaurant. However, by the time I was allowed in, I was hooked, particularly on chemin de fer or vingt-et-un as it is sometimes known. I haven't played it for years but I can still remember my excitement as the 'shoe' containing the cards was pushed towards me when it was my turn to place a stake and run the bank. If you were in luck you could continue to run a winning bank, 'garaging' your original stake if you were cautious like me, or gambling it all if you were Jimmy. Because of the illegality of it, Aspers used to hold private gambling parties every ten days and we would all go. These parties became immensely grand, attracting some of the biggest gamblers in the country.

In order to avoid discovery, he was very careful to change the venue for each game, which on some occasions used to take place in Claus von Bülow's flat, and on others at various friends' houses. Lady Osborne, Aspers's mother, would provide the buffet supper. Her game pie and fabulous desserts became famous and Aspers's gambling friends affectionately knew her as 'Al Capone with a shopping basket'.

On one of these gambling evenings in 1957 in a flat on the north side of Hyde Park, I had left to go home when the game was raided by the police and twenty-one members of the nobility were arrested including the Lords Cavendish Bentinck, Pelham, Hoare, Willoughby and Fane, and taken to the police station. As Aspinall was charged with keeping a common gaming house, the irrepressible Lady O retorted to the officer, 'Young man there was nothing common here until *you* walked in.' This episode led to a court case at Bow Street the following year, which heralded the legalisation of gambling in Britain and the Gaming Act, known informally as 'Aspinall's Law', was passed by Parliament in July 1960.

In the early days of my relationship with Jimmy we spent many evenings together in casinos, mostly at the Clermont but once we went to Las Vegas with Mark and Liz Brocklehurst. We stayed in Caesar's Palace and Liz and I were amused to find that there were even fruit machines in the ladies' loo. While Jimmy made straight for the casino, Mark, Liz and I wandered around the hotel, amazed at the number of live shows and thrilled to discover that Frank Sinatra himself was on the bill. Eventually Liz and I wandered into the casino and put five dollars on the rouge et noir part of the roulette table, and through our modest winnings made enough to move on to the baccarat table. That night I knew instinctively that I couldn't lose and by seven the following morning I had won $4000 and, splitting the winnings with Liz, retired to bed. After only a couple of hours' sleep I was woken by Jimmy, shaking my shoulder. 'Get up,' he said. 'You're on a winning streak' and having barely had time for a piece of toast, we stumbled back to the casino, with Jimmy urging me on: 'Concentrate, I know you can do it.' However, my luck had by then run out and after a few minutes, at my insistence we retreated.

After the legalisation bill Aspers opened his gambling club at 44 Berkeley Square, the only surviving private house built by William Kent, the masterly architect of such jewels as Holkham Hall in Norfolk. He employed John Fowler to decorate the club, filled it with exquisite furniture and paintings, and employed a first-class chef. There, halfway up the beautiful baroque staircase, was the famous Grand Saloon where you could play chemin de fer, roulette, blackjack and, of course, backgammon. With Annabel's in the basement, the combined activities of 44 Berkeley Square soon made it the most fashionable if hedonistic address in London. On one occasion I remember running a winning bank while sitting beside Ian Fleming, as Frank Sinatra hovered behind my shoulder. Everyone came to the Clermont: I would often see Bill Stirling, Archie Stirling, Simon Fraser and Sunny Marlborough and among other regulars (and by them I do not mean people who merely popped in for a few hours' gambling, interspersed maybe with a dance downstairs) was Lord Lucan, known to his friends as Lucky. Rarely did I walk into the Clermont and not see Lucan sitting at a table playing backgammon. To me he was simply part of the furniture. Although he was a friend of Jimmy's I hardly knew him, except for an exchanged and cordial 'good evening' or 'goodnight'.

Lucan, his wife Veronica and their three children sometimes spent part of their holidays at Jimmy's rented summer villas and Cliff Howes, Jimmy's chauffeur, used to tell me what a hands-on and adoring father Lucan was, always playing with his children on the beach. I found this information surprising as even with my limited knowledge of the man it was not a side of Lucan I would ever have imagined.

In February 1973 Jimmy rented a villa in Mexico and invited a few people to stay, among them Lucan, Eric Neilson and my cousin Dominic Elwes. Two friends of mine, Elizabeth Brocklehurst and Victoria Getty, came as well. Liz's husband Mark had tragically died of a heart attack aged barely forty, leaving her with two small children to bring up, Henry and Molly. Victoria, who, much later, married Sir Paul Getty, was one of the most beautiful and witty girls I knew. She was an old girlfriend of Alastair's and we had become close friends. Although it was rather a mixed group, the holiday was a great success. Dominic spent most of his time teasing Lucan about wearing drill shorts and khaki shirts on the beach, making Victoria and me cry with laughter. Lucky was very good-natured about all this teasing with his very British stiff-upper-lip approach to life but I gradually discovered the other gentler side to Lucan. Sometimes in the evening we would sit by the pool and Lucky, who was beginning to feel more relaxed with me as the holiday progressed, would pour out his heart about his children. To describe him as obsessed would not be an exaggeration. He was in the process of getting divorced from Veronica and was determined to be given custody because he felt he would be the better parent. I did not know Veronica at all well, so it was difficult for me to judge, but I could see that Cliff Howes had been right: Lucan simply adored his children and he was terrified of losing them.

Some days we would all go out to lunch or dinner at hotels nearby and there was one rather beautiful hotel on the beach that we went to quite frequently. We would have lunch there at a long wooden table and I clearly remember the usual holiday snaps being taken. By the end of the holiday I had made a new friend in Lucky. From then onwards, whenever I went into the Clermont, he would come and talk to me and I saw that he was getting more and more desperate about his children's future. But in court, despite having argued that his wife was unstable, he lost the case for custody and was inconsolable, and I do not think he ever recovered from this catastrophic blow.

In November 1974 I was watching the television when I heard on the news that Lord Lucan had gone missing after a murder in his house involving his wife and their nanny, Sandra Rivett. According to Ivan Fallon's account in his biography of Jimmy, *Billionaire*, Lucan had booked a table at the Clermont for 10.30 but

> When his guests arrived he was not there. Unknown to them as they were sitting down to dinner, a mile and a half away in Belgravia an hysterical woman, blood pouring down her face, burst into the Plumbers Arms pub and shouted, 'He's in the house . . . the children are in the house . . . he's murdered the nanny.' She then collapsed. It was Lucan's wife Veronica.
>
> Downstairs in the basement of her house in Lower Belgrave Street police found signs of a struggle. There were teacups dropped on the bottom of the stairs, a light bulb was lying on a chair – and the badly beaten body of Sandra Rivett, nanny to the Lucans' three children, had been pushed into a US mailbag. Nearby was the murder weapon, a piece of lead piping wrapped in tape. Veronica Lucan said she had heard a noise in the basement, gone down to investigate and been grabbed by the throat and beaten about the head. She had fought back and when the intruder broke off from her she had dashed to the Plumbers Arms pub next door for help.

Appalled, I rang Jimmy, who was in Dublin on business at the time. He was as mystified as I was. He had been well aware of Lucan's desperation over his children after Lucan had been to see him in Paris a month before, begging Jimmy for a loan to 'buy' his children from his wife. He told Jimmy that Veronica was using the children to 'torture' him and asked Jimmy for £10,000. Jimmy had firm ideas about lending friends money and would say to me, 'Don't lend money, give it, and that way you won't expect it back and it won't spoil a friendship.' But Lucan refused to accept the offer of a gift and Jimmy never saw him again.

I was sure that Lucan, driven by his custody obsession, had intended to murder his wife but because the nanny had changed her day off he killed the wrong person. I have always felt that this dreadful story must have been made worse for the family of the one real victim, Sandra Rivett, the nanny, of whom so little mention was made by the press. Had Lucan succeeded in killing Veronica I believe he would have given himself up knowing that with Veronica dead, Veronica's sister Christina and her husband Bill Shand Kydd, of whom he was very fond, would have looked after the children. Ironically, shortly after his disappearance the Shand Kydds were awarded custody.

Deprived of his children I knew he would have no desire to live and am convinced that he committed suicide. Maybe he jumped off a boat and drowned himself. No one can be sure when and how he died but neither Jimmy nor I at any time believed he was still alive. Some time in the spring of 1975 a detective came to interview me as they had done with all Lucan's friends and acquaintances. I told him I knew nothing and neither did Jimmy, but that I did not believe he could be alive. I could never understand one of the police theories that Veronica Lucan was looked down upon by Lucan's friends because she wasn't good enough for him, as this was such nonsense. No one thought about her in that way; she was simply a reserved and shy woman who must have found it difficult to be married to a gambler like Lucan for whom gambling was a complete way of life.

In June 1975 an article appeared written by James Fox in the *Sunday Times Magazine*. On the cover there was a large picture of Lucan and myself with our heads close together, taken at one of those lunches on the beach during that holiday in Mexico. It was nothing more than a typical holiday snap, with Lucan and me laughing at a joke and had the photograph not been deliberately cropped, it would have shown Jimmy sitting on my other side and Liz Brocklehurst next to Lucan. Unfortunately Dominic Elwes had helped James Fox with the article, which attempted to reconstruct the fateful night of the murder seven months earlier and had even persuaded Aspers to talk to James Fox, having reassured him that the article would be favourable.

The *Sunday Times* had also printed a picture of an oil painting, by Dominic, which showed the gambling set of Lucan, Stephen Raphael, Charles Benson, Micky Suffolk, Aspers, Peter West and Nicholas Soames and Jimmy in the back room of the Clermont. Jimmy was enraged both by the article and by the reproduction of the oil painting, but what really infuriated him was the picture on the cover of the magazine, which strongly suggested an intimate relationship between Lucan and myself. Mark was also furious and Robin, who was at Eton at the time, was badly teased about the picture of me and Lucan, and wrote to James Fox to complain.

I realised that Dominic had been responsible for much of James Fox's article, but I did not believe he had sold the pictures, which included the infamous one of Lucan and me. Although I think he did write to Mark and Jimmy, contrary to what has been said he never approached me in any way at all, but I wish he had because as one of my closest friends I feel sure we could have talked the problem through.

Jimmy refused to speak to Dominic at all and Mark banned him from Annabel's. Neither Jimmy nor Mark was by nature particularly vindictive and in the end the row would have blown over, but Dominic was a depressive and on many occasions had tried to take his life. In September 1975 he succeeded by taking an overdose of barbiturates. Sensing there might be a good story here, Richard Ingrams, editor of the satirical magazine *Private Eye*, wrote an article which was to unleash a sequence of pieces about every aspect of Jimmy's life, both personal and professional, resulting in the most famous libel case of the decade.

THIRTEEN

My Second Family

There came a time in about 1972 when Jimmy started talking about wanting to have children. At first I was too frightened even to contemplate the idea. I knew that if I became pregnant the news would get into the papers and make headlines. I was also terrified of what my Combe relations would say and certain that Patrick Plunket would disapprove. A year later our old go-between and matchmaker John Aspinall took me for a walk round Howletts and said I was making a terrible mistake. He explained that Jimmy was desperate to have more children and speaking to me rather as if I were a Siberian tigress, Aspers said, 'It is time you mated with Jimmy and gave him the children he wants.' He tried to explain that I should consider it a great honour that Jimmy should want to have children with me, adding rather forbiddingly, 'If you don't do this soon, one day the affair will be over and you will be left with nothing.'

I thought and thought about what Aspers had said, and began to understand the value of the commitment that Jimmy was offering me. I concluded that when a man asks a woman to have his child it is a wonderful thing. After Aspers's death in 2000 in the commemorative book about her godfather Jemima wrote, 'I have a lot to thank Aspers for; in fact, I even have to thank him for my own conception, since he was the one who persuaded and coerced my reluctant mother into "breeding" with my father in the first place.'

Although I was already thirty-nine and had not had a child for thirteen years, my gynaecologist Roger DeVere was wildly

With Jimmy and the children at Torre de Tramores, our house in Spain.

Clockwise

My beloved eldest son, Rupert, who tragically disappeared while working in Lomé, in West Africa in 1986.

Robin, in the mid-1990s.

With my three youngest children in my bedroom at Ormeley.

India Jane has inherited her Birley grandfather's creative gift and is an artist of some considerable repute.

Jemima's wedding to Imran Khan, the great Pakistani cricketer and politician, in Richmond in June 1995.

Our much loved nanny, Mimi arriving at Jemima's wedding.

The inimitable and wonderful Mrs White, pictured with Sulaiman shortly after he was born.

With Jimmy and Copper the dog in 1997, during the Referendum campaign, and shortly before Jimmy's death.

Copper, the greatest canine character I ever knew. Here he is dressed as a member of the Mafia, in a photograph I sent as evidence of his innocence when he received a court summons for biting a jogger.

The cover of *Private Eye*, the week after Jimmy died. Despite the disrespect shown to Jimmy so recently after his death, I could not help laughing.

Zac's wedding in June 1999 to Sheherezade Bentley.

Ben's wedding in September 2003 to Kate Rothschild.

The grandchildren

Sulaiman and Kasim

Thyra

Uma

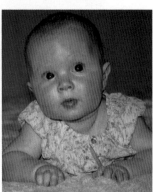

Iris Annabel, *aka* 'The Pudding'

James

I cannot imagine my house without a great number of dogs. Currently there are five in residence – in this picture they surround me on the staircase at Ormeley: Barney, Bindy, Boris, Lily and Daisy.

With Mark at the party we hosted at Annabel's in September 2003 in celebration of the fortieth anniversary of the founding of the club. Behind us is the 1960 portrait of me by Liz Moore.

enthusiastic, encouraging me to have at least twenty more. I was over the moon when I became pregnant almost immediately. At first I told only Jane and Nico and Alastair, who were enormously supportive. Jane was particularly thrilled. She had already had three children with Max, and she was expecting Alexander, her fourth and last child in October. I also confided in Mark, fearing he would read it in the papers and I wanted him to hear about it first from me. I was apprehensive of my Combe uncle Tony's reaction, but after I wrote him a long letter his reply was understanding and loving, although my Combe aunts were less forgiving. I knew Patrick Plunket was desperately worried when he heard, but of all the people I feared telling I was most apprehensive of the reaction of my children.

One very hot day at the beginning of September I took Cosima and India Jane, who were nearly twelve and thirteen, to swim in Jane's pool in Hampstead. As I lay in Jane's garden sunbathing, I could see the girls looking and giggling at me, and I realised they were on to me as although I was still really small, my stomach certainly wasn't concave. In a cowardly way I thought it would be easier to tell the girls before the boys and I heard Cosima say afterwards to India Jane, 'I told you so, I knew she was.' But when I added the further bombshell that it was Jimmy's they were completely astounded as I don't think they had ever quite understood that Jimmy and I were having an affair. Woman to woman, I told them I needed their help in telling the boys. Rupert was nineteen and at Oxford, and Robin, at seventeen, was in his last year at Eton, and I feared my news would undermine the closeness of our relationship. Cosima and Jane agreed to tell them for me.

At first Rupert was angry and incredulous. 'Shut up, how dare you say that about my mother?' he shouted at Cosima. 'And anyway it couldn't be true as they aren't married.' Later he laughed at himself for his naïveté. When I found the courage to explain that the child was a reflection of the depth of my love for Jimmy, they understood and were happy for me.

Mrs White, on the other hand, was horrified. 'I knew you had fallen. I could tell by your eyes,' she snapped. 'And I think it's dreadful. I'm very shocked and frankly, My Lady, I know you done it and I know you are going to have it but don't expect me to even look at it, or even touch it.' Needless to say the moment Jemima was born she was never out of Mrs White's arms.

I had a wonderful pregnancy. I felt serene and well, and I exercised regularly as I was determined to stay trim for Jimmy. The day before the birth, Mark and the girls took me into hospital and when Jimmy arrived that evening, as if in a scene from the Arabian Nights, he pulled from his pockets a lovely ruby and diamond shamrock brooch and a beautiful sapphire and diamond bracelet which he placed on my lap. I don't think I had ever seen him as excited. The next day, 30 January 1974, an exquisite baby was born and we named her Jemima, the female equivalent of James, which means 'little dove' in Hebrew, although I cannot think of a less dove-like person than Jemima.

In the early summer, much to Mrs White's dismay, I had 'fallen' again and this time, while it was unplanned and I knew Jimmy was truly besotted by his girls and adored Jemima, I also knew he wanted us to have a boy. I hadn't expected to be pregnant again so soon. There were no scans in those days but as I was forty I was required to have an amniocentesis test to determine whether the child had any abnormalities, a more common occurrence in older women. As well as reassuring me that the baby was well and healthy, the test would also reveal the sex of the unborn child. I was in Deauville when the hospital rang me to confirm there were no medical problems and asked whether I wanted to know if I was having a boy or a girl. After a little wavering I asked them to tell me. I was to have a boy. Utterly elated, I rang downstairs where Jimmy was playing bridge.

'Darling I'm in the middle of a game,' he started to say.

'It's a boy,' I interrupted.

And he rushed from the room, running up the stairs to find me, clutching a single tulip that he had grabbed from a hotel vase on the way. He was overjoyed.

Zacharias, known as Zac, was born on 20 January 1975, making him and Jemima twins for ten days in the year.

Although domestically Jimmy was extremely happy with our two young children in London, professionally he was becoming increasingly irritated by the attacks he was receiving in a small fringe section of the British press.

On 12 December 1975 a story had appeared in *Private Eye* implying that Jimmy had contributed to obstructing the course of justice by helping Lord Lucan to escape from the police. Jimmy did not at first react but his attitude changed when the next article was published under a month later, suggesting he was involved in shady business dealings with Jim Slater's company, Slater Walker, and attempting to link him to a disreputable businessman called T. Dan Smith whom Jimmy had never even met. The article also claimed that Jimmy had recently been in a Swiss nightclub 'with a variety of lissom young ladies of Ugandan extraction', this expression being *Private Eye* code for illicit sex. Aware that this wholly untrue allegation would be read by all his family, and in particular by me, Jimmy felt he had become the target of a serious attack on everything he cherished. He had been provoked too far and retaliated, issuing sixty-three libel writs against *Private Eye* and its editor Richard Ingrams. If Jimmy had ignored the stories maybe Ingrams would have given up, but instead the writ had the effect of encouraging the magazine to intensify its campaign.

Personally I have always had rather mixed feelings about *Private Eye*. I loved it as a magazine and it often used to make me shriek with laughter. The family has appeared on the cover at least twice. When Jemima and Imran got married, in a reference to the extreme punishments sometimes delivered in Pakistan, there was a picture of Jimmy, Imran and Jemima, with Imran saying, 'May I have your daughter's hand' and Jimmy replying, 'Why? Has she stolen something?'

I was worried about the libel suit, and I was uncomfortable that most of my friends were totally supportive of *Private Eye* and thought it quite the trendy thing to send contributions to the magazine's own appeal, the Goldenballs Fund, which was launched to raise money to cover their own costs of the trial. Although I could see why he chose to sue I knew that the popularity of *Private Eye* was simply too strong for Jimmy to have stood a chance of succeeding and that he should never have attempted it. But Jimmy had never heard of *Private Eye*, let alone read it. The humour, although a source of delight to my own family, was too English to have any appeal to him.

However, I would have supported him in anything he did. So I went with him to court on the opening day of the trial wearing an Yves St Laurent dress that I had had for years. We walked up to Bow Street magistrates court, arm in arm, pub-licly facing the press for the first time during our twelve-year relationship, when a light summer breeze lifted the unbuttoned hem of my dress blowing it wide open in full view of the waiting photographers. There was intense speculation in the newspapers the following day about whether I had been wearing any pants. Probably as a result of this photograph Mrs Ingrams was rumoured to dislike me and think I was a bit tarty, and sometimes I saw her glaring at me in court. I would go every day to be there for Jimmy, often sitting there for hours on my own, hardly daring to look to the right or left in case I caught the eye of Patrick Marnham, the main journalist cov-ering the story for *Private Eye*, or the scowling Mrs Ingrams.

Shortly after the writ was issued Jimmy met the former Labour Prime Minister and his wife, Harold and Mary Wilson, at a dinner party given by the television presenter David Frost, a lifelong friend whom I had first met in the sixties when Jimmy took me to his house in Egerton Crescent. He and Jimmy were so close that it was David whom we invited to introduce Jimmy's memorial service. He was enormous fun, always stimulating and astonishingly energetic, at one time flying to America three times a week. In 1983 he married Carina Fitzalan-Howard (Lady Carina Fitzalan-Howard) and they had three sons, Miles, Wilfred and George. Their exceptional loyalty to me was demonstrated by their insistence, although David was originally Jimmy's friend, that they would only visit Jimmy's house in Mexico when they knew I would be there and for that degree of support I will always be especially grateful. At David's dinner party Jimmy found a ready sympathiser to his cause in Mrs Wilson who had been very upset by the magazine which had run a regular series 'Mrs Wilson's Diary' (one of my own favourite columns in the magazine along with Grovel and the later 'Dear Bill' spoof letters from Denis Thatcher), which professed to tell the readers what she really thought of the goings-on inside 10 Downing Street.

Wilson's personal and political secretary, Marcia Falkender, was also at that dinner. Jimmy had introduced me to her in the early 1970s and although she had a reputation for being temperamental and difficult, I found her instead to be amusing and friendly. When Jimmy's affair with Laure began, Marcia became my confidante and we invited her to be Benjamin's godmother.

In 1986 Jimmy formed a film company called Golden Swan, and made Marcia and the writer and journalist Geoffrey Wansell directors. The first project was adapted from a book discovered by Geoffrey called *When the Whales Came* by Michael Morpurgo. The story was charming but despite Helen Mirren in a starring role, the film was not as great a hit as we had hoped, although I think that if it had been shortened and if the whales had arrived a little earlier, it might have been as delightful as the book. As Jimmy was then spending most of his time in America, he left the running of Golden Swan, the renamed Canvasback Productions, to Geoffrey, Marcia, the actor David Suchet and me, but unfortunately without Jimmy's financial backing the company lost momentum and was eventually dissolved. Marcia, however, remained a great friend and supporter of both Jimmy and me.

While the *Private Eye* case was still being heard, Jimmy was given a knighthood in Harold Wilson's retirement Honours List for 'services to export and to ecology'. His name was included on the controversial 'Lavender List', so called as it had been written out on coloured paper by Marcia in the absence of any typewriters, which had all been packed up in preparation for Wilson's imminent departure from Downing Street. His critics saw this public award as an indication of Jimmy's blatant political ambition, as a socialist prime minister gave an honour to an avowed capitalist, and it provided *Private Eye* with yet more ammunition. At one point the magazine did offer to settle out of court, admitting to factual errors in their original piece, but Jimmy was a stubborn man and his pride prevented him from giving up the fight. Eventually Madame Beaux intervened, persuading Jimmy that the case was occupying and even monopolising his energy. She also knew that he was intent on becoming a newspaper proprietor and that he had already initiated talks with the Beaverbrook empire. The continuing suit with *Private Eye*, together with the mistrust and suspicion with which he was viewed by the rest of the press, was not helping. Eventually, with the aid of Simon Jenkins, then editor of the *Evening Standard*, Jimmy agreed to settle, and *Private Eye* printed a full-page apology and contributed £30,000 to Jimmy's legal costs.

Zac summarises the implications of the entire *Private Eye* débâcle succinctly.

The case immediately became a David versus Goliath epic which was, with hindsight, inevitable. My father was a bigger-than-life character, with all the resources he needed to tackle the publication. *Private Eye* meanwhile promoted an image of defencelessness.

But it wasn't that simple. Daddy was goaded incessantly. He was viciously and maliciously attacked week after week. The humour of initial snipes gave way to something altogether more vindictive and reached such a pitch that Daddy felt he had no choice but to retaliate. And he did with the boundless energy that characterised so much of what he did.

He was right to put the record straight, and in so doing he demonstrated to the wider press that he was not the kind of person to be trampled on by innuendo and false gossip. But without a doubt the repercussions were costly. My father did not fully recognise that it was something of a repository for journalists of every type from every paper. By taking on the journal, he was in effect taking on the press itself.

Right and wrong were lost in the ensuing battle, with journalists and the wider press banding together like football supporters defending a bad tackle from one of their own. He was scarred, and from that time on the *Private Eye* affair was never far from the minds of journalists covering aspects of his work and life.

It has been said to me a hundred times by current journalists that the reason the Referendum Party itself was so poorly covered, despite the passion of its many supporters, was that journalists could not bring themselves to side with what they saw as the enemy of their peers.

Daddy was right to defend himself. But it cost him. It is ironic that only now after his death does the same media give him the credit he deserves for forcing a debate and finally a referendum on the single currency and our wider involvement in the European Union. It is a pity they did not support him at the time.

After Zac was born Mark and I were discreetly divorced while

I was out of the country. At about the same time Jimmy had told me that he wanted us to live together officially and find a house big enough for the whole family. My heart sank, realising I would have to sell Pelham Cottage. I had been there for twenty years and did not think I could bear to give it up. I looked at every possible option that would allow me to keep it and even considered persuading Jimmy to buy another house nearby so we could move between the two. When I did agree to look for one large house, I could find nothing that Jimmy liked. Finally I put Pelham Cottage on the market, with my own housing problem still unresolved. One day on the estate agent's typed list of those coming to view Pelham Cottage I saw the name of Lord Howard de Walden, a prominent racing figure and a senior steward of the Jockey club, whose wife had recently died. I knew he had a beautiful house near Richmond Park called Ormeley Lodge and I had even been there once when our friends David and Jane Westmoreland (the Earl and Countess of Westmoreland) owned it. I also knew he had one or two houses in the country as well as a flat in London and I could not understand why he wanted another home in London. Rather boldly I wrote him a letter asking whether he was selling Ormeley and please to forgive my impertinence. He wrote back straight away to tell me that although Ormeley was not yet officially on the market he was indeed planning to sell it.

Ormeley, a large red-brick Queen Anne house, was as magical as I had remembered and when I saw the glorious cedar tree that dominated the lawn, I knew that I would never find a more perfect place to bring up the children. The house had a tremendous history, having for a short while been the home of Mrs Fitzherbert, the mistress of the Prince of Wales and future George IV. It was at Ormeley that in 1785 after their morganatic marriage the couple were supposed to have spent their honeymoon. Just as I had when I first saw Pelham Cottage, I lost my heart to the place instantly.

Jimmy had wanted a rather grand house while I preferred something smaller and more intimate but I thought Ormeley might be the perfect compromise. I knew that when I filled it with our own things, and when the children and the dogs arrived, I would be able to turn it into the ideal family home. That day I walked over every inch of it. Lord Howard de Walden had used the house in the grand upstairs-downstairs manner but I could see that the butler's pantry would make a perfect children's dining room and the maids' rooms would be wonderful bedrooms for the children. There was a staff flat above the stables which was eventually to become Jemima's when she was eighteen and much later I had the stables themselves converted into a nursery for my grandchildren.

Before showing Jimmy the house I talked to Cliff Howes, Jimmy's chauffeur, who was my ally and friend. The idea of Ormeley suited Cliff down to the ground as he lived at Chessington, only twenty minutes away and for him Ormeley would mean the end of nightmare daily journeys to and from Jimmy's house in Regent's Park. Between us, Cliff and I were determined to convince Jimmy that Ormeley was the right place.

On the day of Jimmy's first visit we said a little prayer together: 'Let us pray the traffic will be light, that the deer will appear from the depths of the park and let there be a glorious sunset. Let everything be absolutely wonderful.'

Cliff, always a genius for picking the best route, brought Jimmy through the park and I was already waiting for him at the front of the house. 'Bit near to the road,' he said as he got out of the car.

Slowly he walked through the entire house, just as I had done a few days earlier, and at first he was somewhat critical and not very enthusiastic. I had grown to recognise that silence at important moments of decision usually signified Jimmy's approval. So I waited and as I showed him the cedar tree he stopped speaking. The prayers had been answered: the traffic had been light, the deer had been grazing, the sunset had been breathtaking. I knew he was hooked.

We started negotiating with Lord Howard de Walden, who stipulated that nothing was to appear in Nigel Dempster's *Daily Mail* column before the deal was done, and that summer while I was abroad in Sardinia with all the children and the teenagers on a particularly squalid holiday in a house with only one bathroom between us, the contract was signed and Ormeley became ours.

Maria Harrison was one of the first people to see the new house: 'Darling it is not for you. No, I can't see you here, darling,' she announced in her heavy Latvian accent.

Crushed, I asked her to explain why, as her taste was the epitome of everything I admired.

'It's too grand.'

'But that's what Jimmy wants,' I said.

'But it's all grey,' she said.

I was rather depressed by what she had said, trying to explain that her reservations were only due to Lord Howard de Walden's decorations, and later as the house began to take shape, she willingly admitted she had been wrong.

I was desolate on the day of the move but the first night I slept at Ormeley I felt I was sleeping at Pelham Cottage. Because Pelham Cottage was so tiny I felt that the whole place had somehow been bodily lifted and set down in my bedroom and sitting room at Ormeley. When I woke up the next morning and heard the birds singing outside my window I knew it had been the right thing to do.

Tom Parr from Colefax and Fowler was in charge of the decorating of the house and in particular my wonderful bedroom. Margaret Anne Stuart (Ducane), my old friend from as long ago as the Brown House days, did the nursery and the spare rooms. Unfortunately my own first shot at decorating the drawing room was not a success as I had not been concentrating and the result was too frilly for Jimmy. I remember him getting into a frightful rage and kicking a pouffe which was intended to be shaped like a clover leaf but instead could have been mistaken for someone's arse, shouting, 'I am not living with a thing like that.' And the whole ground floor had to be redone by Nina Campbell.

Lord Howard de Walden was very helpful with local names and addresses, introducing me to his doctor, Dr Matthew Gardiner, who had come from a whole family line of doctors and turned out to be the best doctor in the world. He and his wife Jean became close friends. Jemima was very happy in a marvellous kindergarten that was also recommended to me and was just round the corner. Based in a church hall, it was run by Margaret Luddington and she was soon joined there by Zac.

Life at Ormeley was like living in London in the country and provided the perfect combination for us as Jimmy was not fond of the real countryside. Once after spending one night in Wiltshire he told me quite seriously, 'Darling, can't you understand that for me after twelve hours in the country every blade of grass becomes a personal enemy.' And he was not at Ormeley all the time either, as he travelled frequently, maintaining his habit of spending weekends in Paris with Ginette. He would usually be with them for Christmas, too, in a rented chalet in Gstaad as Christmas did not mean as much to him as it did to me. I found this arrangement to be perfect because the constant presence of Jimmy could have become somewhat overwhelming and I needed to have time and space for myself. But when he was with us for the weekends our wonderful couple, Isabel and Arnaldo Pires, would prepare great lunches and dinners, and sometimes very grand dinner parties in the huge room that I had made in the basement. We painted it dark red and you could seat about fifty people down there.

One of the most amusing parties we gave was for Annabel Elliot's fortieth birthday in 1989. The idea was for me to give the party but for Simon and Annabel to do all the inviting, as Jimmy was abroad at the time. A few days before the big dinner, I was on my way back from a horse show with Jemima when Simon rang to say that they had invited the Prince and Princess of Wales, who were friends of theirs. I was slightly concerned about this as I worried whether the party would remain as relaxed and informal as it was supposed to be. One of my main worries was the temporary Spanish couple I was employing at the time, Vidal and Rosa. Vidal was a serious alcoholic who habitually though unsuccessfully tried to cover up his alcoholic breath with TCP. I realised that with a dinner party of this magnitude I was going to have to be careful that Vidal was kept away. I put a very nice professional butler called Charles in charge of my table where Annabel, the birthday girl, Nico, Prince Charles and Annabel's father Bruce Shand were all to be seated. Manuel, my housekeeper Maria's husband, was to organise the other table at which Simon would preside with my brother Alastair and other friends including Diana. I told Vidal's wife Rosa very sternly that under no circumstances was he to go anywhere near either of those tables; in fact, I would rather he were kept away altogether.

Dinner began very smoothly. Although I had met Charles, I had never met Diana before, and they both seemed friendly and jolly. Charles was between Annabel and me, and glancing behind my back I could see that everything was fine at Simon's table. The first course was already in front of us and consisted of a delicious chilled soup – so far, so good. Then I happened to glance up while in mid-chat with Prince Charles and saw Vidal approaching the table with the next course, an Oriental chicken dish. He was wearing that well-known drunken leer I had grown to recognise with Frieda so I glared at him but he paid no attention. Having served Annabel with the chicken, instead of coming round the table to serve Prince Charles, he leant over Annabel and with a flicking manoeuvre managed to send the next bit of chicken flying into the air before it landed with a plop on Prince Charles's plate.

I saw Charles raise his eyebrows and hissing 'Get out' under my breath to Vidal I said to Charles, 'I am so sorry but you know what it's like with hired help,' hoping that he would think I had never met Vidal before. Worse was to follow. As the pudding was about to be served I spotted Nico frantically gesturing to me when Vidal appeared again, this time carrying a silver dish piled high with Penguin chocolate biscuits in their shiny multicoloured wrappers. Hot with horror and embarrassment, although I must admit Prince Charles did not seem to notice, or maybe he was too well-mannered to show it, I begged Nico to deal with the situation. She turned to Charles the butler to ask him what the hell was going on to which he replied, 'Madam, I have no idea. I thought it was some kind of an "in" royal joke.' Later Simon told me that the Penguin biscuits were rather a success at his table as Diana scoffed most of them.

Much has been written about this dinner party and the alleged confrontation between Diana and Camilla but I was unaware of any such incident. However, several years later in Andrew Morton's book Diana described what was for her a 'ghastly party'. I knew I had to get rid of Vidal. The final straw came when one evening I was getting ready to go out to dinner, and was running my bath and one of the taps stuck. I asked him to come up and help me turn them off. This time he was so drunk that he fell head first into the bath and had to be pulled out by a security guard. Ben-Ben remembers me saying, 'Get out, you drunken bastard. I never want to see you again.' Despite his alcoholism and although I was not sad to see him leave, he was not a nasty man and I wished him well for the future.

After that rather anxious-making dinner, I met Diana on a couple of occasions with Carina Frost and later at several lunches at Kensington Palace. She was always very light-hearted and as our friendship developed I invited her to Ormeley. I was aware that she came there as much for the security and refuge that she found in the place as for the company of my family and towards the end of her life she came most weekends. Rumour had it that she could be quite manipulative but she never showed that side of herself to me. She would ring asking if I was going to be at home and if she could come and join me. She would land like a butterfly, have lunch and dart off again, sometimes bringing the boys with her, sometimes not. She would drive herself down, usually managing to shake off the press before she arrived, dash through the back door often clutching a present, greet the staff who all loved her, try to evade the mass of dogs yapping at her feet and settle down to amuse us. She gave as good as she got as she was enormously entertaining and few people realised how funny she could be. She used to make Robin, whose sense of humour is thoroughly idiosyncratic, shriek with laughter.

Friends invited to lunch who were meeting Diana for the first time were often overwhelmed by her naturalness and quick wit. Her repartee became an essential part of these Sunday lunches, interrupted occasionally when she vanished to the kitchen to do the washing up. There was no protocol and she felt she was surrounded by people who genuinely liked her. As a family she teased us and we, with an easy intimacy that she encouraged, teased her back. Although I felt she responded more to my surroundings than to me personally, I think she did regard me as something of a surrogate mother. I will always wish she had opened up to me a bit more. As a wife whose husband also kept a mistress, I would have repeated to her the simple question that my lawyer Lord Goodman had put to me, 'Do you want to be a divorced woman or do you want to be married?' to which my own reply had been an unequivocal desire to remain married. But when Diana was unhappy she would mostly confine our talks to descriptions of rows with her own family and, knowing that she was aware of my friendship with Camilla's sister, I did not encourage her to talk about the other side of her private life.

Sunday lunch at Ormeley remains an institution and most of our great friends have been on many occasions. Before they bought Nether Lypiatt, their house in Gloucestershire, the Kents, Michael and Marie Christine, were frequent Sunday lunch guests, although Marie Christine used to joke that there was a jinx on the presence of her family at Ormeley. Their son Freddie (Lord Frederick Windsor) was almost born on my sofa and every time they came to see us it seemed that someone in the family broke a bone. Marie Christine broke her ankle stepping on a ball on the tennis court and Jemima managed to give Freddie a greenstick fracture while throwing him round the lawn when he was a little boy. Ella (Lady Gabriella Windsor) became Ben-Ben's partner in crime and on one occasion they locked the nanny in the rabbit run, where her cries for help were only heard three hours later.

The lunch itself is usually chaotic. There is a huge sideboard in the dining room and all the food from the first course through the main course and the pudding is laid out buffet style and everyone helps themselves. Lunch is eaten so fast that Diana started to time us. 'Right,' she would say, 'today was an all-time record. Fifteen minutes!'

Jimmy is the only person I have ever met who ate faster than me, one terrible defect we had in common. His mother used to get simply furious and say, 'Jimmy, *tu vas ruiner le* stomach and now here comes Annabel who eats just as fast.'

Our friend, the historian Andrew Roberts, was a regular guest at those lunches. During one he was so taken aback to see Princess Diana that he dropped her a low curtsy. She, hugely amused, insisted that he do another for which she awarded him just eight out of ten marks. Andrew well remembers an occasion when we had invited some American business friends and their wives. Shortly after we had first sat down,

Andrew was amazed to watch as Jimmy pushed back his chair and said to me, 'Right, let's go and have coffee. Darling, organise coffee in the study.' Andrew could see that the poor Americans had barely finished their main course while in the same amount of time Jimmy had managed to gobble his way through his first course, main course and his pudding.

But despite his urgency over food, Jimmy was quite capable of relaxing and liked nothing more than sitting with a cigar and a glass of brandy and his family after one of those Ormeley lunches telling story after story. When I was upstairs all I could hear were gales of laughter coming from Robin and Rupert below. He loved entertaining, whether it was at the dinner parties at Ormeley, a ball at the Ritz, an evening at the Café Royal and especially at Laurent, his restaurant in Paris.

Jimmy had begun to spend a great deal of time in America, largely as a result of the difficulties he faced in working in Britain after the *Private Eye* case. Since 1973 he had owned the American supermarket chain Grand Union, which he began to develop, expanding its services. He was also gradually buying up shares in Diamond International, a company that had originally introduced the safety match, which had now diverged into the prepackaging of timber and, among other contracts, was responsible for manufacturing a large share of the paper plates for McDonald's. An oil company in Guatemala called Basic also caught his attention, and with these interests in North and South America, he began selling off his great Cavenham Foods chain in England. His attempt to launch the news magazine *Now* in England had foundered after eighteen months and he was ready to move across the Atlantic.

In 1977 he had met a French journalist called Laure Boulay de La Meurthe, a great-niece of the Comte de Paris who was working for the *Paris Match* office in Paris. I soon realised he had fallen in love again and by the late 1970s he was dividing his time between Ginette in Paris, me in Richmond and Laure in New York. I can hardly pretend that any of the three women in his life was entirely happy with the arrangements because just as Ginette had hated me coming along, so I did not exactly welcome the arrival of Laure and for some time the situation made me miserable.

Despite Jimmy's new relationship with Laure, in 1978 we decided to marry in order to legitimise Jemima and Zac, although neither Jimmy nor I really wanted to get married again, and he made it clear that Ginette would remain as much his wife when he married me and I in turn was to remain as much when he met Laure. He was desperate for the wedding ceremony to be kept private and determined to hold it in Paris, although I felt the choice was insensitive to his family there and thought the Richmond register office, recently chosen by a couple of pop stars for discretion, would have been a better place. However, Jimmy insisted on Paris and Nico, Jane and I were followed there by several English journalists. The whole wedding day was something of a farce with me and Madame Beaux racing up the Champs Elysées trying to catch up with Jimmy who was trying to escape the photographers. Jimmy's anger at the press, never far from the surface after the *Private Eye* case, suddenly erupted and, grabbing a photographer from the *Daily Express*, he wrenched the film from his camera, managing at the same time to break his glasses and bruise his ribs.

Jimmy had made a now famous and frequently quoted remark: 'If you marry your mistress, you create a vacancy' and after our marriage people would ask me how I could bear to be married to a man who had a mistress, to which I would reply 'what goes around comes around'.

As I had caused an enormous amount of pain to Ginette when he was married to her I felt I was quite unjustified in complaining when the same thing happened to me. But he was the only man I can think of who could get away with such behaviour because when he was with each one of us, he was totally protective and kind to us. Just because he had found another woman to love did not mean he changed his behaviour towards or feelings for her predecessor. Jimmy's private life may have shocked and puzzled people but he never made a secret of it. One of the things I most admired about him was his remarkable lack of hypocrisy, as he could not have cared less what people thought about him or may have whispered behind his back. He got away with having three separate families because he compartmentalised his life so effectively.

For a few years I was very unhappy and despite having two small children aged only six and seven, my sadness made me feel broody once again. After Zac's birth I had two miscarriages but at the beginning of 1980 I discovered I was pregnant. I think I was fortunate to have a calm and wonderful pregnancy, and did not feel like a woman of forty-six having a baby, as the births seemed to get easier with each successive child.

I went into labour in the Westminster Hospital in London on the morning of 28 October, attended both by Roger 'Divine' DeVere and by his registrar, Anthony Kenney, who both cracked a series of revolting jokes over my bed in the delivery ward. I remember Roger's excitement because not only was 28 October his own son's birthday but mine was the last baby he was going to deliver before his retirement. Anthony Kenney was to take over as my much loved gynaecologist and in the future he was to deliver my grandchildren. Benjamin was born that evening. We chose a name that means 'last child' in Hebrew.

Jimmy was pacing up and down at Aspinall's at the time. There was no question of him attending the birth, as I knew he wanted all his babies to be handed to him in beribboned baskets as if they had just appeared from the stork, shiny and clean. There was none of this earthy 'holding your hand and watching it come out' stuff for either Mark or Jimmy. Having a late baby was gloriously fulfilling and those five days I spent recovering in the Westminster Hospital were absolute heaven.

I could not believe I had this tiny creature that, at a difficult time, had brought a real ray of hope into my life. I felt as if I had come through a terrible storm and emerged happy.

Zac and Jemima had been given the news about Benjamin at home in the morning and when they came to see us in hospital I gave them the two toy monkeys I had bought as a present from the baby. Although Jemima was at first disappointed about not getting a sister and Zac triumphant because he had the brother he wanted, neither was remotely jealous; instead, they were mesmerised by the baby. I had no need for a monthly nurse as I had Mimi our nanny who took him into her loving arms when he was only five days old. By a happy coincidence, a few weeks after I had discovered I was pregnant with Ben my adored maid Maria Teixeira, who has been with me since 1973, told me that she too was going to have a baby. Her son David was born three days before Ben, providing me with a new godson and the boys each with an instant best friend as they grew up together at Ormeley.

In the new year, a few months after Ben's birth, Jimmy suggested that I fly over for a few days to join him in New York. I loved New York and we had spent a lot of time there together in the early days of our relationship, and had a flat in the Carlyle Hotel on Madison Avenue. I had been looking forward tremendously to being with Jimmy and that first night we had planned to have dinner with Claus von Bülow and his wife Sunny. Just before dinner Jimmy announced that he needed to talk very seriously to me. He told me that he no longer wished to live in England and was planning to move to America for good, explaining that he could not do business in England any more as the press had made his life there a nightmare. 'I am afraid that if you want us all to be together you must think of moving the children here,' he ended, as I burst into tears saying I did not think I could possibly do as he asked. I cried all the way through dinner, which must have been very disconcerting for Claus, and went back to England to think seriously about Jimmy's ultimatum. He had presented me with probably the most agonising choice of my life.

I was acutely aware of the importance of the presence of Laure in New York, and I knew that if I decided not to join Jimmy there and stayed in England, thousands of miles away, I would be severely compromising my marriage. On the other hand if I decided to leave England I would be abandoning everything else that was important to me. Life without my sister Jane would be unbearable as well as living without Alastair, their families, my many friends and Ormeley. I would be exchanging all this and uprooting myself to go to start a new life in somewhere like Connecticut (as I would never have wanted to live in New York itself). I knew the whole idea was unthinkable and that I would not be able to go through with it. I had once told Henry Ford that I thought I was an incredible mother, rather a good mistress, but not a very good wife and, reluctantly, I gave Jimmy my decision, aware that in doing so I was relinquishing some of my hold on the man who had been my lover and husband for the last seventeen years. But if I had to take the same decision again I would not change it.

However, life did go on and I began to have a wonderful time at Ormeley, mostly because the children were so happy there in what was a sort of paradise for them. We had a swimming pool and a tennis court, and both the older children began to learn to ride at the nearby riding school, Manor Farm. I was delighted to realise that Jemima had inherited my love of riding and over thirty years later I suddenly found myself leading the same kind of equestrian life I had led at Wynyard. By the time Jemima was ten, she and I began to spend nearly every weekend in the horsebox going from horse show to horse show up and down the country. All these shows were potential qualifiers for the Horse of the Year Show which was held at Wembley each October and Jemima, under the expert tutelage of Richard and Marjorie Ramsay, became like my childhood friend Angie a really good rider and won everything. Although these shows were great fun and seeing Jemima winning was a great source of pride for me, they entailed a great deal of hard work on her part. While most of her friends were attending teenage parties at weekends in the winter, she would be down at the Ramsays' yard every Saturday and Sunday, riding out and preparing for the qualifying shows that started in the spring. Jemima still has very happy memories of those teenage years but there came a time when she felt she was missing out on being with her friends and by the age of seventeen, having passed her A levels, she admitted she had finally grown out of horse shows altogether.

Academically, life was equally successful for Jemima, who was delighted with her new school, the Old Vicarage, and quickly made masses of friends. Zac started at Kings House, which was less good so I moved him to the Mall at Twickenham where Ben went later. But while little girlfriends of Jemima's were pouring in and out of the house as her school was on Richmond Hill less than a mile away, the Mall was not so close and there did not seem to be many boys living near us. Zac was therefore living at home in a predominantly female society, which worried Jimmy. After Rupert and Robin left St Aubyn's I had always vowed that I would not send another child away to prep school, but I relented under Jimmy's insistence and took Zac to look at Hawtreys near Marlborough. Hawtreys is a Palladian house standing in the Savernake Forest and it is a dream to look at. Mr Watts, the headmaster, could well have provided the original idea for Mr Chips as he had a real presence, inspiring great confidence in boy and parent. But although he was just the sort of headmaster in whose hands you would choose to put the well-being of your child, Zac was still not quite nine, which seemed a heartbreakingly young age to be sending him away to school. Without telling Jimmy, I paid the Mall a whole year's tuition in advance so they would keep his place open, just in case homesickness overwhelmed him and he wanted to leave. I did get the odd miserable letter from him that first term and he will still tell me now how unhappy he was, but Ben Elliot, Zac's best friend since they were at Hawtreys together, tells me that Zac's sob stories were exaggerated and that they both had rather a good time. At the end of term, unlike the local day school boys, a happy, healthy-looking boy full of country air would come home to me. Most of the boys Zac met at Hawtreys went on to Eton with him afterwards and are his friends today.

While all the younger children were happily settled in their schools, I began having trouble with the hip that had been so badly fractured in the Boswell Hazy accident when I was very little. Although the hip had been set immediately after the accident the job had not been well done and in my thirties it had begun to hurt again. The pain may have been exacerbated by the fact that I was quite athletic, rode a lot and had had three children by the time I was twenty-six, but when I was in my late forties a further X-ray showed the bones had never really set and in my early fifties I was advised to have a hip replacement. Sir Rodney Sweetnam did the operation in the King Edward VII Hospital, and after the initial pain, I rather enjoyed myself. No longer in my first youth, I felt like a spring chicken there among all the other hip replacements who were in their seventies and eighties.

I would advance into the hydrotherapy pool sporting the tan I had acquired in Barbados a few weeks previously, wearing a rather low-cut bathing suit which showed off my bosom to advantage. Usually there were a few elderly gentlemen method-ically doing their exercises in the warm pool, pretending not to stare at my cleavage and I would be put through a rigorous routine which left me exhausted. I longed to get well and go home, and was triumphant if I managed to lift my leg to the correct angle, made easy in water because of the weightlessness. I became friendly with some of the other patients on my wing (they all seemed to be men) and I organised a sort of sports day along the passage down which we all hobbled as fast as possible with the help of our sticks. This self-devised entertainment was not popular with the nurses and our behaviour resembled that of boarding-school inmates with a lot of whispered asides: 'Cave, Sister's coming!'

After all the exercise I would collapse into my bed, and wait for the children to come and visit me. Zac was away at Eton, but Robin and India Jane would come from work; Jemima, who was by this time at Frances Holland School in Chelsea, would arrive at the end of her school day and celebrated her fifteenth birthday while I was in the hospital; and my youngest son Benjamin, then aged eight, arrived with his nanny Mimi, and hurled himself into my arms. He used to feel important as it was his job to collect and take my laundry home to be washed, but being as naughty as I was at his age, he would trick Mimi into waiting for him in the car while he would commandeer the lift riding up and down, unwittingly preventing other visitors from reaching their relations and friends.

Jimmy adored his children and was constantly in touch with them by telephone. He often came back to Richmond on visits and would always turn up for holidays, delighting us all with his infectious capacity for excitement and fun. The children loved being with him, whether they were all playing Twenty Questions together or going on exotic trips in a boat. One summer when Ben was about three years old Jimmy suggested that we might buy a holiday house in Europe and I thought it was a lovely idea. He had recently been renting various houses for the Easter holidays on the southern Spanish coast near Marbella because the climate was so wonderfully dry. We started to look for a house in that area and once again we couldn't agree on anything, but I will always be indebted to a great friend, Jean Hill, the mother of Jemima's school friend Rebecca, for ringing me one morning to tell me about a beautiful house she had seen advertised in the property pages of

Country Life. As soon as I saw the photograph I realised that it was Jaime and Jeanetta de Parlade's house in the mountains above Marbella, and I grabbed Jean and Nico and we all flew straight over to look at it.

Torre de Tramores is a unique and glorious house dominated by a huge fifteenth-century Moorish lookout tower which, when I first saw it, was a crumbling ruin. I had once visited the paradise that Jeanetta and Jaime had created there, and never forgotten it. With his impeccable taste, Jaime had transformed a collection of old cowsheds into a beautiful and comfortable house, while Jeanetta had made an extraordinary garden, on a series of ascending terraces, filling them with rare and amazing shrubs, and they had only decided to sell because Jaime had recently inherited his father's ancestral house nearby. With some difficulty, unable to get a proper perspective owing to the different levels on which it is built, I tried to capture the elusive spirit of the house with my video camera, exclaiming on the voice-over, 'Oh look! An avocado tree and look at all those oranges and lemons.' I hoped that all this exotic planting would impress Jimmy but when I showed him my amateur film he could not have been less interested, so reluctantly I tried to put Tramores out of my mind.

However, a year later when we were on holiday in Spain I heard that the house was still on the market and persuaded Jimmy to come and look at it with me. That day, as we stood on the terrace, looking out over the mountains at the astonishing view, with no other sign of human habitation, and at nature at its most simple and dramatic, Jimmy fell silent. For a long time we stood there together, not saying a word. I realised he was totally taken with it and in the spring of 1986 it became ours.

We knew we would have to build on at the back to provide more bedrooms for our large family and that there was quite a lot of work to do. Only in 2003 did I at last finish restoring the tower which gives the house its name, but within a year of buying the house the bulk of the work was complete and in 1987 we had our first holiday there. We also built an adjoining guest house enabling us to have our own friends and those of the children to stay. Our first guests were Aspers and his new wife Sally, followed by the entire Frost family and since then the Frosts have become an integral part of our annual holiday scene at Tramores.

FOURTEEN

Rupert

Shortly after we bought Tramores, the greatest tragedy of my life occurred, an event from which in some ways I have still not recovered and probably never will.

On 17 June 1986 I received a telephone call from Mark asking whether he could come down to Ormeley to see me. He sounded slightly strained but otherwise normal, and I assumed that he was thinking of walking his dogs in the park and calling in on me at the same time. I remember thinking his behaviour was slightly unusual but I did not worry about it unduly. Mark arrived about thirty minutes later and I was showing him round the garden when he said, 'Let's go and sit on that bench.' Rather haltingly he started attempting to tell me something and I remember going cold with horror, trying to make sense of what he was saying. Holding my hand, he told me that Rupert, our oldest son, had gone missing.

Rupert had been working in Lomé, in West Africa, building a terminal for Burkina Faso for the purpose of supplying grain to Nigeria. He had been there for a couple of years and I knew he was not happy. Despite his incredibly funny letters describing life in Lomé (I have included one of my favourites in this book), he longed for his work there to be over and to leave what Mark has described as 'a bloody miserable place'.

That morning Mark told me that neither Rupert's colleague Tony Andrews nor anyone else had any idea where he was. He had quite simply vanished overnight. I had never imagined hearing anything quite so terrifying and I found myself clawing wildly at Mark, begging him to go out and find Rupert, imploring him to tell me this dreadful news was not true.

The previous autumn I had received an urgent call from Tony Andrews telling me that Rupert had been fooling around on a motorbike doing really dangerous manoeuvres, presumably to impress his girlfriends, when he lost control of the bike and it fell on top of him, crushing his leg from the knee down. By the time Tony Andrews had rung me Rupert was being flown back to London on a Swiss Red Cross plane. When he finally arrived in the middle of the night, I had arranged for an ambulance to bring him straight to the Parkside Hospital in Wimbledon and while the doctors gave him pain-killing drugs they had literally to cut off his jeans.

As I had suspected, his injuries were terrible and his leg from the knee down was so badly shattered that bits of bone were sticking out. Although he was in agony, he still managed to joke with Robin and me. He was lucky to have Roger Vickers as his orthopaedic surgeon who did an incredible job on his leg (and who seemed to spend the next years mending the rest of my family's broken bones, including Zac's foot, my knee and my niece Cosima's broken ankle). Rupert was soon strapped up and although he was in terrible pain for the first week he brightened up as a queue of beautiful girls became constant visitors. His room was always full of laughter and once, while he was fooling around with his girlfriend, he managed to break the bed.

He was rather depressed at the thought of going back to Lomé and I did not want him to go, but he had to return one last time to tidy up his affairs. I tried every way I could to dissuade him but I was somewhat comforted by the knowledge that it would be a few more months before he was allowed to leave Parkside. Even when he eventually came out after Christmas he could only walk with the help of a stick, which he was still using when he went back to Lomé in the spring. He rang me several times after his return and continued to send his usual flow of amusing letters to me, Robin and to his great friend Justin Frewin. The last time I spoke to him was on 11 June, my birthday.

By the 17th he had gone missing and theories about his disappearance were multiplying. In the beginning there was talk of kidnap as the most likely reason and then, because Rupert, who was fluent in Russian and had spent some time in Moscow working for the *Herald Tribune*, the sighting of a Russian ship anchored in the harbour gave rise to rumours that he might have been a spy. Every theory was explored, however far-fetched, but sometimes the most obvious solution is the hardest to accept.

Mark and Robin, accompanied by Rupert's great friend Tony Bromovsky, flew straight out to Lomé where Mark hired a firm of private investigators and I found myself waiting by the telephone every evening for Mark to call me, a time of day he told me later he dreaded because he never had any news to give me and I could not or would not allow myself to believe that he was dead.

We were told that Rupert was in the habit of going swimming every morning on a particularly dangerous beach where the currents were strong and vicious, and local people were frequently swept out to sea. Rupert would undress and, leaving his clothes and watch in a heap, would ask the beach guard to look after them while he swam. That early-morning swim was important to him as his leg was still not healed and it was his only exercise. On the day he disappeared the red flag was up, forbidding swimmers to enter the sea. Rupert was attracted by danger, loved taking risks and found beating the elements a particular challenge. That morning he had followed his daily routine of leaving his clothes together with his watch in a pile on the beach and had as usual tipped the guard to look after them until his return from the swim. The guard, although fully aware of what had happened, was too afraid to admit the truth when questioned, in case he lost his job for failing to prevent

Rupert from swimming at a time when the danger flag was flying. They searched for days but never found his body and finally I had to face the fact that not only would I never see my beloved son again, but that I would have no grave to visit. I can understand precisely the anguish of the relations of those who died in the collapse of the World Trade Centre on 11 September of whom there is no trace and for whom there could be no grave.

At the time of Rupert's disappearance I considered flying out to Lomé to see the place from which he set out on that final swim but I knew that any gesture such as the throwing of a flower into that grey and hostile sea would have been pointless. Nothing then would have eased my sense of emptiness and loss. Some time later the possessions that Rupert had left on the beach were returned to us, and Robin gave me his wallet and his watch, and I get much comfort by simply holding the watch in my hand. And of course I have his letters, which help to bring back his voice to me.

It was several months before I could accept the truth completely. It was something that I had to work out for myself and I could not talk about it for years. Although Robin tried to conceal his feelings from me, his grief must have been unbearable as he and Rupert were as close as Siamese twins. He was the person Robin loved most in the world and to this day he carries Rupert's passport photograph in his pocket.

On the day Mark came to tell me the news Robin, without saying anything to me, had driven around collecting my three younger children from their schools: Jemima from Frances Holland in London, Zac from Hawtreys in Gloucestershire and Benjamin from his nursery school in Richmond. He must have hoped that by the spontaneous act of kindness of surrounding me with my family the blow would somehow be softened. His instincts were right because in the weeks to come, having three young children who needed my attention and love forced me to pull myself together, although I felt like a zombie for years as I went about my daily life completely empty inside.

Rupert was my first child, born when I was barely twenty-one, and he had grown from an enchanting baby into a beautiful and clever little boy. It seemed almost unfair that any child could have been born with so many gifts. He was brilliant, beautiful and funny, and I absolutely adored him. In those days all his friends and contemporaries went to boarding school as it was the done thing, but both he and Robin hated it and longed to live at home. I remember them both, but particularly Rupert, clinging to me when the time came to leave for a new term, begging me not to let them go, and now, when I read his letters from school, which are so full of love and homesickness, I cannot understand how I could have sent them away.

From his prep school at St Aubyn's in Rottingdean, where he excelled, he went to Eton, which he loathed. From Eton he won a History exhibition to Oxford where he read History and Russian at Christchurch College. At Oxford he met and fell in love with the German Ambassador's beautiful daughter, Bettina von Hase, who rapidly became one of the family. We all adored Bettina, particularly Zac and Jemima who looked upon her as a sister. Sadly they had met too young, and when they broke up I really missed Bettina. The first time Rupert dared to bring his new girlfriend, Isabel Zumtobel, down to Ormeley for the night, Zac and Jemima burst in on them in the spare room and were very rude to Isabel. They were furious to find Rupert with a strange girl, and had pulled the bedclothes off and told her what a big bottom she had, and that she was ugly – all quite untrue, but they were fiercely loyal to Bettina.

When he left university Rupert found it hard to settle into a job and he never really discovered his true vocation, but I think in time he would have become a writer. He once told Mark that an ability to write was the only thing he felt he had learned from university.

He went to Moscow to work for Ed Stevens, the editor of the *Herald Tribune*, and wrote me hilarious letters about the goings-on in the Stevens household. While he was working in Vienna, involved in east–west trading, Jimmy, making an exception to his rule that he would never employ anyone with a university degree, was desperate to recruit him for Banque Occidentale. Rupert declined the offer feeling that if he were to work for either his father or stepfather he would be denied the chance to succeed on his own merits.

In September 1986, with the final acceptance that Rupert really was dead, we held a memorial service at St James's Piccadilly. Mark took care of all the arrangements and although everyone told me afterwards how moving the service had been, it remains a blur for me. I *was* there sitting in that church, but I felt the curious detachment of an observer, as if I was not really part of it or even actually present. I do remember holding Robin's hand throughout and then walking down the aisle at the end of the service without noticing or recognising any of the faces on either side until I saw the wide reassuring smile of both my doctor's wife and neighbour, Jean Gardiner, and another friend and neighbour, Sue Tobias, and feeling happy that they were there. The church was packed to the hilt, with many sobbing females among the congregation. I recollect answering the condolence letters which arrived en masse by writing that Rupert had been 'an almost perfect human being' and that is how I will always remember him.

Letter from Rupert   Lomé
                                                   1 July 1984

Darling Mum,

Just a short note to let you know that I am installed in a huge suite in Hotel 2 Fevrier (so named because the President's Plane crashed on the 2nd February 1974 and he survived) which is decorated in mauve plush and which is full of gadgetry, none of which works.

I'm beginning to get the hang of life in Africa: you need *incredible* patience and the ability to laugh at anything –

whatever happens. The first evening in the hotel restaurant the waitress picked up a plate under from which scuttled three huge cockroaches. Far from looking abashed she screamed with laughter and then called the head waiter who burst into giggles as well.

I was invited to a typical African lunch yesterday and have not looked at food since. I was invited for 1 o'clock and duly arrived on time. No food whatsoever and a gaggle of Africans all talking animatedly in a mixture of French and dialect. First drinks: a butler wearing a very tattered smock whose legs were covered in huge scabs appeared with a tray of something called Pom Pom which is dark green, fizzy and so revolting I was almost sick on the spot. Then on with the video: a 1960s French soft-porn number called 'Passion' with no sound except a low crackling noise whose plot consisted of long conversations (inaudible) between a very fat blonde with huge knockers and a very slimy looking Georgie Best look alike. Every 15 minutes exactly there would be the same scene of his white bottom bobbing up and down and of her face showing an expression of ecstacy. At this stage the crackling and the hissing from the video would get much louder (presumably music) and there would be roars of approval from the Africans, '*Ah illes travaillent, quoi*', and (groan) more Pom Pom would be ordered. This went on until 4.30 by which time our host had generously opened a bottle of a liquor called GBOMA ABRICOT of which I was forced to drink endless glasses.

Finally the food was brought in by a succession of very fat African ladies. The main course was served in what looked like a huge dustbin lid, and as the guest of honour I was given a massive helping. The ingredients consisted of goats balls in bright orange grease, tripe and cows skin (still covered in hair) – all washed down with a tumbler of Pom Pom.

I bought one of those huge Japanese Jeeps as the roads here are riddled with potholes the size of bomb craters. I have also hired a very sweet African called Cisse as a driver. Cisse describes himself as a rally driver and wears an apple green bomber jacket and a pair of size 15 Turkish slippers (with curly toes) in white patent plastic (bought specially for the job). He is enormously proud of the car which he polishes feverishly every morning.

Needless to say he has already had a crash. He came to pick me up one morning and I noticed he was unusually subdued. He confessed that he had had a small accident but that the other driver was completely to blame. Unfortunately for Cisse the other driver was a Frenchman who immediately sent a very detailed telex to our insurance company outlining what had happened. As the owner of the car I was summoned with Cisse to give our version of the story. According to Cisse the Frenchman had pulled out to overtake him just at the moment that about 4 cars were coming the other way. To avoid a head on collision with the oncoming traffic, Cisse in true rally driver style had simply pulled across the road thereby demolishing the front of Mr Defou's Mercedes.

'Well, Cisse,' I asked, 'what did happen?'

Cisse looked slightly taken aback by the scowling insurance man and then thought deeply for about ten minutes. Finally his face lit up as he had remembered what had happened. The road was completely empty at the time and he had moved into position to overtake the Mercedes. Just as he was overtaking the stupid Frenchman had accelerated on purpose and smashed into him. This was recorded on the claim form in illiterate French. Cisse could not understand about drawing a sketch of the accident for the form and insisted on producing a profile of the jeep.

There is nothing to do in the evening apart from going to the cinema (Bruce Lee and *Jesus of Nazareth* have been showing for the last two years).

Tennis is quite fun, particularly as the ball boys (of which there seem to be about 60) do everything for one. Because I have been quite generous with tips, they have decided that I should be given hearty vocal support whenever I play. The worse I play the louder the squeals of support become.

'*Bien joué, Rupert,*' 60 little voices chant, as yet another ball goes sailing out of the court. All this to the great annoyance of the extremely professional French four on the neighbouring court who are completely ignored and who have to shout to make themselves heard above the din. Things are beginning to get out of control as the ball boys have now discovered when I go swimming and have taken to invading the pool swarming like ants over a lot of very well oiled French women to ask me when I am playing.

Will be back at the end of July.

Love

    Rupert

FIFTEEN

The Referendum Campaign
and Jimmy's Illness

It is impossible for me to write about Jimmy's extraordinary and courageous campaign for a public referendum on Britain's involvement in Europe without simultaneously describing his courageous and final fight against the terrible illness that killed him. Apart from Laure and Ginette, for a long while I was alone in knowing that he was suffering from cancer. During that last year, perhaps the finest of his life, political and personal bravery were undeniably merged and at his memorial service Lady Thatcher summed up that final achievement. 'It takes courage of a high order to lay yourself open to the taunts and sneers of lesser men who try to diminish your character and it takes a well-nigh superhuman brand of bravery to do all this knowing you are mortally ill, without a shred of self-pity or complaint, feeling your strength ebbing, fighting back the pain,' she said. The depth of passion that he felt for the principles behind the Referendum Party kept him alive, even while he was dying.

Several years earlier he had had a dramatic vision, in which he saw himself standing on the summit of a mountain from where he could see a railway line far below him and on the track a train containing his family. The train was heading swiftly towards a landslide that was obscured from the driver by a bend in the track. From his vantage point Jimmy could do nothing except watch the inevitable crash with mounting horror. For Jimmy this nightmarish image was a seminal moment and it became a metaphor for the disastrous consequences he foresaw if Britain were to join a European state. He regarded his campaign for a referendum as nothing less than a crusade to save Britain.

Initially I was surprised by the approach he took to his final illness because for as long as I had known him, Jimmy had been a committed hypochondriac. The slightest sign of a cold would be seen as the onset of a dreadful flu and a headache translated into a brain tumour. In 1985 he had been feeling off colour and had a series of tests including a check-up at the Mayo clinic in America but nothing was found. One morning at Ormeley in 1986 he confessed to me that he was feeling particularly ghastly and very tired. I called in Dr Gardiner who confirmed on the spot that he had developed adult diabetes. However, he did not prescribe Jimmy any medication and as it was possible to treat the condition with diet, Jimmy was not unduly worried. After cutting out all sugary and other things he was not supposed to eat, the diabetes did not seem to affect his way of life.

But six years later Jimmy rang me in a highly agitated state from Paris to tell me that his French doctor thought he had liver cancer. Although the diagnosis had not been confirmed he swore me, along with Ginette and Laure, to secrecy. I said I would find a liver specialist in Britain for a second opinion and Dr Gardiner suggested Roger Williams, by reputation a first-class liver specialist and now well known as the consultant who treated George Best. Jimmy arrived in London and was rushed under a false name into the Cromwell for a biopsy. He had asked me to arrange for Isabel, our cook at Ormeley, to make his favourite meal of cold roast chicken, salad, apple purée and yoghurt, but I was not allowed to tell her or anyone else whom I was taking this huge meal to. It was packed into a hamper and I was driven to London by Mike Burns, by then Jimmy's driver as Cliff Howes had sadly retired with heart problems. On arrival at the Cromwell, Mike leapt out of the car and lugged the huge hamper out of the boot but explaining that the large wicker basket was for a friend, I said that I wanted to carry it myself. While Mike stood watching bemused, I staggered into the Cromwell with the hamper and lurched into Jimmy's room to find Laure waiting for Jimmy to return from the biopsy. We had never met before but, united through our concern for the same man, we managed to make conversation, if rather awkwardly, while waiting for Jimmy to return.

Eventually Jimmy was wheeled in looking rather cheerful and grabbing a drumstick with both hands he tucked into the chicken with relish, and when Roger Williams, a charming and gentle man, arrived he tried to reassure me. When the test results came through later that month, they revealed that there was indeed a minuscule malignant tumour but that although Jimmy would have to have an operation on his liver he would be fine.

The thought of the operation was appalling to Jimmy and his instinct was to refuse to have it, but he was persuaded by Ginette, Laure, Sam Pisar his lawyer and me that it would be safer to remove the tiny tumour. I wanted Roger Williams to do the operation in London but Jimmy preferred to have it done by his French surgeon Henri Bismuth in Paris, where he would feel more private. He had the operation in the American Hospital there and although he must have been a trying patient everything went smoothly and the tumour was removed.

Jimmy recovered in time to give a great party at Laurent in Paris, in joint celebration of Jemima's nineteenth and his six-tieth birthday. All seemed well and this is where I hoped his health problems would end.

But in 1994 I spotted a mole on his chest and didn't like the look of it. I urged him to have it checked but for a few months he did nothing about it. When he did finally go to the doctor the mole proved to be of no consequence but in the hospital there was a new scanning machine and as a precaution Jimmy volunteered to be tested on it. While he was having the scan the doctors discovered another very small but primary tumour on his pancreas.

This time Jimmy rang me to tell me calmly but defiantly that he was not going to have another operation as the first one had been too painful. Once again he was persuaded to have the tumour removed. He gave instructions that on no account were any of his children or his staff to be told of his illness. He was determined to carry on as normal.

In 1992 Jimmy had published *The Trap*, an unflinching look at the problems of global society, including unemployment, increasing violence, environmental deterioration and a feeling that something fundamental was going wrong. The book was a bestseller in France and when it appeared in England it became a focus for animated debate. With the grandson of Charles de Gaulle, he had already established a political movement in France, L'Autre Europe, with the purpose of fighting the 1994 European elections with eighty-eight candidates to cover France. The campaign was successful and Jimmy was elected as a Member of the European Parliament.

In the autumn of 1994 Jimmy invited Jim and Mark Slater to stay for the weekend at Montjeu, his French house in Burgundy, and there he broached to them his idea of founding a British party that would declare itself before the next election and which would have only one policy: to recommend a referendum in Europe. If it succeeded in getting the main parties to adopt a referendum as part of their manifesto, then Jimmy's party would disband. He was not seeking party political power, merely power on behalf of the people. The Referendum Party was above party politics.

Patrick Robertson, a public relations consultant who had worked with Jimmy in promoting the English edition of *The Trap*, had impressed Jimmy with his dedication and effectiveness, and Jimmy invited him to become the co-ordinator and public relations adviser for the Referendum Party. Patrick was an excellent choice as he was of invaluable help to Jimmy throughout the campaign and remains a great friend of our family today.

While Patrick was attending to every detail of the political side of launching the party, Jimmy's personal assistant Charles Filmer was responsible for making all the practical and personal arrangements for Jimmy and the family. Charles had come to work for Jimmy in 1985 at the age of twenty-six, after a career in the army and more recently as aide to the King of Jordan. Jimmy relied on Charles to such an extent that we used to joke that he was incapable of brushing his teeth without consulting Charles on the choice of toothpaste. However, after Jimmy's death the joke was on us as, having founded his own company, Charles became an indispensable friend and adviser, managing all our business concerns with the perfectionism for which he is well known.

Shortly after that weekend at Montjeu, without revealing his serious physical condition, Jimmy went on *The Frost Programme* to launch the idea of a Referendum Party. After that interview he went on one programme after another, including three further appearances with David Frost over the next twelve months.

As well as being preoccupied by his illness and the launch of the Referendum Party, Jimmy also had his family to think about. In 1994 Jemima had fallen in love with the great Paki-stani cricketer Imran Khan. Although I had been aware of their love affair and their plans to marry for some time, I was nervous about telling Jimmy as I knew he would be worried about the difference in cultures and concerned that Jemima was only twenty-one and in the final year of taking her English degree at Bristol University. When I finally told Jimmy about their romance, he was initially furious but after meeting Imran he discovered that he liked him enormously and sharing a mutual respect, they became great friends.

A far more difficult challenge than telling Jimmy about Jemima's engagement occurred when I realised I would have to tell Mrs White the news. I knew the press would go mad when the announcement was made and I wanted to break it to Mrs White myself before she read it in the *Daily Mirror*, her favourite paper. She had continued to live in her much loved flat for many years, but after Reg's death her usual good health began to decline. She began having dizzy spells and after one of a series of falls, she broke her hip and had to go to hospital. She never really recovered her strength. I found people to come and look after her in the day but it was difficult to find night carers and she needed twenty-four-hour attention. I became used to her saintly neighbour George ringing me up to tell me she had had another fall but when she broke the same hip again and returned to hospital I braced myself to tell her that she would have to go into a home for her own safety. I knew she would hate this but she was too proud to agree to the children's and my wish that she come and live at Ormeley. Eventually I found a lovely private nursing home in Putney called the Elmbank, which was near enough for regular visits, where she could have her own room with her own furniture around her.

Telling Mrs White that her beloved Jemima was marrying a Pakistani was bound to be somewhat problematic, as I had been aware for some years that Mrs White had faintly racist leanings and Robin went as far as to describe her as 'Alf Garnett in a frock'.

When Jemima was a baby I employed a charming Anglo-Jamaican girl called Terry as a part-time nanny. She had been adopted by a white family in the north of England and spoke with a strong northern accent. One day I had been having lunch in the kitchen with Terry and Mrs White, with Jemima beside us in her high chair. Terry had been shopping to buy herself a wig and trying it on she asked me what I thought of it. I told her that although I quite liked it I thought her own ethnic hair suited her better. I turned to Mrs White to ask her opinion, realising the moment I did so that it was a mistake. Mrs White, her false teeth chomping on a lamb cutlet, looked up briefly and said, 'Me, well I prefer 'em in wigs.' Luckily Terry had such a wonderful sense of humour that she burst out laughing.

The week before Jemima's engagement was to appear in the newspapers I rang Mrs White in the nursing home. 'Wags,' I said. 'Do you watch much sport? I mean like cricket?'

'No, I can't be doing with that,' came the answer.

'I see,' I said rather lamely, watching one explanatory avenue close, as Wags clearly would not know that Imran was a cricketing hero.

'Wags,' I said, mustering up a voice full of enthusiasm. 'Guess what? Jemima's engaged to a wonderful man and Sir James and I are thrilled to bits.'

There was silence on the line.

'His name is Imran Khan,' I said rather hesitantly.

'I see,' she said. 'What kind of a name is that? Is he Jewish?'

'No,' I said. 'He is a, er, a Pakistani.'

There was a long silence then she said rather grudgingly, 'Well, as long as she's happy.'

Jemima and Imran were married in June in Richmond and looking at the wedding pictures now I can see how frail Jimmy then was, and realise how tired and weak he must have felt.

On the day of the June wedding, reporters and television cameras besieged the house. I arranged for Mrs White, dressed in her best clothes, to be brought to Ormeley in a wheelchair for Jemima's wedding party. She looked so happy and was so pleased to see all the family together and to be a part of it. Most of Imran's family thought she was Jemima's grandmother and made a big fuss of her. Before she left I pushed her wheelchair to the gate where all the photographers were gathered, as they were not allowed inside for the party, and she had her photograph taken with me by *Hello!* magazine. She had a big smile on her face and I knew this would be an enormous boost to her morale and definitely one up on all the old ladies in the home, most of whom she disliked intensely.

Although the children and his close friends knew Jimmy had had an operation they thought it was simply a routine procedure for diverticulitis and had no idea of the truth. I, on the other hand, began to marvel at the extraordinary courage of a man who had always quailed at the merest toothache.

Later that year in October the doctors found that the cancer had spread and they removed his spleen and upper pancreas, and encouraged him to have radio and chemotherapy, which he loathed. In 1996, just before Christmas when Jemima's first son Sulaiman was only a few weeks old, we all went on one final holiday to Mexico where Jimmy was unable to conceal any longer the terrible pain he was suffering and I was not surprised when Jemima came to me and said, 'Mum, I have to know the truth.'

Although I still tried to avoid telling her and thereby breaking my word to Jimmy, she was insistent. Eventually I told her that although Jimmy had indeed had cancer, he was recovering, but as I was telling her I was aware that by concealing the whole truth I risked the chance of Jemima being denied the farewell to a parent that, in the secrecy surrounding my mother's illness, had been denied me. I could not imagine what I would say to her or the other children if Jimmy died without them having a chance to say goodbye and I knew they would never forgive me. But Jimmy continued to insist on secrecy.

Meanwhile Patrick Robertson had rented offices in Horseferry Road round the corner from the Houses of Parliament in Westminster on the second floor of an old office building, staffed by about 200 party workers. The candidate selection had begun and a cross-party group of responsible, non-eccentric men and women were selected.

Unlike the then serving Prime Minister, John Major, his predecessor Margaret Thatcher was a strong ally for the Referendum Campaign and she, together with Denis, became close friends of us both. In the autumn of 1995 Jimmy and I were invited to attend Lady Thatcher's seventieth birthday party at Claridge's. It was an evening I am unlikely to forget not so much for its historical significance as for my dreadful faux pas. Margaret Thatcher and Denis were standing together while receiving their guests. She was keeping an eye on the entrance door where at any moment the Queen and the Duke of Edinburgh were expected. I knew they were coming as we had all been asked to be there in advance of the royal party. There is no doubting the fact that Margaret Thatcher is very regal and although I had met her several times before, my mind must have strayed towards the Queen's imminent arrival. Without thinking, I dropped a deep curtsy in front of Mrs Thatcher. Realising my hideous mistake I tried to struggle to my feet but having dropped so low, I found it impossible to get up again. Mrs Thatcher seemed to have taken the curtsy for granted but Denis, ever the gentleman and seeing my predicament, hauled me to my feet and, kissing me on the cheek, said, 'Gosh, we *are* honoured!'

Crimson, I turned to Jimmy and said, 'I cannot believe I did that,' to which he replied rather tersely, 'Well, you did.' Looking round, I saw my great friends Vicky and Evelyn de Rothschild roaring with laughter and as I rushed over to them I wondered how many other people had witnessed this shameful event.

About a year before the 1997 election Jimmy had started having secret meetings with John Major at Downing Street. Alan Clark was the middleman responsible for organising these meetings, motivated by the wish to be given the credit for getting rid of the Referendum Party, which was increasingly threatening to erode the Conservative vote. At one stage the Conservatives estimated that the Referendum Party was stealing as much as 15 per cent of their support and it was easy to see why Major was grateful for Alan's intervention. It was even rumoured that Jimmy might be ennobled as a reward for disbanding his party, although Jimmy laughed at the thought that he could be bought off with a peerage.

Patrick vividly remembers being on Jimmy's aeroplane as we flew down to Tramores for the 1996 Easter holidays. Jimmy was changing his shirt in his bedroom and, clearly excited, called Patrick in, hinting that John Major was on the brink of agreeing to adopting a referendum as part of the Conservative manifesto for the election. In the end Major decided that he could not offer a full referendum as it would have led to a split in his party so instead he offered a diluted version focusing on the single currency. Jimmy had wanted a much fuller proposal, which would have included questions on the Maastricht Treaty, on reforms of the agricultural policy and even whether to stay in Europe or not. Major's referendum had left out most of the issues that Jimmy felt were important, but by offering a concessionary referendum, Major hoped that the threat Jimmy and his party posed would simply evaporate. He was wrong and the Conservatives continued to regard Jimmy's party as enough of a problem for them to feel it necessary to hand out stickers and leaflets in Huntingdon, Major's constituency, stating 'WE are the real Referendum Party'.

Alan Clark never admitted to his role as go-between as he himself was trying to get back into Parliament by standing for the safe Conservative seat at Kensington and Chelsea. By an odd coincidence my son Robin had been selected as the Referendum candidate for the same seat and this presented Jimmy with an uncomfortable personal dilemma. Reluctantly he explained to Robin that Alan was an old friend against whom he did not want to put up any competition and somewhat puzzled (as Alan had not made his views on Europe widely known) Robin agreed to stand down, making his announcement at a Referendum Party meeting in a church in Pont Street which was attended by several hundred very well-heeled people. If you had been a Conservative at that meeting you would have been thoroughly alarmed as it was packed with people who should have been diehard Tories but who had become supporters of Jimmy's campaign.

The Conservatives' announcement presented a problem for the Labour Party who until then had agreed with their rivals that neither would talk much about Europe in the run-up to the election because they knew that it was not a popular issue with the electorate. In order to maintain this low-priority emphasis on Europe Gordon Brown, the Shadow Chancellor, announced a referendum on the single currency three or four months after the Conservatives, so that there would be no difference on the question of Europe between the two main parties. This left the Referendum Party in the really awkward position of having to fight harder to communicate what was special about them, a challenge which was exacerbated by Jimmy's odd reluctance to define the question that would be put to the public vote until two months before the election and when he finally did, there were three parts to it, making it complicated and cumbersome to explain.

If we were privately concerned about positioning the party, the experience of the Brighton Party Conference in October 1996 left us in no doubt of our impressive level of support. There were 5000 people queuing to get into the Grand Hotel and Lord Tonypandy, the distinguished former speaker of the House of Commons, although terminally ill himself, had recorded a video for the conference in which he spoke particularly passionately of his conviction that joining Europe would question 'whether this nation survives with its cherished liberties'.

Although the Brighton conference was one of the most moving occasions I can remember, Jimmy's illness also made it a particularly worrying time. The night before Jimmy was due to speak from the platform Carla Powell, the political hostess and a tremendous supporter of Jimmy's ideals, gave a dinner party for Jimmy's friends and supporters. As he was getting dressed he confessed he was feeling dreadful and made me promise that night to fulfil a wholly unfamiliar role of nagging wife by making him go to bed early. I promised I would and three-quarters of the way through dinner I interrupted the party and took him upstairs. The following day he delivered a magnificent speech, although when watching the recorded footage I can see clearly that while he had lost none of his formidable powers of oratory, physically some of the flamboyance and energy of his usual public performance was missing.

Early in the new year the focus of Jimmy's active life switched from Paris to London for the build up to the Referendum Campaign, although every weekend he would go to Paris for exhausting chemo sessions. I knew by then that Jimmy was not going to make old bones but even I had no idea how close to death he was. To me, as to everyone else, he seemed invincible.

I realised the best way I could show my loyalty and demonstrate my belief in the party was to canvass. For six weeks I pounded the pavements of Putney, knocking on every door and climbing endless steps to council flats. The weather was wet and miserable, and despite the odd coffee break in the Putney Café Rouge, I soon realised that with very few exceptions canvassing is a thankless job. One feels desperately intrusive and in my case, self-conscious, and although occasionally I received a warm welcome I was always anticipating a snub. One woman, while emphasising how much she was in favour of the single currency, answered the door clearly in the middle of carving her Sunday roast and, wielding a very large and threatening knife, made her impassioned points while waving the knife about wildly, barely an inch from my face. Some people were openly hostile, others were warm and full of praise for Jimmy, but I was constantly asked why Jimmy was not seen more on the streets of Putney. This put me in a difficult position as I knew people were frustrated by his absences and yet I was forbidden to give the real reason why he spent each weekend in Paris.

Whenever he felt well enough he did go out on to the streets to canvass himself and people were generally so pleased to see him although there was one slightly difficult moment when an old lady became convinced that Jimmy was her own beloved but long since deceased husband and, grabbing hold of him, would not let him go.

The Putney office was run magnificently by Charlotte Blacker and under her direction we decided that it was better to tackle people towards the evening when they were home from work. This, of course, was exactly the time when they wanted to be left alone to relax so our knocks on the door felt even more invasive. One evening a small blonde girl answered her door to me. I asked if her mummy or daddy were in and for a moment she vanished inside, only to reappear saying, 'Mummy says she's in the bath and Daddy says he's out.'

I remember one wonderful couple who apart from being fervent admirers of Jimmy had two huge black Newfoundland dogs with whom I inevitably fell in love. I went back two or three times to visit them, taking Jimmy with me on one occasion, and I still have a photograph beside my bed of Jimmy and the couple flanked by the dogs.

I would arrive back at the end of the canvassing day, wet and exhausted, and Jimmy would ask me how it had gone. I tended to make it a bit more upbeat than it actually was and he loved hearing the funny incidents.

As Mike Burns was chauffeuring Jimmy during the day, I was being driven by a charming man called Brian Bond, who entered into the canvassing spirit with gusto and would sprint from door to door announcing as he emerged, puffing and out of breath, 'Another one signed up, Lady A!' I was slightly suspicious about the number of 'signed-ups' that Brian professed to have accumulated but I did not wish to dampen his enthusiasm. One day he and I were canvassing on opposite sides of the same street when I heard a loud altercation coming from one of Brian's houses. I hurried over to find a very annoyed couple who, when I enquired what the matter was, snapped back, 'If he's the sort of person Sir James employs to work for his party then we doubt Sir James will have much success.' Mystified, I pressed them for a further explanation, only to learn that Brian had earnestly explained to them that if they didn't vote for Jimmy there would be 'hundreds of those flaming gits pouring in from all over the Continent'. However, I could not be annoyed with Brian as he was so kind and well-meaning, and he worked as hard as, if not harder than, any of us as he raced up and down the terraced streets with bundles of stickers under his arm. His energy was inexhaustible and we all loved him.

A week after Jimmy died, Brian achieved fame when he appeared on the *Private Eye* 'Farewell Sir Jams' cover. The photograph they used had been taken a while before when I was going in to the Portland Hospital in the rain, to visit my newborn grandson Sulaiman. On the cover the speech bubble has me saying, 'Let me through, I'm his wife,' to which Brian, pictured holding an umbrella over my head, replies, 'there are four of those in there already, Madam.' Despite the disrespect shown to Jimmy so recently after his death, I could not help laughing and rang Brian to tell him to go and buy the magazine, but he had already done so, being too kind-hearted to tell me, fearing it might upset me.

On one occasion that spring Jimmy fulfilled a long-standing invitation to speak at the Eton Political Society, an engagement he was particularly anxious to accept as Benjamin was at the school. Jemima and I went down to Windsor with him and on the way he had to stop the car to give himself an insulin injection for his diabetes. I honestly wondered if he would be able to make the debate at all, feeling as ill as he did, but we had dinner with the Provost who did not seem to notice anything wrong. Before he began to speak, Jimmy swayed slightly on the platform and with Jemima beside me I was stiff with apprehension. But he managed to put up a spirited performance and afterwards took questions from the floor. One boy said that the last speaker they had heard on the subject of the European Union had been Nicholas Soames, the Conservative MP, who had declared that Jimmy Goldsmith spoke 'a lot of hot air'. Jimmy paused and with that wonderful smile of his replied, 'Ah, Nicholas Soames. Charming fellow. He used to work for me a few years ago.' And went on to the next question.

If Brighton had been a public success, the rally held at Alexandra Palace in March six weeks before the election was a triumph.

Patrick remembers going to see the Palace a month before with Alistair McAlpine (Lord McAlpine), the party chairman. 'We drove up in Alistair's car,' Patrick told me, 'and as we walked into that vast, empty, cold building, I looked up to the left and to the right and burst into laughter because we realised we had just committed ourselves to filling this huge place!' He need not have worried as, costing £1 million, it turned out to be the biggest political rally since the Second World War with 12,000 people present. There were two main ideas behind the rally. The first was Jimmy's recognition of the importance of raising morale. Every single candidate was brought on to the stage, and every supporter and every regional party chairman had a chance to be there. We even had our own song recorded, the 'Referendum Song', sung by Nico's husband Georgie Fame.

Secondly Patrick thought the rally would get some television coverage as a news story alone. But the BBC argued they didn't have to give any new party any political coverage at all, even a 650-candidate, £30 million-backed party with a proven 5 per cent support in the polls. We did not get one second of coverage on British National TV. Meanwhile the Conservative Party, who had had 1500 people in a half-full Albert Hall, got the usual full network attention.

On election night we all went to Wandsworth Town Hall

where the results for several local constituencies, including Putney, were to be announced. There was a wonderful mixture of candidates standing against Jimmy for Putney. Apart from David Mellor, the defending Conservative MP, there was a man who had been driving round the streets with a huge hand made of papier-mâché strapped to the top of his truck with one finger pointing towards the sky. He was collecting votes for the Hand Party. And there was a pretty model from *Vogue* standing for the Beautiful Party. As the result was announced the atmosphere was electric. Tony Coleman, the Labour candidate, had ousted David Mellor, the Conservative MP. When Mellor came to the microphone he began by thanking the returning officers and the party supporters but then, turning round to face Jimmy, he continued, 'As for Sir James Goldsmith and his Hacienda La Referenda Party, you can all go back to Mexico, together with all your zoological society friends,' a back-handed reference to Aspers. There was a sense of shock in the room as people looked at each other, appalled at such a personal attack. Then Jimmy's great friend Taki shouted an obscenity directed straight at Mellor and started a slow hand-clap, which was picked up by everyone in the room. Jimmy was not quite sure what was happening, but thought he should join in and inevitably the cameras slanted the incident to look like Jimmy's bad grace in defeat. That particular clip continues to be aired on every programme that contains a rerun of the highlights of the 1997 election.

In the end the Referendum Party got nearly 1 million votes, including 12,000 in the south-west of the country, and John Aspinall alone got 7000 in his constituency. In England we polled 5 per cent of the vote, costing the Conservative Party eighteen seats, and the legacy of the Referendum Party and the effects of Jimmy's campaign are felt acutely today as the burning issues of Europe, the single currency and the question of a referendum continue to ride high on the political agenda.

★

About a week after the election Jimmy invited all the party staff to lunch at the Waldorf Hotel in the Aldwych. It was a very hot day in mid-May and Patrick, unaware that Jimmy was shortly going to have another operation in Paris, remembers that he appeared uncharacteristically flustered. He went straight from that lunch to the airport and took his plane down to Corsica where he had chartered a boat. Jemima and Sulaiman and Zac joined him, and they had a wonderful weekend together, and it still makes me happy to know he had that last really good time with the children because thereafter things went downhill very quickly. He returned to Paris in terrible pain and was rushed to hospital. I flew over immediately. In the late afternoon Ginette rang Jemima and me in the car to say the operation had not been a success. Jimmy was in bed in intensive care, looking up at us with an expression of great courage and benevolence. He told the children that he had been operated on for the last time and that the conventional doctors could do nothing more through surgery. However, with Zac's help he said he was determined to try alternative medicine and would not give up the fight. I remember Jemima's voice breaking as she spoke to her father but Zac appeared to be remarkably controlled and seemed to have become the head of the family overnight.

I left it to Zac and Teddy to find the best alternative doctor but I am not sure they found the right one because Jimmy was treated by an Indian doctor whose particular cure, involving the consumption of various metals combined with a strict no-meat diet, might have worked for some people but did not suit Jimmy and he became desperately thin. As soon as he had recovered enough to travel he went to Montjeu and all the children stayed there with him. I used to fly over whenever possible to spend the day there. On the first visits as my helicopter landed in front of the beautiful façade I would see the familiar tall figure of Jimmy wearing an overcoat and a Cossack hat, standing at the top of the steps on the terrace waving to me in greeting. While I was making those sad expeditions, it always seemed to be raining and as he became weaker the figure in the coat was no longer waiting on the steps when I arrived.

But if he was worried about the slowness of his rate of improvement he never showed it except when, looking for reassurance, he would say privately to me, 'Have I got the look?' In the early days of his illness I made a chance remark that he did not have the unmistakable and distinctive look in his eyes of a terminally ill cancer patient and he had fastened on to this as a barometer of hope. He would tell everyone that the doctor was confident he would be well by September, which I found infuriating as he was obviously fading away and without telling the doctor I instructed the cook to let him have some lamb.

In the last few days he had a longing for the sun and although he was in terrible pain and most of his organs were failing, he decided he would fly with Laure to join me in Spain. He took a helicopter from Malaga airport up to the mountains of Tramores but the journey had proved too much for him.

One of the last things he asked me to do was to look after the children and using his own special name for Sulaiman he added, 'Darling, please take care of Jemima and the Turnip.'

He died two nights later and despite my intense sadness, I was also glad that he was not going to suffer any longer. He was cremated in Spain the following day in accordance with Spanish law and at his own request his ashes were scattered later by the children, over the sea in Mexico.

It was very difficult to accept the reality of Jimmy's death because he was the puppet master in all our lives, and I still find myself longing on countless occasions to be able to turn to him and ask for his unique perspective and interpretation on current and world events, or some controversy that might be dominating the headlines. Although I might not necessarily have agreed with him, he always had something illuminating and thought-provoking to say and his mind had been to me an inexhaustible source of stimulation.

A few months after his death we held a memorial service on 13 November in St John's Smith Square. Over 700 people came and David Frost introduced the service with the promise that it was to be a service of celebration and not a specifically religious, but rather a spiritual occasion.

I was determined to have at least one Christian hymn but Aspers thought otherwise and I think this was the only occasion on which Aspers and I had a serious disagreement. In the end I insisted that we at least had 'Jerusalem', although I would have liked others as well, but the mixture of music, readings and personal tributes amounted to a highly original, unforgettable and deeply moving ceremony.

We invited five people who, through their different roles in Jimmy's life, knew him best. Aspers, his oldest friend, refusing to take Jimmy's own advice that he should 'stick to the text', spoke at length but eloquently and with barely a note. Teddy, Jimmy's only brother, recalled that from the age of four Jimmy was already managing to combine his business sense with an ecological awareness when he set up a bartering system on a Bahamian beach, trading his collection of stamps for Teddy's cache of seashells. He summed up what so many of us were thinking when he said, 'Although we know when someone dies that they are dead, we don't necessarily believe what we know.'

David Frost also refused to acknowledge completely that Jimmy had gone by saying that 'death is not a full stop but a comma in the work of Jimmy'.

Lady Thatcher called Jimmy 'a giant among men, great in his qualities and great in his impact', adding that he was 'one of the most powerful and dynamic personalities that this generation has seen'. She paid tribute to his extraordinary generosity both to politics and the environment as well as to individuals. When speaking of the Referendum Campaign she said she believed that he had shown the same intellectual clarity in politics that he had brought to business. After she had spoken, she had to leave the service early to go and attend at the service for Lord Tonypandy, the great champion of the Referendum Party who had died in September.

Henry Kissinger's words were in a way the most affecting of all as, clearly moved himself, he described the conversations he had had with Jimmy up until only a few days before his death, during which Jimmy still refused to admit how much pain he was in. He compared him with 'a knight errant in a medieval romance doing battle with dragons and monsters and protecting even those who did not know they needed protection'. He also told a wonderful story about his own elderly mother who, on being introduced to Jimmy for the first time, told her son that Jimmy was the most charming and intelligent man she had ever met. While accepting 'most charming', Kissinger felt compelled to challenge her. 'Most *intelligent*?' he enquired, slightly hurt.

'Yes,' she confirmed, 'most intelligent.'

There was an unscheduled though welcome speaker when Chief Mangosuthu Buthelezi, head of the Zulu Inkhata Party, took to the podium. Jimmy had become particularly friendly with him when staying with Aspers in South Africa and he delivered his own unique tribute before leading his people, splendid in their black and yellow tribal dress, in a profoundly affecting Zulu funeral chant.

Three of Jimmy's daughters read tributes and for me the most difficult moment of the service came when I had to struggle to maintain my composure as Jemima stood in front of me, beautiful, sad, but calm and read a poem she had chosen to illustrate the way her father had always encouraged his children to take risks in life. The poem is so perfect a choice that I reproduce it in full here.

To laugh is to risk appearing a fool,
To cry is to risk appearing sentimental and soft,
To reach out to another is to risk involvement,
To show up and expose your feelings is to risk exposing your
    inherent self,
To place your idea, your dreams, your desires before people,
    is to risk their loss,
To love is to risk you might not be loved in return,
To live is to risk dying,
To show strength is to risk showing weakness,
To do is to risk failure,
The greatest hazard in life is to risk nothing,
The person who risks nothing, gets nothing, has nothing, is
    nothing.
He may avoid suffering, pain, sorrow
But he does not learn, he does not grow, he does not live, he
    does not love.
He has sold, forfeited freedom, integrity
He is a slave, chained by safety, locked away by fear, because
    only a person who is
Willing to risk not knowing the result is free.

Interspersed between the speakers was a musical programme that could only have been designed for a service for Jimmy Goldsmith including a glorious song by Duke Ellington, Verdi's stirring March of the Hebrew Slaves and Gershwin's gorgeous 'Summertime'.

Most memorable of all, perhaps, were the Mariachis who had always performed at Jimmy's parties in Mexico and who had flown over especially for the service. Wearing their distinctive blue and white suits and fringed sombreros, with their lead singer big-bellied and grand-gestured, they played their hearts out, fulfilling the motivation behind the service that it should be a celebration.

The service ended with 'When the Saints Go Marching In',

during which the entire congregation rose to its feet and clapped in time to the rhythm, in a mood of collective energy, vitality and appreciation that Jimmy would have loved.

SIXTEEN

Children and Grandchildren

With five loving children I consider myself one of the luckiest women alive. Although I have a large circle of friends it is my family, including my sister and brother, who matter most in the world to me. My life has been packed with incident, but it has never been lonely as my family have always been there to share times of great happiness and to sustain me when sometimes things have not been so easy.

Dogs, too, have played a fundamental role in my life. Having grown up with the little stone monuments to dogs and horses in the Peace Garden, the family pet burial ground at Mount Stewart, and those that are scattered around the grounds at Wynyard including the grave of that great racehorse Hamletonian, I now have similar memorials at Ormeley commemorating my love for my own dogs that are buried in the garden there. A dog's love is unconditional and its companionship unsurpassed and I cannot imagine my house without a great number of them, and whenever I have been away, my return is made happy by the welcome they give me.

Robin, my second son, has inherited my love of dogs and a few years ago when my two Norfolk terriers Barney and Bee had four puppies, Robin rang me and told me to look in the births column in *The Times*. 'To Mr and Mrs Arthur Barnes,' it said, 'three beautiful daughters and a bouncing baby boy', followed by the full address at Ormeley. Eager to capitalise on the prospect of a new really substantial quadruplet account, a hamper-sized supply of disposable nappies arrived for me the following day, courtesy of a well-known shop specialising in baby goods.

Currently there are five dogs in residence. The three Norfolk terriers, Barney and two of his children Bindy and Boris, and they have been joined by Lily (named by Sulaiman) who is officially a Grand Basset Griffon Vendeen which simply means she is a large white shaggy French gundog. This breed is famous for its friendliness and good nature and Lily is no exception. It is unthinkable for her to greet my visitors without bringing them a present, sometimes one of my shoes or, more frequently, a pair of my pants she has retrieved on her regular forays into the laundry basket.

Shortly after Lily's arrival, I had paid a visit to Rigby & Peller the lingerie shop in Knightsbridge to buy some new and rather large bras. At about the same time, the trial of Paul Burrell, Princess Diana's butler was approaching and I had agreed happily to talk to Paul's lawyer Andrew Shaw because although I had very little to contribute, I liked Paul and knew that Diana had been very fond of him.

While Mr Shaw and I were deep in earnest conversation, I noticed the door opening very slowly and into the study came Lily, slowly wagging her tail, with something dangling from her mouth which she laid lovingly at his feet. I saw to my horror that it was one of my vast new bras, a purple one to boot. She laid it out in all its tremendous colourful glory, resembling as my brother Alastair said when spotting it hanging on the washing line 'a parachute masquerading as a brassiere'.

Crimson in the face, I tried to reclaim it but playfully Lily snatched it back, running round the room pulling it by the straps and showing it off from every angle. When I finally managed to wrench it away from her I found it almost impossible to bring myself to look at Mr Shaw's bemused face.

The most recent addition to my dog family is Daisy, Lily's baby sister. But my mongrel Copper, whose intelligence far outshone any lack of blue blood breeding, was the greatest character I ever knew.

One winter afternoon a few years ago I took Copper and my Norfolk terriers for a walk on the golf course adjoining Ormeley, a walk I often took by arrangement with the golf course after all the golfers had finished playing. Half an hour later I returned with the terriers, leaving the gate open as usual to allow Copper to return in his own time. Ten minutes elapsed and he still had not returned, so I took a torch to go and look for him. My search would have been pointless when Copper was younger, as he was a law unto himself; a famously free spirit who came and went at will. I searched for him in silence, as by then he was stone deaf, his only concession to old age. Thinking he might have found a hole in the fence and escaped, I got in my car and drove up Ham Gate Avenue, parallel to the golf course. I thought I had spotted a dead fox lying by the side of the road and was about to avert my eyes when a terrible thought struck me. There was my beloved dog lying in a pool of blood. He must momentarily have lost his instinctive road sense and been hit by a car. No words can adequately describe the feelings I experienced when I found my own dog run over and tried to accept the awful violent end of a life as I gathered up his frail body and wrapped it in a towel. At fifteen, Copper was an old dog and I had known he would not live more than another two years, but I had hoped he would die peacefully on the sofa in my bedroom wrapped in his Colefax and Fowler duvet.

I had found him in a butcher's shop, not on the meat counter with the legs of lamb and joints of beef, but in a pen surrounded by his siblings, a multitude of puppies of indeterminate colours and dubious origins. I am not sure why I chose him above the others, but I know he was copper-coloured and floppy, and that when I first saw him he was lying on his back. Against my better judgement I had promised Jemima I would give her a puppy if she passed her Common Entrance, and while I had no way of knowing what he would grow up to look like, or how large he would become, I took him home with me and placed him in Jemima's arms. She fell in love with him on the spot and as he was so small she would sing him to sleep in her hands. Within a few months he had left puppyhood behind and as he grew bigger the distinctive curly tail of a mongrel appeared. With his dignified beard he had become a young dog.

Rather like the hero of one of the children's favourite films, *The Belstone Fox*, Copper became a living legend in the neighbourhood, notorious for his exploits. By his first birthday he had learned the bus routes to Richmond and Kingston. However hard I tried to keep him in, he would escape to Richmond Park, chasing joggers, rabbits and anything that moved, and when he felt a bit peckish he would take the number 65 bus into town, stopping off at the Dysart Arms on the way, where if he was lucky he would be given lunch. Sometimes he would be accompanied on the bus by my black cat Jessie. Copper was equally partial to a pub on the outskirts of Kingston and more than once he was spotted by one of my friends sitting up at the bar, lunching with an unidentified elderly man. He was also seen in pubs as far away as Surbiton and East Molesey.

At dusk he would make his way home, trotting through the woods, waiting by the pedestrian crossing on the busy Petersham Road, where he would pause, holding up his paw quite pathetically until the cars stopped, when he would cross over with a heavy limp and on reaching the other side scamper off home. I did not want to lock him up as that would have made him miserable and as the years went on I became less worried about his expeditions because he always made it home in time for bed.

His amorous adventures were in a class of their own. He must have fathered more puppies than the highest paid stud dog and could smell a bitch on heat from miles away. I will never forget one incredibly cold and beautiful winter's day when the snow lay thick on the ground, the pond on Ham Common was frozen over and the branches were heavy with snow and dripping with icicles. Zac and Jemima put on their skates and joined the other children on the pond. Copper was amusing himself by pulling Benjamin round the pond on his sledge until, getting bored with the game, he wandered off.

As I was watching this idyllic scene I was joined by a very snobbish lady, whom I vaguely knew, who lived nearby. She was the proud owner of a very well-bred white standard poodle bitch, a regular entrant at Cruft's dog show. She told me in a breathy whisper that in a few days' time she would be sending her beloved pet to stud, that she had a queue of people wanting puppies and that each puppy would be worth hundreds of pounds. She even mentioned the intended pedigree sire's name, which was particularly long and pretentious. As she droned on I happened to glance behind me and saw that Copper had mounted the white poodle behind the sycamore tree. Terrified at the possibility that the owner would turn round and see what was happening, I engaged her in frantic conversation, pointing out interesting sights on the pond in front of us, feigning disapproval at some of the younger skaters' bad language, while furtively I peeped over my shoulder and could see that by now the two dogs were 'tied' back to back, a sure sign of a successful mating. I managed to keep the white poodle owner distracted, wondering how on earth she had failed to notice that her dog was already on heat until eventually the dogs separated and the poodle raced around clearly delighted with herself and her new conquest, while Copper emerged looking bedraggled and exhausted. Luckily the white poodle owner's family moved away shortly afterwards, but I have often imagined the look on the owner's face when the poodle's puppies were born.

Copper soon moved on to India Jane's own mongrel Dushka. Dushka did not fancy him as much as the white poodle but she had little choice in the matter as she managed to get herself stuck in the cat flap while trying to escape Copper's attentions and he moved in fast. Whether or not he was the father of the two puppies she produced remained a matter for conjecture, but I think a dachshund must have got there first. Neither of the puppies looked much like Copper but he became very attached to the one we called the Platypus who was black with a very long body and short little legs. Soon the Platypus was accompanying Copper on his adventures, but unable to keep up the pace because his legs were too short, he would be dumped by Copper on the nearest doorstep. I was getting at least two calls a day from people asking me to come and collect him.

Finally Copper took the Platypus to Brighton for the day. Trotting down the side of the A3 they were given a lift by a charming lady who had an antique shop in Brighton who, on seeing this extraordinary duo by the side of the road, had thoughtfully called my number which was printed on the inside of Copper's collar. After that the Platypus went to a good home in Herefordshire and Copper resumed his solo roaming.

But soon his freedom was curtailed when he was accused of biting a jogger outside the house. A summons arrived and I prepared for Copper's day in court. I found an excellent barrister and took masses of photographs of the driveway where the offence allegedly took place. Among the pictures I enclosed for the magistrates as evidence of his innocence was one of Copper looking rather rakish, dressed as a member of the Mafia, wearing a hat and dark glasses, a cigar clamped between his teeth. In court I watched as the magistrates tried to suppress their grins when they saw the picture and, helped by many character witnesses including dear Jilly Cooper (who had loved him ever since she judged a charity dog show in my garden and had found him to be the naughtiest dog in the show), Copper's life was spared although the penalty was that he was no longer permitted to roam free.

As the years went by he settled into a contented old age, spending much time asleep wrapped in his duvet. We buried him in the wild garden at Ormeley and Alastair composed the following words for his tombstone.

Copper
1983–1998
In loving memory of the professor
A true gentleman of the road,
Tragically removed from our midst
By cruel fate but never to be forgotten.
As the poet has said,
'They are not dead who live in hearts
They leave behind.'

But not even the companionship of dogs can rival the joy I receive from my children. They are a source of enormous pride to me as individually they have excelled in their own fields. Robin continues to go from strength to strength. Having spent a year in New York working for Jimmy's supermarket chain, Grand Union, he found the experience to be invaluable when he started his chain of Birley Sandwich Bars in the City, which have proved to be a huge success, and with India Jane he has now taken over the running of Annabel's from his father. A passionate follower of Jimmy's political beliefs, he was determined that Jimmy's vision would not die with him and although Jimmy had left no instructions, Robin and I decided to continue as best we could with his campaigning work on the Referendum Party. Four years ago Robin set up the Democracy Movement, a thriving Eurosceptic grassroots organisation.

India Jane has inherited her Birley grandfather's creative gift and is an artist of some considerable repute. She has been described as 'an absolutely dedicated painter and dazzling talent' and without being accused of boasting, I can call her beautiful because she does not look like me but resembles the Birleys with her large blue eyes and dark hair. She is the best company in the world and wonderfully eccentric. Aged twenty-one, having vowed never to marry as young as me, she married Jonty Colchester, a friend of Rupert's, and for a time they lived in the cottage at Ormeley. Sadly, the marriage did not work out and after they separated she spent what she called 'her wild years' before marrying Francis Pike in October 1993. For several years they lived in Bombay and India Jane's tales of life there in an apartment in the red light district never fail to make me laugh, but I was very happy when they returned to London. Francis has always been unmercifully teased by Jane, which he takes with his usual good nature. I once wrote him a birthday party poem about butter with which he was obsessed and of which he ate far too much. It was read out on his birthday in the private room at Annabel's by India Jane's best friend, Bettina von Hase:

> *The Butter Party*
> In February nineteen fifty-four
> Francis rendered his first snore;
> His mother's eyes were filled with joy
> For he was such a bonny boy.
> One day to Mrs Pike's dismay,
> Whilst crawling on the floor at play,
> The first words Frank was heard to utter
> Not Ma or Pa but butter, butter.
> Poor Mrs Pike was quite unable
> To stop him climbing on the table,
> All she could do was stand and splutter
> While Francis stuffed his mouth with butter.
> As years rolled on and Francis grew
> (A lovely youth, good-looking too)
> His parents naturally were wary
> He'd spurned the city for the dairy

He much preferred the butter churn
To boring sums he could not learn.
By night, exhausted, he would dream
Of pitchers full of double cream.
At thirty-eight he chose his bride
In shimmering yellow by his side
As they exchanged their marriage vows
His thoughts were full of grazing cows.
He hoped that Jane was keen on butter
Although he thought he heard her mutter
'I hate the nasty greasy stuff',
Her dulcet tones becoming tough.
Thank heavens for his lunchtime break,
And hidden slices of cream cake,
With endless packs of Tesco's best
Concealed inside his winter vest.
Happy birthday Francis Pike
Tonight you may eat what you like
Lots of butter, rich and yellow,
Fit for such a charming fellow.

Born when I was thirty-nine, Jemima was everything I could have asked for in a new child: pretty, lively and intelligent. At school she was an academic like Rupert, and I never had to worry about her homework because she was so ambitious and wanted to do well.

Like her sister India Jane, she also told me that she never intended to marry young but happily her plans changed when she met and fell in love with Imran Khan at the age of twenty. I greatly admired her courage when prior to her marriage she readily took on another culture and adopted another religion. When she moved to Pakistan she was deeply affected by the evident and urgent need for funds for Imran's cancer hospital in Lahore and, wanting to do something to help, she set up her own business employing a team of Pakistani women to sew and bead dresses of her own design that she sold in various shops all over the world. The dresses were hugely successful and became highly coveted, and she gave all the proceeds directly to the hospital.

Jemima has been made a special representative to Unicef UK and has set up her own charity to support Afghan refugees in Pakistan, which distributes food, emergency supplies and clothes, and which funds specialist paediatric and obstetric clinics in the camps. In 2002, seven years after giving up her university studies to get married, she decided to return to the University of Bristol to complete her Bachelor's degree in English. Mimi and I were bursting with pride when we watched her step up on to the university hall platform wearing her black gown, to be awarded a 2:1 degree. She is now doing a Masters degree at LSE in International Relations and plans to go on to complete a doctorate. Sadly after nine years Jemima and Imran's marriage came to an end in a civilised and dignified manner and they continue to remain friends with one another.

Zac has been the biggest surprise. He never really settled in any school and, like Jimmy, loathed any kind of authoritarianism. Although he made friends easily, I am not sure whether Eton was the best school for him but his burning ambition to save the environment manifested itself soon after he left. In 1998 he took over the editorship from his Uncle Teddy of the *Ecologist Magazine*, already then deemed a considerable source of authority for those with an ecological interest, and through Zac's dedication and immense hard work he has managed to turn the magazine into an important and recognised platform for many international issues. By making the articles accessible and stimulating, even to the less ecologically aware reader, he has greatly increased the circulation. He has described for me his response to those people who suggest there is a divergence from his father in the ethic of his environmental work.

I am often asked whether or not I see the irony in my involvement in protecting the environment when at least part of my father's fortune was built on exploiting it. The answer is that I cannot think of a single fortune that wasn't. The difference, though, is that my father spent the last chunk of his life funding key environmental campaigns that other funders would not touch. They would focus on path-of-least-resistance charities on the basis of how it would make them appear. My father would focus instead on 'funding the unfundable'. The result is that what were radical groups at the time grew and have become mainstream. He rarely mentioned his donations, but in truth much of today's environmental movement owes its success to him.

Zac has also helped to set up a new campaigning organisation called 'Farm', which represents small family farmers in the United Kingdom. He has given numerous television and radio interviews discussing environmental issues and is a frequent contributor to the editorial pages of the national press. He is one of the most thoughtful and gentle people I know, and his amazing affinity with animals reminds me of his brother Rupert. My great hope is that he will follow his father and go into politics. In June 1999 he married Sheherazade Bentley, a wonderful girl who has integrated happily into this mad family. She is a great linguist being fluent in Italian, French and Spanish, and is therefore an enormous help to me in running things at Tramores.

Ben-Ben, my last and late child, is only twenty-three, but he is already showing signs of being a chip off the old block, having inherited Jimmy's entrepreneurial energy. Marvellous with and adored by all ages from the youngest child to the oldest of my friends, in 2003 he married a delightful girl, Kate Rothschild, a kindred spirit for me in her love of children and dogs. Ben, like Zac, is passionate about the environment. He is setting up a venture capital fund called WHEB Ventures, to invest in early-stage companies that have developed exciting technologies in the areas of clean energies, waste, water, and agriculture.

When my Birley children were young I used to pray that they would reach the age of eighteen before I died. Having lost my mother and seeing what it did to the family, I could not bear the same thing to happen to them. Thirteen years later when my second family began to arrive I had to make the same prayer all over again. Although obviously I find them all beautiful and talented, I remember Jimmy teasing me whenever I would brag *too* much about them all, by bringing me down to earth with the old saying, 'The donkey in the eyes of its mother is a gazelle.'

From the age of twenty until the present day, I have been fortunate to have been blessed by the presence of a continuous flow of children. By the time my youngest child by Mark, India Jane, had reached thirteen, I had given birth to Jemima, followed by Zac a year later and then by Benjamin in 1980. While Benjamin was still a schoolboy at Eton my first grandchild appeared, the first of the next generation.

With three children born by my twenty-sixth birthday I could have been an early grandmother, something I had always wanted to be. As the years rolled on I became used to the casually dropped remarks by my friends, most of whom already had more than one grandchild, commiserating with me on this missing element in my life. However, with a thirteen-year gap between my first and second family, there was plenty of room for hope and in 1996 this hope was fulfilled when my youngest daughter Jemima, who to me still seemed a child herself, gave birth to Sulaiman. I stayed with her throughout the birth, which was one of the most wonderful experiences of my life. To be able to see your first grandchild born and to have been able to participate in that experience has to be one of the most uplifting and euphoric moments in any woman's life, almost akin to giving birth oneself. No one had ever told me how overwhelmed I would feel when that baby was born. During the day my feelings had veered from anxiety, love and fear for Jemima until the moment he was born when I finally arrived at a state of triumph and awe.

Before Sulaiman's birth Jemima had promised Mrs White that she would show her the baby as soon as she came out of hospital. Shortly after Jemima and Sulaiman returned home to Ormeley, I received a telephone call from the Elmbank nursing home to say that Mrs White had had a stroke and was not expected to live through the night. When I told Jemima she burst into tears saying, 'I cannot break my promise to Wags. I must show her Sulaiman.' With Sulaiman in her arms, I drove Jemima to the nursing home where we found Mrs White lying pale and unconscious in her bed. Jemima put the baby on her chest and talked to her gently, telling her his name, even though there was no response. The next morning Helen, the matron, rang to tell me that Mrs White had made a lightning recovery and was sitting up in bed grumbling that her breakfast was late. I rushed round to see her and asked if she could recall the events of the night before, and she astonished me by not only remembering the visit of Jemima and the baby, but also that the name of the baby was 'something foreign'. The following year she had a series of small strokes and died after her ninetieth birthday, which we all celebrated with her, gathered round her bed.

Within three years of Sulaiman's birth he was joined by his brother Kasim and I have to face the fact that they must spend a certain amount of time in Pakistan and it is right that they should do so. But the sadness I feel at their absence is tempered by my knowledge of their extended and loving paternal family, and of the sunshine and freedom that fills their lives there. No matter how many times I have met them at the airport on their return to England, their arrival never fails to excite me, when they dash out to greet me as I lean against the barrier waiting for them. Imran tells me that they start asking when they are going to see me even before they take off from Islamabad.

Sulaiman and Kasim have very different personalities. Sulaiman is gentle and sensitive whereas Kasim, charming and cheeky, is more extrovert, but they are inseparable. In that difficult period of adjustment and sibling rivalry that most mothers experience after the arrival of a new baby, I remember telling Jemima, 'Wait and see; your workload will be halved as Kasim gets older.' And sure enough they are now content to amuse each other, and I love listening to the conversations between them and the different games that Sulaiman invents for them to play.

In April 2000 Uma Romaine was born to Zac and Sheherazade. I was happy to have a little granddaughter to join the boys and she has proved to be another delight. She is already showing a pleasingly eccentric streak, having adopted the identity of her next-door neighbour's cat, Benson, to whose name she always answers, preferring to lap her lunch out of an ashtray while delivering a wet lick when asked for a kiss.

In 2002 Thyra appeared, another girl for Zac and Sheherazade, a sister for Uma. Their third child James and Ben and Kate's daughter Iris Annabel *aka* The Pudding has brought my current grandchild total to six, although I suspect this may not be the final tally.

I had intended to be called Grandma by all of them but when Sulaiman was very small he began to call me Mum because he heard Jemima, Zac and Ben calling me Mum and when Kasim learned to speak he copied Sulaiman. With the boys this didn't matter because the Urdu for mother is amma and abba for father, but when Uma arrived, although we tried to start her with 'Grandma', I rapidly became 'Mum' again. I am now resigned to the fact that I will always be known as Mum, although occasionally I get odd looks from people listening to the children calling out to me in shops. I imagine them thinking, 'She's far too old to be their mother', and wondering whether I have been treated by Dr Antinori, the Italian doctor who has been known to help women become pregnant in their sixties.

God willing I will be part of my grandchildren's lives for a long time to come. They all have very loving parents but I believe, like every other child, they need their grandmother, that we grandparents have an important role to play in our grandchildren's lives and I take my responsibilities very seriously. We are older and wiser and, most importantly, unlike many busy parents we have the gift of time, time to play with them and time to talk to them. For their part, flattered by our interest in them and willingness to listen to them, most children seem to have an intuitive liking for older people. This sense of continuity of family life remains for me an endless source of pleasure.

My favourite room at Ormeley has always been my bedroom. It is the loveliest and lightest room in the house with its four great floor-length Queen Anne windows, through which on one side I have a wonderful view of the garden and on the other Ham Common, with the sight and sound of horses taking their morning exercise below me. Surrounded by woodland and greenery, there is not another building in sight. The room was added on to the house by Mrs Fitzherbert in the late eighteenth century and I love the romantic assumption that it may have been a love nest for her and the Prince Regent for several years before their marriage. Since the days of Pelham Cottage I have always spent a great deal of time in my bedroom and consider it the core of the house, whether in the long sun-filled days of the summer or during winter evenings when the room is filled with the flickering of firelight. Because I brought most of my favourite furniture and even the mantelpiece from Pelham Cottage with me, the spirit of that place continues to fill my room at Ormeley. When I am home it is in this room that I read, write letters, watch television, talk on the telephone and it is also the place where I keep my favourite books, most of my photographs and drawers full of precious papers including letters not only from my parents but from all of my six children as well as their drawings and school reports that I have saved over all these years. The room is dominated by the same huge four-poster bed on which I once sat with Mrs White, discussing how strange it was that 'men had to have their way'.

I find I am still sharing the bed, as I so often have over the last several decades, with a jumble of children and dogs. It was on this bed that my children used to gather at Pelham Cottage to do their homework and to watch Popeye on a small black-and-white television set, and it is on to this bed that my grand-children and a new generation of dogs now choose to throw themselves. These days we are usually tuned in to the Dis-covery Channel with its amazing wildlife programmes in which cheetahs are filmed travelling at thrilling speed across the African bush in pursuit of their prey. This happy and contented existence seems a long way from the days when I sat with my own grandmother on her bed, as together we turned the pages of her black prayer book.

Acknowledgements and thanks

I am grateful to the following authors and their books which have provided me with invaluable background information:

Anne de Courcy, *Circe, The Life of Edith Marchioness of Londonderry*
Ivan Fallon, *Billionaire*
The Countess of Fingall's Memoirs, *Seventy Years Young*
Edith Londonderry, *Retrospect*
Brian Masters, *The Passion of John Aspinall* and *Wynyard Hall and The Londonderry Family Guidebook*
H. Montgomery Hyde, *The Londonderrys*
Ben Pimlott, *The Queen*
Geoffrey Wansell, *Tycoon*
Alan Whicker, *Within Whicker's World*

And I would like to thank the following for their help:

Naim Attallah
Billy Dudley
Geordie Greig and the staff at *Tatler*
Shaun Plunket
Gavin Rankin and the staff in the Annabel's office
Patrick Robertson
Ed Victor
The staff at Wynyard
My publishers, Ion Trewin, Victoria Webb and George Weidenfeld

My patient secretary Judith Naish who had the unenviable task of deciphering my illegible handwriting

Last but not least my wonderful editor Juliet Nicolson, without whom I would have lost the incentive to struggle on with the book. I will always be grateful for her resourcefulness in the research for the book including her visit to my old home, Wynyard, in order to remind me of the chapel, a journey I could not bring myself to do. And I will not forget the countless times we spent laughing and crying over different incidents in the book.

Index

Index

Index